"This book is a testament to the power of rigorous historical research paired with empathy for a vulnerable woman who was victimized by her rapist, the Baptist leaders in charge of her care, and the Southern Baptist institutions that privileged their own reputations over their responsibility for Antônia Teixeira. Indeed, Parsons and Chaves demonstrate the long-standing interest missionaries in Brazil and Texas Baptist leaders shared in upholding the triumphalism and prowess of their Southern Baptist legacy through habits of selective silence and ethnic pride. These habits first minimized both the scandals and successes of Antônia's father as a Brazilian ex-priest turned Baptist pastor, then mounted a campaign to discredit Antônia's claims as a rape victim, and finally worked to excise Antônia's very existence from local and denominational history. Chaves and Parsons leave no stone unturned in telling this harrowing tale of injustice, which is relevant to recent Baylor University history and current international #MeToo and #ChurchToo movements."

—**Laura Rodgers Levens**
Baptist Seminary of Kentucky

"This impressive history book sheds light on themes such as mission and power, manipulation of memory, religion and race, and sexual abuse. Modeling a transnational historiographical approach, it excavates a memory that has been forcibly forgotten. Mikeal Parsons and João Chaves uncover the tragic story of Antônia Teixeira and excavate racialized theological assumptions that justified covering it up. The book exemplifies the work of world Christian historians at its best, challenging hagiographical accounts of mission, while bringing to light uncomfortable facts that force the reader to face the paradoxical nature of Southern Baptist mission in particular and of modern Christian history more broadly. The authors also help to achieve justice for a violated body and soul, bringing this migrant woman of color to the center stage of a story that remained unknown until now. This well-documented history of Baylor University, the Southern Baptist Convention, and its Foreign Mission Board is revealing and valuable in its own right. Yet this book also has wider significance as it encourages the reader 'to explore ways in which power was [and continues to be] used by key players in major religious institutions to reconstruct memories and suppress inconvenient truths.'"

—**Raimundo C. Barreto**
Princeton Theological Seminary

Remembering Antônia Teixeira

A Story of Missions, Violence,
and Institutional Hypocrisy

Mikeal C. Parsons
and João B. Chaves

William B. Eerdmans Publishing Company
Grand Rapids, Michigan

Wm. B. Eerdmans Publishing Co.
4035 Park East Court SE, Grand Rapids, Michigan 49546
www.eerdmans.com

© 2023 Mikeal C. Parsons and João B. Chaves
Published 2023
Printed in the United States of America

29 28 27 26 25 24 23   1 2 3 4 5 6 7

ISBN 978-0-8028-8309-4

Library of Congress Cataloging-in-Publication Data

A catalog record for this book is available from the Library of Congress.

Photographs marked (TC) are courtesy of The Texas Collection, Baylor University, Waco, TX; photographs marked (IMB) are courtesy of International Mission Board, Richmond, VA.

In honor of the Baylor regents, administrators, faculty, students, staff, and alumni who have been, and continue to be, allies of and advocates for the marginalized, forgotten, and abused

Contents

Contents

Foreword

I n the introduction to his memoir *The Sacred Journey*, the late Presbyterian minister and writer Frederick Buechner asks, "How do you tell the story of your life—of how you were born, and the world you were born into, and the world that was born in you?"[1]

Those questions, which Buechner applied to his life and identity in the world, seem applicable on an even broader scale to *Remembering Antônia Teixeira: A Story of Missions, Violence, and Institutional Hypocrisy*. In its most basic sense, this book is a memoir of the long-overlooked life of Antônia Teixeira, the adolescent Brazilian girl who, in 1892, was taken to the United States by Southern Baptist missionaries to become a student at Baylor College in Waco, Texas, where she was essentially the ward of Baylor president Rufus Burleson and his family. The story of her life presented here comprises as much of a memoir as the authors, Mikeal C. Parsons and João B. Chaves, were able to discern and document from the limited details available. The professors trace Antônia's journey from her native Brazil to Texas, a saga that began with great promise and welcome but deteriorated into profound sadness, a tale of exploitation, abuse, and rejection, much of it initiated by persons and institutions that initially claimed to nurture her to salvation in this world and the next.

Yet the book is also something of a memoir for a group of individuals and institutions that understood themselves as paragons of Christian (and Baptist) orthodoxy and intent but were born of a world that interpreted Antônia Teixeira and the events that overtook her in ways that contradicted the very gospel they

---

1. Frederick Buechner, *The Sacred Journey* (New York: Harper & Row, 1982), 9.

professed. The Southern Baptist missionaries who "took the gospel to Brazil" sought to anchor a particular type of Christianity there, transforming its culture through their witness and that of their Brazilian converts. What the missionaries failed to recognize was that they also brought with them the world into which they had been born, a society where White supremacy and racial stratification were undergirded by biblical authority. As this study indicates, those Southern Baptists, both at home and in Brazil, seemed unable to separate their biblical hermeneutic on faith and salvation from the racially engendered hermeneutic that birthed the Southern Baptist Convention in antebellum America. That interpretation, which began with support of chattel slavery, continued to inform racially related attitudes and actions long after slavery's political demise. The biblical hermeneutic set forth by Richard Furman, pastor of First Baptist Church, Savannah, Georgia, in 1822 established the interpretative principle. Furman wrote, "Had the holding of slaves been a moral evil, it cannot be supposed, that the inspired Apostles, who feared not the faces of men, and were ready to lay down their lives in the cause of their God, would have tolerated it, for a moment, in the Christian Church. . . . But, instead of this, they let the relationship remain untouched, as being lawful and right, and insist on the relative duties. In proving this subject justifiable by Scriptural authority, its morality is also proved; for the Divine Law never sanctions immoral actions."[2] That racist biblical hermeneutic became normative in the founding of the Southern Baptist Convention in 1845 and endured through the Civil War, only to be adapted as Lost Cause support for White supremacy and what became Jim Crow culture in the South.

In his earlier book *The Global Mission of the Jim Crow South*, published in 2022, Professor Chaves explores the way in which those racial-oriented biblical and cultural interpretations impacted the theology and practice of Southern Baptist missionary endeavors, issues particularly evident in the mission to Brazil. He writes: "In the case of Southern Baptists, the mission to reach the Brazilians with the message of Christ was simultaneously the mission of the Jim Crow South, and a mission that developed in a national environment that was mostly receptive to the White supremacist dispositions of Southern Baptist missionaries."[3]

2. Richard Furman, "EXPOSITION of the Views of the Baptists, Relative to the Coloured Population in the United States in a Communication to the Governor of South-Carolina," in Bill J. Leonard, *Early American Christianity* (Nashville: Broadman Press, 1983), 382–83.

3. João B. Chaves, *The Global Mission of the Jim Crow South: Southern Baptist Missionaries and the Shaping of Latin American Evangelicalism* (Macon, GA: Mercer University Press, 2022), 23.

This hermeneutic extended into the twentieth century, as evident in the approach of James Franklin Love, executive secretary of the SBC Foreign Mission Board, 1915–1928. Missiologist Robert Nash writes that during Love's tenure, "the basic premises of Anglo-Saxon supremacy were adopted with considerable intentionality as mission strategy. In an effort to encourage Baptist expansion into Europe, Love argued that world evangelization could be accomplished more quickly if the aggressive white races were evangelized first."[4] In laying out his strategy for that kind of White-dominated evangelism, Love wrote: "Let us not forget that to the white man God gave the instinct and talent to disseminate His ideals among other people and that He did not, to the same degree, give this instinct and talent to the yellow, brown or black race. The white race only has the genius to introduce Christianity into all lands and among all people."[5]

The saga of Antônia Teixeira illustrates the enduring presence of a racially focused biblical hermeneutic articulated by Richard Furman as early as 1822. Recognizing that hermeneutic is central to reading and reflecting on the events and issues described in this insightful study. It is indeed "a hard lesson" throughout, documenting actions and attitudes that undermined the attested Christian commitments of leaders related to missionary and educational endeavors in the Baptist past.

It is "a hard lesson" for our present as well, cautioning us to acknowledge that our claims of orthodoxy will not absolve us from the sins that can so easily beset us. Indeed, *Remembering Antônia Teixeira* reminds us that our claims to "believe the Bible" do not mean that we are incapable of ignoring the gospel.

Bill J. Leonard

---

4. Robert N. Nash Jr., "Peculiarly Chosen: Anglo-Saxon Supremacy and Baptist Missions in the South," *Perspectives in Religious Studies* 38, no. 2 (Summer 2011): 164–65.

5. James Franklin Love, *The Appeal of the Baptist Program for Europe* (Richmond, VA: Foreign Mission Board of the Southern Baptist Convention, 1920), 14–15, cited in Nash, "Peculiarly Chosen," 165.

Abbreviations

BBC	Brazilian Baptist Convention
FMB	Foreign Mission Board
FMJ	*Foreign Mission Journal*
IMB	International Mission Board
SBC	Southern Baptist Convention
WMB	World Mission Board of the Brazilian Baptist Convention

Prologue: Bloody Cotton

Everybody who was anybody in Texas, as well as lots of folk who were not, attended the grand opening of Waco's Cotton Palace in early November 1894. Waco residents had raised over $40,000 for the construction of the exhibit hall intended to celebrate the city's significant place in the cotton industry. A suspension bridge and two railroad systems in the 1870s and '80s had linked Waco's cotton farmers with industries and consumers across the country, so that by 1893, 120,000 bales of cotton had been bought and sold in the city market.[1] The Cotton Palace also hoped to draw tourists and new residents as the town struggled to keep up with the growth of Dallas, its rival city to the north. Waco's 1880 population of 7,295 had nearly doubled by 1890 to 14,445, but Dallas's had nearly quadrupled, going from 10,358 in 1880 to nearly 40,000 in 1890.[2] Thus opening night at the Cotton Palace was both a grand

---

1. "Waco History," Waco—Heart of Texas, accessed July 1, 2021, https://wacoheartoftexas .com/wp-content/uploads/2017/05/Waco-History-2017.pdf; Roger N. Conger, "Cotton Palace," in *Handbook of Texas Online* (Texas Historical Society, 1954), updated December 1, 1994, https:// www.tshaonline.org/handbook/entries/cotton-palace.

2. These figures are taken from "City Population History from 1850–2000," in *Texas Almanac*, accessed July 1, 2021, https://texasalmanac.com/sites/default/files/images/CityPopHist%20web .pdf. In 1880, Waco had the sixth-largest population in Texas, behind only Dallas, Austin, Galveston, Houston, and San Antonio (Galveston being the largest at over 22,000). By 1890, the population gap between Waco and these other cities had widened considerably, and today the city, with slightly less than 140,000 in population, is the twenty-sixth largest city in Texas, dwarfed by metropolitan areas like Houston, San Antonio, Dallas–Fort Worth, Austin, and El Paso, all of which approach or exceed one million residents.

gala celebrating Waco's place in the "heart of Texas"—both geographically and economically—and a more or less futile attempt to cling to its fading place in Texas legend and lore as "Six Shooter Junction."[3] The town pulled out all the stops for the grand opening, and it was by all accounts a spectacular affair. Texas Governor James Stephen Hogg was on hand to christen the place and crown the first "King Cotton" and "Queen Texas." Also present were the president and first lady of Baylor University, who had attended a wedding planned in conjunction with the Cotton Palace opening.

Of course, not everyone was welcomed. While Black people lined the streets to watch the big parade, they were not allowed to attend the coronation.[4] The very invocation of "cotton," which had gone hand in hand with chattel slavery in antebellum Texas, must have touched raw nerves among Waco's Black residents, many of whom had been enslaved only thirty years earlier and were now bound to landlords as impoverished sharecroppers still raising cotton or otherwise engaged in the cotton industry as mill workers.[5] The Cotton Palace celebrated what Black Wacoans still mourned: the bloodshed and lives sacrificed by themselves, their parents, and their friends for "mighty King Cotton."[6]

3. This first effort was short-lived. The original Cotton Palace burned to the ground in January 1895, only six weeks after its opening. It reopened in 1910 and had a successful run as an exhibition hall until it became a casualty, like so many other institutions, of the Great Depression.

4. See Amanda Slamcik Lasseter, "Politics, Patriotism, Pageantry: Performing Power at the Texas Cotton Palace, 1910–1930" (master's thesis, Baylor University, 2014), 30. In the later iteration of the Cotton Palace (1910–1930), according to Lasseter's interview with Rubie Wilborn Evans, an African American Waco resident who attended the Cotton Palace exhibit, Black persons were allowed to roam the grounds and participate in the parades (mostly as grooms for the horses) but were still prohibited from attending the coronation ceremonies.

5. By 1860, there were 3,799 White persons and 2,404 enslaved persons in Waco's McLennan County. Karla Price, "Slavery in Waco," Waco History Project, accessed July 1, 2021, http://waco historyproject.org/Slavery/slaveryshadows.htm.

6. See Neil Foley, *The White Scourge: Mexicans, Blacks, and Poor Whites in Texas Cotton Culture* (Berkeley: University of California Press, 1997); and Sven Beckert, *Empire of Cotton: A Global History* (New York: Alfred A. Knopf, 2014). Certainly, African American residents of Waco today still resent what the Cotton Palace represents. Myrtle Thompson, a former president of the McLennan County chapter of the NAACP, commented, "I do believe that the Cotton Palace Pageant is insulting to many African-Americans, it's very insensitive to African-Americans. . . . I have never seen an African-American Cotton Palace King or Queen. I doubt if I ever will if this event continues. It symbolizes a period of history when cotton was king and this is not something we take pride in." Price, "Slavery in Waco."

Nor in attendance was the first family's domestic servant, a native Brazilian who was also a part-time student at the college. She was home with the first lady's eighty-five-year-old mother. And there was at least one other person who had skipped the festivities. He lingered in the shadows outside the president's home, waiting.[7]

Around 9:00 p.m., the servant girl stood washing dishes when she heard someone walking in the back yard. Then she heard her name called out by a voice she recognized: "Come out and have something sweet to drink." She moved to the back door, which suddenly flung open. A hand grabbed her by the arm, pulling her out of the house and into the yard. As he held her, the man compelled the girl to drink a sweet white liquor from a glass bottle he drew from his pocket; it had a dizzying effect. The man forced her to the ground and pulled up her dress of light cotton linen to finish what he had set out to do. He yanked her undergarments aside and penetrated her, hurting her. She tried to call out, but the weight of her assailant crushing down on her emptied her lungs of air. She struggled, but to no avail. He overpowered her. Finally, finished, he disappeared into the dark without speaking a word.

She stumbled back into the house, shaking and alone. The old grandmother was fast asleep in bed. By the kitchen's lamp light, she examined herself and saw blood—her blood—on her cotton dress. Her undergarments were ripped. She sat alone in the kitchen, numb and confused, before finally going to bed.

The young woman's name was Antônia Teixeira. This is her story.[8]

7. Given the disputes over Antônia's testimony of this event, it is important to state here that at least one witness, Mr. Ed Norris, a boarder of a nearby neighbor at the time, testified he had seen the accused "in Dr. Burleson's back yard at night." While unable to remember the exact date, he stated that it was in "November or December." Testimonies, case 1165, The State v. Steen Morris, Fifty-Fourth District Court in McLennan County, McLennan County Archives.

8. The preceding paragraphs were derived from an interview with Antônia that appeared in the June 16, 1895, edition of the *Waco Morning News* and her trial testimony, taken on July 24, 1895 (case 1165, McLennan County Archives). These events will be examined in more detail in the pages that follow. The parties could not agree on the date of the Cotton Palace opening; finally, they settled on November 6, 1894. All other accounts place the date on November 8, 1894. Still, it was the event and not the date on which it happened that the parties agreed marked the alleged first sexual assault on Antônia Teixeira.

Introduction

Power and Transnational Histories

The cultivation of a common memory is important to the identity and functioning of any social group, so the construction, imposition, and protection of memory are crucial to the exercise of power in that group. More broadly, access to institutions of cultural production, such as media outlets, printing presses, universities, and newspapers, help shape what is remembered. This is as true in religious institutions as anywhere else. As the Oxford historian Diarmaid MacCulloch argued in his Gifford Lectures—notably, on the history of Christian silence—the perceived need for evasion and the willful avoidance of truth has, at crucial moments in church history, driven people to remain quiet. To quote his apt coinage, church officials have both "monopolized noise" and "gathered silences of shame and distortion of the truth," and they have done so for purposes of power.[1]

This disposition can often join forces with more aggressive moves to erase memories that are particularly inconvenient. When effective, such processes both draw from and help maintain structures that benefit directly from the meanings so established, all the more so when they happen out of sight. As the social theorist Steven Lukes puts it, "power is the most effective when least observable"; the most powerful constructions of memory are those that do not feel constructed at all, the ones in which what is remembered does not include that which was intended to be forgotten.[2]

---

1. Diarmaid MacCulloch, *Silence: A Christian History* (New York: Penguin Books, 2014), 3–7.
2. Maria Paula Nascimento Araújo and Myrian Sepúlveda dos Santos, "History, Memory and

The story told in this book was not supposed to be remembered, and it took place between the worlds of the US South and Brazil. It is the story of Antônia Teixeira, a young immigrant woman who was raped by a powerful man in Waco, Texas, where she had been taken by a Southern Baptist missionary who had met her in Brazil. It is a story that many people in both her worlds tried to forget because of what it threatened to reveal about US foreign missions, Christian universities, and their long entanglements with violence, racism, and xenophobia. Thus Antônia Teixeira's story is also a story about how powerful men in Texas and Brazil tried to forget her, and how forgetting her long allowed them to construct their image in ways that distorted not only who they really were but also aspects of the institutions they represented: Baylor University, the Southern Baptist Convention (SBC), and its Foreign Mission Board (FMB). The case of Antônia Teixeira's rape at Baylor University is important in and of itself but also because it enables us to explore ways in which power was used by key players in major religious institutions to reconstruct memories and suppress inconvenient truths.

Problematic Memories in Southern Baptist History

Historical selectivity has been a common phenomenon in Baptist life across the Southern United States. The particular value of Antônia Teixeira's story lies in presenting a unique and powerful case study that illustrates how such a disposition could carry across borders. The SBC has often presented itself to the world in a skewed and self-congratulatory manner, making the control of collective memory especially important to the SBC's institutional self-understanding. SBC intellectuals long resisted reinterpretation of its myths and canonical stories.

White denominational historians have done this from the very founding of the SBC in Augusta, Georgia, in 1845. Their narratives have deliberately obscured the role slavery played in that event. Between blaming Northern Baptists for infringing on the denomination's constitutional documents and rights, stating that slavery was but a minor point among more important issues in its birth, and admitting that slavery was central while minimizing its impact, the real place of slavery was whitewashed from the prevailing denominational

---

Forgetting: Political Implications," *RCCS Annual Review* 1, no. 1 (September 2009): 77–94; Steven Lukes, *Power: A Radical View* (New York: Palgrave Macmillan, 2005), 1.

creation myth until after the Civil Rights Movement.[3] That it took so long for SBC historians to confirm what has always been clear from the primary sources is so surprising that Walter Shurden and Lori Varnadoe had to comment in an essay covering the historiography on the topic: "Most non-Southern Baptist church historians would doubtless ask, 'Is it not obvious that slavery was the decisive factor in the formation of the SBC?' The answer: 'No, it has not been obvious to white Southern Baptist church historians that slavery was the primary issue in the formation of the SBC.'"[4] From the very beginning, SBC intellectuals were invested in crafting innocent versions of their denomination's trajectory while simultaneously ignoring clear historical facts deemed to be impractical for the memories they hoped to construct.

Some Southern Baptist historians tried to digress from such triumphalism only to practice other distortions themselves. William Whitsitt, a one-time president of Southern Baptist Theological Seminary, offers a prime example. On the one hand, he suffered the consequences of disputing the Landmarkist myth that traced the origins of the SBC directly back to the New Testament. In the resulting Whitsitt Controversy, this corrective led many of his critics to charge him with "heresy" and led to Whitsitt's resignation from his presidency in 1899.[5] If he thus became the victim of one of the more famous purges in SBC history, Whitsitt was hardly a historiographical innocent. He held a largely ahistorical stance as to the place of slavery in the SBC's origins and strongly supported the Lost Cause mythology that legitimized racial violence in the post–Civil War South. It has been difficult indeed to avoid the SBC's selective memory entirely.[6]

The Civil Rights Movement did start exposing a number of cracks in this fortress so that, while various whitewashed versions remain predominant, a

---

3. Walter Shurden and H. Leon McBeth were among the first White Southern Baptist historians to identify slavery as the factor for the 1845 schism. See Walter B. Shurden, *Not a Silent People: Controversies That Have Shaped Southern Baptists* (Nashville: Broadman Press, 1972); and H. Leon McBeth, *The Baptist Heritage: Four Centuries of Baptist History* (Nashville: Broadman Press, 1987).

4. Walter B. Shurden and Lori Redwine Varnadoe, "The Origins of the Southern Baptist Convention: A Historiographical Study," *Baptist History and Heritage Journal* 37, no. 1 (Winter 2002): 71.

5. C. Douglas Weaver, *In Search of the New Testament Church: The Baptist Story* (Macon, GA: Mercer University Press, 2008), 158–59.

6. For Whitsitt's stance on the role of slavery in the origins of the SBC, see Shurden and Varnadoe, "Origins." Regarding his involvement in promoting Lost Cause mythology, see Christopher C. Moore, *Apostle of the Lost Cause: J. William Jones, Baptists, and the Development of Confederate Memory* (Knoxville: University of Tennessee Press, 2019).

few insiders, former insiders, and outside critics have been righting a number of historiographical wrongs. Studies on the relationship between the SBC and Southern racial violence have revealed how deeply the SBC has been involved in shaping Southern forms of White supremacy and deploying forms of racial violence.[7] Recent biographies of Southern Baptist figures have started to move beyond the hagiography that once characterized the denomination's literary projects to take critical stances revealing the complex and often problematic entanglements of denominational luminaries.[8] Other scholars have addressed the long and continuing history of SBC resistance to offering space for full gender equality.[9] More generally, historians of Christianity in the United States have uncovered the SBC's central role in shaping broad social, cultural, economic, and political realities in the United States.[10]

7. John Lee Eighmy and Samuel S. Hill, *Churches in Cultural Captivity: A History of the Social Attitudes of Southern Baptists* (Knoxville: University of Tennessee Press, 1987); Paul Harvey, *Redeeming the South: Religious Cultures and Racial Identities among Southern Baptists, 1865–1925* (Chapel Hill: University of North Carolina Press, 1997); Charles Reagan Wilson, *Baptized in Blood: The Religion of the Lost Cause, 1865–1920* (Athens: University of Georgia Press, 2009); Robert P. Jones, *White Too Long: The Legacy of White Supremacy in American Christianity* (New York: Simon & Schuster, 2020); Anthea Butler, *White Evangelical Racism: The Politics of Morality in America* (Chapel Hill: University of North Carolina Press, 2021); J. Russell Hawkins, *The Bible Told Them So: How Southern Evangelicals Fought to Preserve White Supremacy* (New York: Oxford University Press, 2021).

8. Barry Hankins, *God's Rascal: J. Frank Norris and the Beginnings of Southern Fundamentalism* (Lexington: University Press of Kentucky, 1996); A. James Fuller, *Chaplain to the Confederacy: Basil Manly and Baptist Life in the Old South* (Baton Rouge: LSU Press, 2000); Steven P. Miller, *Billy Graham and the Rise of the Republican South* (Philadelphia: University of Pennsylvania Press, 2011); Grant Wacker, *America's Pastor: Billy Graham and the Shaping of a Nation* (Cambridge, MA: Belknap Press, 2014); Moore, *Apostle of the Lost Cause*; Mikeal C. Parsons, *Crawford Howell Toy: The Man, the Scholar, the Teacher* (Macon, GA: Mercer University Press, 2019); Jonathan D. Redding, *One Nation under Graham: Apocalyptic Rhetoric and American Exceptionalism* (Waco, TX: Baylor University Press, 2021).

9. Susan M. Shaw, *God Speaks to Us, Too: Southern Baptist Women on Church, Home, and Society* (Lexington, KY: University Press of Kentucky, 2008); Elizabeth H. Flowers, *Into the Pulpit: Southern Baptist Women and Power since World War II* (Chapel Hill: University of North Carolina Press, 2012); Eileen Campbell-Reed, *Anatomy of a Schism: How Clergywomen's Narratives Reinterpret the Fracturing of the Southern Baptist Convention* (Knoxville: University of Tennessee Press, 2016); Elizabeth H. Flowers and Karen K. Seat, eds., *A Marginal Majority: Women, Gender, and a Reimagining of Southern Baptists* (Knoxville: University of Tennessee Press, 2020).

10. Bethany Moreton, *To Serve God and Wal-Mart: The Making of Christian Free Enterprise* (Cambridge, MA: Harvard University Press, 2010); Darren Dochuk, *From Bible Belt to Sunbelt: Plain-Folk Religion, Grassroots Politics, and the Rise of Evangelical Conservatism* (New York: W. W.

These sorts of contributions are welcome and essential for a better understanding not only of the SBC's history but also of the history of US Christianity in general. Yet, approaches that are largely confined within national borders can fail to address the deeply transnational nature of US Christianity in general and US evangelicalism in particular. The SBC, after all, has been a transnational institution from the start, and transnational institutions are best understood via transnational histories.

The United States, Brazil, and Baptist Transnational Histories

While this mandate of producing transnational histories is broadly accepted today, scholarly acceptance has not always led to scholarly practice. Writing the history of Baptists from primarily national perspectives remains the dominant model in the English-speaking world. This is a particularly important limitation for Baptists because the SBC has not only been aggressively involved in foreign missions since its founding but has been significantly influenced by its global footprint. Writing about the historiography of missions after World War II, Dana Robert noted a few decades ago that US historians were increasingly entering into collaborative projects with scholars from other parts of the world so that projects could move beyond the monolingual limitations that have historically characterized the discipline.[11] A few years later, Catherine Albanese identified the increasing importance of immigrant groups in the historiography of US religious history.[12] In addition, the growing attention to globalization in US religious history has become so evident in the last few decades that Benjamin Park's introduction to the *Wiley Companion to American*

Norton & Company, 2012); Axel R. Schäfer, *Piety and Public Funding: Evangelicals and the State in Modern America* (Philadelphia: University of Pennsylvania Press, 2012); Matthew Avery Sutton, *American Apocalypse: A History of Modern Evangelicalism* (Cambridge, MA: Belknap Press, 2014); Amanda Porterfield, *Corporate Spirit: Religion and the Rise of the Modern Corporation* (New York: Oxford University Press, 2018); Daniel Vaca, *Evangelicals Incorporated: Books and the Business of Religion in America* (Cambridge, MA: Harvard University Press, 2019); Darren Dochuk, *Anointed with Oil: How Christianity and Crude Made Modern America* (New York: Basic Books, 2019).

11. Dana L. Robert, "From Missions to Missions to Beyond Missions: The Historiography of American Protestant Foreign Missions Since World War II," in *New Directions in American Religious History*, ed. Harry S. Stout and D. G. Hart (New York: Oxford University Press, 1997), 362–93.

12. Catherine L. Albanese, *American Religious History: A Bibliographical Essay*, Currents in American Scholarship Series (Washington, DC: US Department of State, 2002).

Religious History begins by emphasizing not only how the US has affected the religious history of other nations but how other nations have also shaped the contemporary religiosity of US populations, White and otherwise.[13] Yet, Baptist historiography published in English largely lacks transnational approaches that take into serious consideration sources in languages other than English or events that happened outside the US-UK axis.[14] When historians of Baptists in the US and the UK give their renditions of global or transnational Baptist history, they often rely on a limited selection of sources and methods and treat the denomination's global history from an almost exclusively US or British point of view.

A few examples may suffice in illustrating the point. William Brackney's *Baptists in North America* practically ignores Baptists outside the United States and Canada and therefore overlooks the rich history of Baptists in countries whose language may not be English but still qualify as North American, such as Mexico and Puerto Rico.[15] Standard works, such as David Bebbington's *Baptists through the Centuries*, Robert E. Johnson's *A Global Introduction to Baptist Churches*, and Anthony Chute, Nathan Finn, and Michael Haykin's *The Baptist Story*, offer better accounts of Baptists outside Anglophone boundaries, but more approaches from a transnational perspective are needed.[16] The story of Antônia Teixeira as told here uses such a lens. It offers a methodological and historiographical model for collaborative work in which scholars from the two different worlds

13. Benjamin E. Park, "The Centrality, Diversity, and Malleability of American Religion," in *A Companion to American Religious History*, ed. Benjamin E. Park (Newark, NJ: John Wiley & Sons, 2021), 1–6.

14. For other examples that emphasize the importance of transnational studies, see Derek Chang, *Citizens of a Christian Nation: Evangelical Missions and the Problem of Race in the Nineteenth Century* (Philadelphia: University of Pennsylvania Press, 2010); Janel Kragt Bakker, *Sister Churches: American Congregations and Their Partners Abroad* (New York: Oxford University Press, 2014); David A. Hollinger, *Protestants Abroad: How Missionaries Tried to Change the World but Changed America*, illustrated ed. (Princeton: Princeton University Press, 2017); Melani McAlister, *The Kingdom of God Has No Borders: A Global History of American Evangelicals* (New York: Oxford University Press, 2018).

15. William H. Brackney, *Baptists in North America: An Historical Perspective* (Oxford: Blackwell Publishing, 2006).

16. David Bebbington, *Baptists through the Centuries: A History of a Global People*, 2nd ed. (Waco, TX: Baylor University Press, 2018); Robert E. Johnson, *A Global Introduction to Baptist Churches*, Introduction to Religion (New York: Cambridge University Press, 2010); Anthony L. Chute, Nathan A. Finn, and Michael A. G. Haykin, *The Baptist Story: From English Sect to Global Movement* (Nashville: B&H Academic, 2015).

involved—the United States and Brazil—partner to draw on each other's bibliographical bases, linguistic strengths, and ways of knowing. In turn, because the story told here has value for both the nations involved, this book is designed to be released in both English and Portuguese. In short, we hope that this project, beyond the value of the narrative it transmits, may model a way of writing history not commonly seen in US or Brazilian Baptist historiography.

A Road Map

In light of its complex and transnational nature, Antônia Teixeira's story will be told in two main parts. In part 1, we outline the fascinating set of events that culminated in Antônia's transit to Waco, Texas. Beyond her own significance, Antônia was the daughter of a popular and controversial ex-priest who was also Brazil's first native-born Baptist pastor. By the time Antônia arrived in Waco, her deceased father had already become one of the SBC's most significant agents in Brazil. The Baptist mission in Brazil was organized by exiles from the failed Confederacy, and it was immensely aided by the accession to its cause of Antônio Teixeira de Albuquerque. From his side, already a renowned and controversial figure at that moment, Antônio's Baptist ministry provided a space for a new career and the continued growth of his public persona. All this went into the effort of the Southern Baptist missionary Zachary C. Taylor, Antônio's former co-worker, to bring Antônia to Texas after her father's death. Antônio's significance to the Southern Baptist missionary legacy helps explain why there was so much effort to purge Antônia's story from the denominational record lest it taint the narrative that missionaries told their US audience about the Brazil mission.

Part 2 will focus on the rape of Antônia Teixeira and its aftermath. Her preliminary hearing and jury trial presented spectacular twists and turns that will be recounted in detail. In addition, the public war of words between Baylor University President Rufus C. Burleson and the controversial local journalist William Cowper Brann—nicknamed "The Apostle of the Devil"—reveals the public and polemical import of these episodes. Thus, while the story of Antônia's rape, and Antônia herself, were eventually forgotten, the legacies of the individuals and institutions that played major roles in her fate were not only remembered but celebrated. These celebrations need critical commentary in their own right, especially in light of Antônia's expungement.

Part 1 begins by offering an account of the missionary enterprise that lies behind Antônia's story. Chapter 1 focuses on the first decades of SBC missions in Brazil, featuring a missionary being accused of trying to organize a slave insurrection, Confederate exiles who went to Brazil to recreate the old South after the US Civil War, and missionaries who brought to Brazil the White-supremacist anxieties of Jim Crow society common in the US South. The story then picks up locals, such as Antônio Teixeira de Albuquerque, who chose to link up with Baptist missionaries and eventually partner with them in a transnational, expansionist project. In light of Antônio's centrality to this story, chapter 1 reviews how he was memorialized by Brazilian and US historians who romanticized and capitalized on what he came to represent—to the Baptist mission in particular and to Brazilian Protestantism in general. This chapter thus breaks new ground by providing an assessment of how Antônio Teixeira's story was constructed and deployed in Brazilian Baptist historiography.

Chapters 2 and 3 build on scholars both in Brazil and in the United States who are revisiting the origins of the missionary presence in the country in order to better understand the development of Brazilian national identity, on the one hand, and the development of the religious Right across the borders of the United States and Brazil, on the other.[17] The history of Antônio Teixeira de Albuquerque has been revisited in this light by Brazilian historians who have produced new studies of this iconic figure.[18] Yet such histories contain

17. For a few recent titles, see Erika Helgen, *Religious Conflict in Brazil: Protestants, Catholics, and the Rise of Religious Pluralism in the Early Twentieth Century* (New Haven, CT: Yale University Press, 2020); Benjamin A. Cowan, *Moral Majorities Across the Americas: Brazil, the United States, and the Creation of the Religious Right* (Chapel Hill: University of North Carolina Press, 2021); Anthony D'Andrea, *Reflexive Religion: The New Age in Brazil and Beyond* (Leiden: Brill, 2018); Martijn Oosterbaan, *Transmitting the Spirit: Religious Conversion, Media, and Urban Violence in Brazil*, 1st ed. (University Park: Penn State University Press, 2019); Amy Erica Smith, *Religion and Brazilian Democracy: Mobilizing the People of God* (Cambridge: Cambridge University Press, 2019); Eric Miller and Ronald J. Morgan, eds., *Brazilian Evangelicalism in the Twenty-First Century: An Inside and Outside Look*, Christianity and Renewal—Interdisciplinary Studies (Cham, Switzerland: Palgrave Macmillan, 2019).

18. For examples of recent treatments of Teixeira de Albuquerque's history, see Josemar Valdir Modes, "Antonio Teixeira de Albuquerque: O Ex-Padre Facilitador e Potencializador das Capacidades de Bagby e Taylor," *Revista Via Teológica* 20, no. 39 (July 2019): 15–35; Pedro Henrique Alves, "Primórdios Batistas no Brasil: Abertura de Igrejas e Formação da Equipe Missionária (1881–1886)," *Mosaico* 12, no. 18 (2020): 162–83; Jovesi de Almeida Costa, *O Evangelho Chega à Terra de Alagoas: Primeira Igreja Evangélica Batista de Maceió* (Maceió: Poligraf, 2017).

major gaps that this book will begin to fill. First, Brazilian historiography on Protestant beginnings has rarely engaged with both sides of the Protestant-Catholic polemics that infused Antônio's life and writings. Second, Antônio Teixeira's national and international impact, as well as his life beyond his role in Baptist beginnings, have been either overlooked or distorted by historians of various persuasions. These two chapters take up these issues; in addition, they provide a fresh account of the man and his family's complex relationship with US missionaries.

Antônia herself enters the picture here. As well-known as her father is, she remains largely unknown in Brazil. While some of her siblings' names have been recorded in connection with their father, Antônia is at best known as "the first born," and her journey to the US South is not recorded at all. Yet Antônio Teixeira's centrality in Brazilian Protestantism underscores the importance of Antônia's story—for religious history in Brazil and for the history of SBC missions there. Chapter 4 closes part 1 of the book by recounting Antônia's voyage to Waco, Texas. After the death of her father, the financial difficulties of the Teixeira family prompted SBC missionaries Kate and Zachary C. Taylor to step in and bring Antônia to study at Baylor University. The Taylors themselves had decided to return to the States for treatment for Kate Taylor's declining health, and their connection to Baylor University helped provide an opportunity for Antônia to study there. But to turn the Old Testament story of Joseph and his brothers on its head, what may have been meant as a blessing to Antônia soon turned into a nightmare.

Chapters 5 through 8 constitute the second part of the book, relating in detail the story of Antônia Teixeira's serial assaults in Waco and their scandalous aftermath. Eminent figures from various domains enter in at this point, including Baylor's president at the time, Rufus Burleson; the controversial journalist William Cowper Brann; and the alleged rapist, Steen Morris. Their connection with Antônia's story casts aspects of their own stories in a new and likely discomfiting light. Chapter 5 narrates Antônia's assaults and the preliminary hearing of the alleged rapist, Steen Morris, a relative of Rufus Burleson. Chapter 6 tells the story of how two local giants—W. C. Brann and Rufus Burleson—clashed via conflicting accounts of Antônia's rape and its meaning, with direct consequences for Burleson's career. Chapter 7 covers the jury trial. Together, these chapters offer a detailed look at one of the great sex scandals in Waco's history and at how Antônia was not only assaulted physically but oppressed, shamed, and discredited by the most powerful people in town. Then she was deliberately and thoroughly erased.

By contrast, chapter 8 details how other major players in this saga were memorialized. Rufus C. Burleson, Zachary C. Taylor, and other leaders in SBC missions and educational enterprises have been celebrated for decades—a celebration dependent on the active expungement of records such as Antônia's. Such episodes have involved, beyond sexual scandals, illegal activity, unethical behavior, and immoral convictions on the part of Christian leaders and missionaries. This chapter confirms the impression that D. L. Hamilton, a Southern Baptist missionary to Brazil, once shared with his mother about his colleagues: "It is not well for everybody to know this, but it is a fact that foreign missionaries have no wings."[19]

Indeed, this book demonstrates that heroes celebrated in traditional religious accounts are very often no angels. It outlines the broader conceptual and practical lessons to be learned from the history of Antônia's rape and its aftermath. *Remembering Antônia Teixeira: A Story of Missions, Violence, and Institutional Hypocrisy* challenges us to go beyond condemning or criticizing individual players in her story and to consider the narratives of institutional goodness constructed from the images of false heroes who serve as proxies for institutional and collective legacies. As the epilogue reflects on the particular institutional legacies into which our own history as authors is grafted, it becomes clear that *Remembering Antônia Teixeira* is not a "neutral" project of scholarship, if any such thing exists. Rather, it stands as another installment in a lifelong process of individual self-reflection toward communal awareness. The history in this book is not designed, and is unlikely, to make the reader feel good, no matter whom you love or what you hate. It has a more important goal than that.

19. D. L. Hamilton to Lydia Hamilton, January 24, 1908, IMB Archives. Unless otherwise noted, all correspondence of Southern Baptist missionaries is available in the IMB Archives in Richmond, Virginia.

Part 1

Transnational Context

1

Brazilian Baptist Memorialization:
The Myths about Antônio Teixeira de Albuquerque

The Brazilian Baptist Convention (BBC) is today one of the most successful examples of Southern Baptist missions in the world. Out of the over 240 Baptist conventions on the Baptist World Alliance list of members, the BBC is one of the largest—and *the* largest outside the United States and Africa. The BBC includes almost ten thousand churches and is approaching two million members. The denomination also has theological seminaries, national and transnational mission boards, educational associations, and numerous social initiatives across the world. Beyond such quantitative measures, the convention has played a role in shaping Brazilian national identity, racial imagination, religious dynamics, and political trajectory—sometimes via missionary interventions, sometimes via Baptists elected to political office.[1] This grand journey, however, began in a Southern Baptist dream that dawned in a group of disgruntled exiles from the failed Confederacy. They would be aided by a Brazilian ex-priest, Antônio Teixeira de Albuquerque.

Antônio Teixeira came into a particular missionary context and gave rise to particular ways of memorialization both in Brazil and the United States. Thus, before retelling the story of Antônia and her family in Brazil, we need to provide a picture of the broader missionary enterprise into which her father was incorporated and gauge the role that his particular memorialization played

---

1. For more on the BBC and its relation to the SBC, see João B. Chaves, *The Global Mission of the Jim Crow South: Southern Baptist Missionaries and the Shaping of Latin American Evangelicalism* (Macon, GA: Mercer University Press, 2022); Benjamin A. Cowan, *Moral Majorities across the Americas: Brazil, the United States, and the Creation of the Religious Right* (Chapel Hill: University of North Carolina Press, 2021).

for missionaries and Brazilians alike. Then the next two chapters will flesh out the story of the Teixeira family with aspects that both missionaries and locals chose to conceal.

Antônio Teixeira was more important for Brazilian Protestantism than the picture that SBC missionaries created of him. His towering historical presence and his place in the construction of SBC missionary memory were crucial for the triumphalist transnational history Baptists composed on both sides of the border. For those purposes, however, the full story of his journey had to be heavily edited by locals and missionaries alike. Both parties understood well the problems that would arise if the potentially problematic aspects of Antônio Teixeira's story made it into official denominational histories. SBC missionaries were committed to a story of their Brazilian success and therefore shaped Antônio Teixeira and his family to fit the strategies they had for the country and their careers.

Brazil Enters the SBC Missionary Mind

The SBC mission in Brazil began with disgruntled Confederate immigrants who arrived in Brazil after 1865, their egos and finances destroyed by their loss in the US Civil War. But Brazil had been pondered as a potential SBC mission field already in 1850, just five years after the denomination's founding.[2] The following year the SBC annual convention cast favorable resolutions to that end.[3] The missionary periodical *The Commission* added a twist to that sentiment. The anonymous article, while framing South America negatively as "one of the strongholds of popery," thought it would nonetheless make sense to invest in a missionary enterprise there because of geographical proximity, US commercial interest, and Southern Baptist acquaintance with the Spanish language, which, the author claimed, "is generally spoken here."[4] Though Brazil did not qualify on the latter count, its place in the market for Black flesh was not lost on the author.

---

2. "Board of Domestic Missions: From Our Missionaries," *Southern Baptist Missionary Journal* 4, no. 12 (May 1850): 310.

3. Annals of the Southern Baptist Convention (1851), 11. Unless otherwise noted, all sources from the Foreign Mission Board can be found in their digital archives at: https://www.imb.org /research/archives/.

4. "Missions to South America," *The Commission* 3, no. 5 (May 1851): 1.

In 1855, Thomas Bowen—then a missionary in Nigeria but later the first SBC missionary to Brazil—viewed the matter from a different angle, that of the devastation caused among Yoruba-speaking peoples by the slave trade. In a report to *Home and Foreign Fields*, Bowen wrote:

> I have counted eighteen sites of depopulated towns in a journey of sixty miles. That district is now a desert, or rather a huge forest. Most of the towns visited by the Landers are now in ruins, including Awyow (Katunga or Eyeo) the capital. The slave trade has done this. Vast numbers of Yorubas have been exported, and vast numbers have perished in the battle and siege. Many are now in Brazil, Cuba, Sierra Leone, & etc. . . . Sometimes they purchase their freedom in America and come home.[5]

Yet when Brazil was mentioned as a potential mission field at the Foreign Mission Board (FMB) national meeting in 1859, its role as a slaveholding country counted as an advantage. From then on, the differences between the Brazilian and the US forms of White supremacy would inform the ambiguity with which SBC missionaries saw the country and its inhabitants. Brazil was deemed a country with great natural resources but a population lacking in character, quite manifest in its saturation with "popery." Yet slavery was celebrated as a hopeful ground of White transnational solidarity.

The 1859 report that took Brazil's slaveholding status as positive was drafted by the Committee on New Foreign Fields, which included such influential SBC leaders as J. B. Jeter, J. M. Pendleton, J. E. Dawson, and William C. Crane. Crane would become president of Baylor University from 1864 to 1885 and would develop a close relationship with the eventual founder of the first Baptist church in Brazil, Richard Ratcliff, before Ratcliff even considered going to South America.[6] The 1859 report forthrightly combined principle and pragmatism:

---

5. Thomas J. Bowen, "Yoruba-Central Africa: Letter from Rev. T. J. Bowen," *Home and Foreign Fields* 4, no. 10 (April 1855): 39.

6. For an example, see the transcribed letter that Ratcliff sent to Crane while the former was en route to Brazil in Betty Antunes de Oliveira, *Centelha em Restolho Seco: Uma Contribuição para a História dos Primórdios do Trabalho Batista no Brasil*, 2nd ed. (São Paulo: Edições Vida Nova, 2005), 152.

Brazil is, like our own, a slaveholding country. No missionary can go thither, from any portion of the Christian world but this—who would not probably feel himself called on, either by his own feelings, or by the demands of the public at home who sent him, to broach this vexed question—and to war, either openly or covertly, with the domestic institutions of the land. A missionary from the southern states of America would be free, at least, from this liability to embarrassment. He would have nothing to preach to them but the gospel of Jesus Christ—and need not commence by laying a foundation either of practical or theoretical abolitionism.[7]

Even though *The Commission* announced that a missionary had been appointed to Brazil in March 1859, FMB officials continued to treat the matter as prospective.[8] Rev. Dr. Abraham Mayer Poindexter, who held a number of important positions in the SBC, including assistant secretary of the FMB, solicited letters about Brazil's potential as a missionary field from acquaintances who lived there.[9] In such letters, which were also published in *The Commission*, a correspondent who went by the pseudonym Theophilus predicted that Brazil would quickly become "the most enviable portion of the New World."[10] Brazilians were generally cheerful, if prone to drunkenness and irresponsibility, and superstitious because of Roman Catholic influence.[11] Happily, Theophilus also espied Rome's key strategic weaknesses there: a lack of priests, disunity, and growing inability to recruit and educate clergy. He assured readers of *The Commission*: "Surely, in no country in Christendom is there a greater demand for an efficient and evangelical ministry. Let a Baptist church be once constituted here, 'and the streams that make glad the city of God, will flow forth.'"[12] Others joined in the chorus for an SBC mission to save Brazilians from Ro-

7. Foreign Mission Board, *Foreign Mission Board Report*, May 6, 1859.

8. "New Missionaries Under Appointment," *The Commission* 3, no. 9 (March 1859): 286.

9. For more on Poindexter, see Archibald Thomas Robertson, *Life and Letters of John Albert Broadus* (Philadelphia: American Baptist Publication Society, 1910), 52–53; William Cathcart, *The Baptist Encyclopædia* (Philadelphia: L. H. Everts, 1881), 923–24.

10. Theophilus, "Brazil as a Missionary Field: No 3," *The Commission* 4, no. 4 (October 1859): 102.

11. Theophilus, "Brazil as a Missionary Field: No 1," *The Commission* 4, no. 1 (July 1859): 10–12; Theophilus, "Brazil as a Missionary Field: No 2," *The Commission* 4, no. 2 (August 1859): 39–40; Theophilus, "Brazil as a Missionary Field: No 3."

12. Theophilus, "Brazil as a Missionary Field: No 2," 39.

man Catholic oppression, including the rising denominational statesman and educator Basil Manly Jr.[13]

It was in this context that in November 1859 *The Commission* mentioned Thomas Bowen as a missionary to Brazil, even though his credentials were suspect. For one, Bowen clearly wished to go back to his mission to the "Yoruba people," particularly in support of the Abbeokuta who fought for the abolition of the slave trade.[14] The Brazilian historian Alverson de Souza argues that such defiance of denominational policy and practice, not ill health as alleged by the SBC, constituted the real reason that Bowen was kept from returning to Nigeria.[15] Bowen would eventually try to be a missionary both to Brazil and to the Yoruba, a possibility raised by Brazil's outsized investment in the slave trade. Brazil received around 5 million of the 12.5 million Black bodies shipped to the Americas, making it second only to Bowen's Nigeria as the country with the most Black people in the world.[16] For the moment, however, still mourning his inability to return to Nigeria, Bowen sailed to Brazil, arriving in the country for a short, controversial stay in May 1860.[17] He immediately faced suspicion for preaching to slaves in fluent Yoruba, which led authorities to suspect he was an abolitionist trying to start a slave rebellion. He also did not receive appropriate financial support from the FMB. Thus, after little more than eight months, Bowen and his family returned to the United States—again, supposedly for reasons of health, even though Bowen lived on for another fifteen years. There are strong indicators that his dissension from the slaveholding commitments of the SBC was the main reason for his lack of support.[18]

Soon after Bowen's return to the United States, the Civil War began, draining the SBC's financial resources and keeping it from investing further in a Brazilian mission. Paradoxically, the Confederacy's eventual loss rekindled the dream. In light of the failure of their political rebellion as well as Recon-

---

13. Basil Manly Jr., "Is Brazil Missionary Ground?," *Home and Foreign Journal* 8, no. 10 (April 1859): 39.

14. "Brazil Mission," *The Commission* 4, no. 5 (November 1859): 148.

15. Alverson de Souza, *Thomas Bowen: O Primeiro Missionário Batista no Brasil* (Brasília: Novos Diálogos, 2012), 18–24.

16. Laurentino Gomes, *Escravidão*, vol. 1, *Do Primeiro Leilão de Cativos em Portugal até a Morte de Zumbi dos Palmares* (Rio de Janeiro: Globo Livros, 2019), 23–24.

17. "The Year of 1860," *The Commission* 4, no. 7 (January 1860): 217–18; "The Brazil Mission," *The Commission* 4, no. 8 (February 1860): 249; Souza, *Thomas Bowen*, 28.

18. Souza, *Thomas Bowen*, 25–41.

struction's gestures towards racial equality, some White Baptist brethren of the South despaired of the United States' future. Ironically, they could have soon counted on the help of a Northern majority that agreed that the South had been "reconstructed" too fast and followed its own forms of White supremacist commitments. For its part, Brazilian imperial policy did encourage immigration from the defeated South but did so partially as a response to the numerous inquiries made by Southerners themselves.[19] Among the eight to ten thousand Southern families who went to Latin America following the Civil War, about four thousand emigrated to Brazil.[20]

Brazil's continuing commitment to slavery (it did not abolish the institution until 1888, twenty-three years after the end of the Civil War) provided a strong motivation for this move, but at the same time the complexity of Brazil's multiracial context presented a challenge to the social imagination of these former Confederates. They were often shocked by the relative freedom Brazil's dominant groups granted to free Blacks as well as by the perceived leniency Brazilian slaveholders showed their slaves.[21] Thus, the erstwhile Confederates, whether Baptists, Presbyterians, or Methodists, at times adapted to their new country by segregating themselves into distinct enclaves with stark racial-ethnic boundaries.[22] It was in one such enclave, Santa Bárbara D'Oeste,

---

19. For a longer treatment on this topic, see Chaves, *Global Mission*. Célio Silva studied Yankee and Confederate immigration to Brazil by way of the letters sent by Americans who wanted to go to Brazil after the Civil War. See Célio Antonio Alcantara Silva, "Confederates and Yankees under the Southern Cross," *Bulletin of Latin American Research* 34, no. 3 (2015): 370–84.

20. Silva, "Confederate and Yankees," 370–84; Judith Mac Jones, *Soldado Descansa! Uma Epopéia Norte-Americana sob os Céus do Brasil* (São Paulo: Fraternidade Descendência Americana, 1998); Laura Jarnagin, *A Confluence of Transatlantic Networks: Elites, Capitalism and Confederate Immigration to Brazil* (Tuscaloosa: University of Alabama Press, 2008), 25–27; Cyrus B. Dawsey and James M. Dawsey, "Leaving: The Context of Southern Emigration to Brazil," in *The Confederados: Old South Immigrants in Brazil*, ed. Cyrus B. Dawsey and James M. Dawsey (Tuscaloosa: University of Alabama Press, 1998), 18–19.

21. José Carlos Barbosa, *Slavery and Protestant Missions in Imperial Brazil: "The Black Does Not Enter the Church, He Peeks in from Outside,"* trans. Fraser G. MacHaffie and Richard K. Danford (Lanham, MD: University Press of America, 2008), 4–6.

22. There is some debate about the role of slavery as a motive for Southern migration to Brazil. Eugene Harter, Judith Jones, Frank Goldman, and Ana de Oliveira downplay the importance of the possibility of purchasing slaves in Southern immigrants' decision to migrate, suggesting that the relatively low number of slaves purchased by Confederate exiles demonstrated either their lack of interest or lack of purchasing power. See Eugene Harter, *The Lost Colony of the Confederacy* (College Station: Texas A&M University Press, 2006); Jones, *Soldado Descansa! Uma Epopéia Norte-*

that the SBC began its permanent mission, opening a new journey in a strange new land.[23]

The first Baptist church in Brazil was founded within a cohesive community of US citizens who wanted to re-create the old South there. Its first pastor was Richard Ratcliff, who had served in the Confederate Mindem Rangers during the Civil War and who, fittingly enough, had been converted in a sermon preached by Thomas Bowen several years earlier. Like his father in the faith, Ratcliff had originally been appointed missionary to Africa in 1860, another post foreclosed by the US Civil War. Ratcliff received strong support and preparation for the job from William C. Crane, thus forging an early connection between the Brazilian mission and Baylor University.[24] Crane had moved to Texas from northern Louisiana in 1863, after the Confederate army began using Mount Lebanon University—for which he was serving as president—as a hospital.[25] The next year he was named president of Baylor University and served in that office until his death in 1885. Present at the creation of the SBC's Brazilian mission, Baylor only became more involved over the years via the training of students who went on to Brazil as missionaries, the training of Brazilian students who became influential voices in that country in and beyond Baptist circles, the appointment of former missionaries to Brazil as professors at the university, and the keen interest in Brazil shown by Baylor graduates even though they never served as missionaries there.

Americana sob os Céus do Brasil; Frank Goldman, *Os Pioneiros Americanos no Brasil: Educadores, Sacerdotes, Covos e Reis* (São Paulo: Pioneira, 1972); Ana Maria Costa de Oliveira, *O Destino (Não) Manifesto: Os Imigrantes Norte-Americanos no Brasil* (São Paulo: União Cultural Brasil-Estados Unidos, 1995). More recent research, however, indicates that the possibility of perpetuating the Southern lifestyle through slavery or, in the case of poor White Southerners, the possibility of acquiring slaves in Brazil were major factors in the Southern migration to Brazil. Gerald Horne, *The Deepest South: The United States, Brazil, and the African Slave Trade* (New York: NYU Press, 2007); Célio Antonio Alcantara Silva, "Capitalismo e Escravidão: A Imigração Confederada para o Brasil" (PhD diss., Universidade Estadual de Campinas, 2011); Silva, "Confederates and Yankees." On the issue of former Confederates' stance on Brazilian miscegenation, see Silva, "Confederates and Yankees," 379; and Charles Willis Simmons, "Racist Americans in a Multi-Racial Society: Confederate Exiles in Brazil," *The Journal of Negro History* 67, no. 1 (1982): 35–37.

23. See Oliveira, *Centelha em Restolho Seco*, 148. Oliveira gathered a wealth of primary sources in this volume, in which she also traces short biographies of US and Brazilian Baptists, focusing primarily on the Confederate colonies that served as the beating heart of Baptist beginnings in Brazil.

24. Oliveira, *Centelha em Restolho Seco*, 144–52.

25. For more on William C. Crane, see Cathcart, *The Baptist Encyclopædia*, 289–90.

Ratcliff returned to the United States in 1879. Rev. E. H. Quillin, another disgruntled Confederate who had migrated with his whole family to Brazil soon after the Civil War ended, would then become a major representative of the SBC in Brazil. He was appointed missionary by the FMB and actively recruited other heartbroken Southerners to join him.[26] It was during Quillin's ministry that Antônio Teixeira de Albuquerque's journey intersected with the Baptists'. He began working and ministering among his Confederate hosts in the state of São Paulo in June 1880, before the arrival of the missionaries who would be credited with laying the foundations for the long-term success of the SBC mission in Brazil: William and Anne Bagby and Z. C. and Kate Taylor.[27] These parties would help build the legend of Antônio Teixeira as an ex-priest, missionary assistant, and first Brazilian-born Baptist pastor in the nation. In reality, he was a much more accomplished, complicated, and controversial figure.

Race, Evangelism, and Institutional Foundations

Antônio Teixeira's connection to the SBC's Brazilian mission began indirectly in March 1881, when William and Anne Bagby arrived as Baptist missionary appointees.[28] That November, William Bagby was introduced to Teixeira with the help of a Confederate-exile translator. Then, in March 1882, Z. C. and Kate Taylor joined the Bagbys in the city of Campinas, São Paulo. To accelerate their acquisition of Portuguese, the two men decided to recruit Antônio as a language instructor.[29] Yet for the next six years, until his death in 1887, he functioned as much more than that: he was a translator, language instructor, missionary, preacher, church planter, anti-Catholic polemicist, Bible salesman, and symbol of Protestantism's alleged superiority to the Roman Catholic competition. Thus he became important for Brazilian religious life well beyond Baptist concerns.

26. William Clark Griggs, *The Elusive Eden: Frank McMullan's Confederate Colony in Brazil* (Austin: University of Texas Press, 1987), 37.

27. A letter written by E. H. Quillin dated June 1880 was forwarded on July 12, 1880, by the clerk of the Baptist Church in Santa Barbara to Dr. Henry Tupper, executive secretary of the Foreign Mission Board. The original letter is reproduced in Oliveira, *Antônio Teixeira*, 77, appendix 2.

28. Anne Bagby diary, folder 20, Luther Bagby Collection, Texas Collection, Baylor University.

29. Bagby and Taylor to H. A. Tupper, March 27, 1882, IMB Archives; Kate Taylor diary, March 22, 1882, Taylor materials, Texas Collection, Baylor University. Bagby penned the section regarding Teixeira.

All that said, his success and that of the Brazilian ministers and missionaries who followed in his footsteps was not enough to overcome Southern condescension. The racial imagination of Southern missionaries persisted for decades, as amply manifested in missionary correspondence and articles published in English and Portuguese. From William and Anne Bagby's casual dependence on slave labor to carry their luggage upon arrival in Brazil to the missionaries' resistance to granting locals the right to lead the denomination, there were few surprises regarding how White southerners saw themselves, their new Brazilian context, and the locals they sought to proselytize, Americanize, and civilize. Missionaries' racial imagination was foundational to their modus operandi in Brazil, shaping the core of their behavior and denominational structures. For now, it affected Antônio Teixeira's ministry in Brazil; in the future, it predicted the way his daughter Antônia would be treated in Texas. The Southern Baptist mission in Brazil was simply saturated with notions of White superiority and US nationalism.

The correspondence and publications of pioneering missionaries show an immediate consequence of this disposition—the deeply racialized ways in which, to quote Edward Said, they "clarified, reinforced, criticized, or rejected" notions about Brazilian culture.[30] For example, the pioneering William Bagby, writing to *Foreign Business Journal*, gave this profile of Brazilians at the very same time that he was asking Antônio Teixeira for language instruction:

> In the vast region I have been describing, there is a population of 12,000,000 souls. Of these millions, the majority are of Portuguese descent, and speak that language. Besides these, there are many Indians in the far interior, untaught, and uncivilized, and living in a manner even more rude and animal-like, perhaps than our North American Indians. The negros form a large portion of inhabitants of the country, of whom some are slaves and some are freemen. The races are very much mixed, and all shades of color are daily seen in any of these cities, from coal black, up though brown and olive, to

---

30. Edward W. Said, *Culture and Imperialism* (New York: Knopf, 1993), 9. For more on this topic as it relates to Southern Baptist–missionary racial imagination, see João B. Chaves, "Expanding the Fear of the Mongrel: Baptist Missions in Latin America and Transnational Racist Cross-Pollination," *Baptist History and Heritage* 54, no. 2 (2019): 81–91.

mulatto, and yellow, and white. Of course, where such unnatural unions exist, all kinds of deformities appear and many hereditary diseases are known.[31]

The "miscegenation" (broadly practiced in Brazil) which Bagby here underscored was likewise condemned by his employer Henry Allen Tupper, who served as corresponding secretary of the FMB from 1871 to 1893 and helped infuse institutional White supremacy in the FMB.[32] He had fought for it in the Civil War, serving as a chaplain of the Ninth Georgia Infantry and thereafter avidly promoted Lost Cause mythology and Anglo-Saxon superiority.[33]

The same attitude appeared in the booklet *Missionary Catechism on Brazil*, published after Antônio Teixeira's death and prepared by the Bagbys, the Taylors, and another missionary couple, the J. A. Bakers, to acquaint other missionaries with the Brazilian context: "Q: Describe the inhabitants of Brazil. A: Brazil is inhabited by whites, blacks, and Indians. The Brazilians are chiefly descendants of the Portuguese. The negroes number several millions, and the majority of them were slaves until May 13, 1888. The Indians are found in the forests of the great interior, and many of them are cannibals. The true white Brazilians are the dominant race. They are intelligent, progressive people, emotional, nervous and impulsive."[34] Blacks by contrast suffered from backwardness and lack of vision. As Taylor would put it in his unpublished autobiography: "The negro in Brazil, as everywhere, lives for the present as the Chinese live in the past and the Caucasian for the future." Still, Brazilian

---

31. W. B. Bagby, "Brother Bagby on Brazil and Its People," *FMJ* 13, no. 12 (1882): 3.

32. Robert Norman Nash Jr., "The Influence of American Myth on Southern Baptist Foreign Missions, 1845–1945" (PhD diss., The Southern Baptist Theological Seminary, 1989); Adrian Lamkin Jr., "The Gospel Mission Movement within the Southern Baptist Convention" (PhD diss., The Southern Baptist Theological Seminary, 1979); Bill Leonard, *Baptist Ways: A History* (Valley Forge, PA: Judson Press, 2003). Nash's and Lamkin's are compelling studies that show how deeply the SBC was commited to the Southern cause during the Civil War and to the Lost Cause after the South was defeated. According to Bill Leonard, "in the search for ways to cope with defeat, Southern Baptists and other Southern Protestants looked to the 'religion of the Lost Cause'—the idealization of the South's culture and religion. Defeated politically, the South turned to the cultural superiority of its mythic past." See Leonard, *Baptist Ways*, 204.

33. See John Wesley Brinsfield Jr., *The Spirit Divided: Memoirs of Civil War Chaplains* (Macon, GA: Mercer University Press, 2006), 12; H. Allen Tupper, *Armenia: Its Present Crisis and Past History* (New York: John Murphy & Company, 1896); and Nash, "Influence of American Myth," 95.

34. W. B. Bagby et al., *Missionary Catechism on Brazil* (Baltimore: Maryland Baptist Mission Rooms, 1889), 4.

Whites, such as Antônio Teixeira de Albuquerque, did not rate as fully equal, being "emotional, nervous and impulsive."[35]

In the same year that the *Catechism* came out, the FMB published a volume by William Bagby that went into further detail on the matter. The locals' "moral condition is fearfully dark and sad," he wrote. "Educated in worldliness, frivolity and sin, children grow up to manhood and womanhood with ideas utterly at variance with all Christian morals and live stained by constant indulgence of every sinful passion and desire. Purity is entirely unknown among men, while among women ideas of propriety and morality are far below the Bible standard."[36] Moreover, Brazilians—especially the Roman Catholics among them—were almost invariably liars. Bagby's conclusion? "How sad and terrible is their condition of ignorance, sin and wretchedness!"[37]

This racialized sense of Southern superiority would continue to appear consistently and broadly in missionary publications and correspondence up to the second half of the twentieth century. In Brazil, SBC missionaries, such as W. E. Entzminger, A. R. Crabtree, Rosalee Mills Appleby, and others, would carry on the pioneers' notions of the country's inhabitants.[38] The missionaries' standard cure for this condition was conversion to Protestantism and racialized reordering of sociocultural norms. White Brazilians such as Antônio Teixeira de Albuquerque worked from some advantage on this score but still had a long path to climb to reach the missionaries' ideal.

Institutionally, the Brazil mission overcame initial challenges and thrived between the Bagbys' arrival in 1881 and 1892, the year Z. C. Taylor took Antônia Teixeira to Waco. Pioneering missionaries learned the language, helped develop material to introduce future missionaries to Brazil and Brazilians, recruited locals to help lead the work, started churches, sold Bibles, developed mechanisms of anti-Catholic polemic, and strengthened connections with a number of local leaders and politicians.[39] They laid the foundations for the

---

35. Zachary Clay Taylor, "The Rise and Progress of Baptist Missions in Brazil: An Autobiography" (unpublished manuscript), 48.

36. W. B. Bagby, *Brazil and the Brazilians* (Baltimore: Maryland Baptist Mission Rooms, 1889), 9–10.

37. Bagby, *Brazil and the Brazilians*, 9–10.

38. See João B. Chaves, *O Racismo na História Batista Brasileira* (Brasília: Novos Diálogos, 2021).

39. For more on these dynamics, see H. B. Cavalcanti, "Southern Baptists Abroad: Sharing the

later success of the Brazilian Baptist Convention (BBC), which followed a pattern of development parallel to that of the Baptists on the US frontier, the organization of "churches, associations, schools, colleges, seminaries, and a convention in Brazil."[40]

First, several mission outposts were created—in Bahia (1882), Rio de Janeiro (1884), Alagoas (1885), Pernambuco (1896), Amazonas (1897), and Piauí (1903). When the number of churches in a particular area reached a certain level, missionaries organized them into a cooperative association, such as those in Rio de Janeiro in 1894, in the northeast in 1900, in São Paulo in 1904, and in the Amazon in 1906. The Brazilian Baptist Convention itself was created in 1907, after brief discussion about whether Brazilian workers or only missionaries were to be included in the national organization.[41] In 1908, the FMB divided the Brazilian field into the north and south. At the same time, the Brazilian Baptist Convention began to spread its influence internationally. The World Mission Board (WMB) of the Brazilian Baptist Convention established a missionary presence in Chile in 1908 and in Portugal in 1911—reverse mission came early in Brazilian Baptist life.[42] In terms of macro-organizational dynamics, therefore, Brazil followed the pattern established by Southern Baptists and had implemented the general contours of denominational organization by the end of the first decade of the twentieth century.[43] Antônio Teixeira de Albuquerque was a key figure in this foundational phase both via his work and by what he represented as an ex-priest. He was extremely important to Brazilian Baptists and is remembered as such.

Memories of Antônio Teixeira de Albuquerque: Missionary and Local

Baptist memory in Brazil, as in the United States, depended on mutual reinforcement between denominational publications and theological education. Books,

---

Faith in Nineteenth Century Brazil," *Baptist History and Heritage* 38, no. 2 (2003): 52–67; Alves, "Primórdios Batistas no Brasil"; Chaves, *O Racismo*.

40. Daniel Lancaster, *The Bagbys of Brazil: The Life and Work of William Buck and Ann Luther Bagby* (Austin: Eakin Press, 1999), xv.

41. Antônio Neves de Mesquita, *História dos Baptistas do Brasil*, vol. 2 (Rio de Janeiro: Casa Publicadora Baptista, 1940), 20–24.

42. Mesquita, *História*, 2:116–17.

43. For a longer analysis of these dynamics, see Chaves, *Global Mission*.

magazines, and pamphlets were so central in forming denominational identity that W. E. Entzminger, one of the leaders in this enterprise, let the FMB know that if they defunded publishing out of budgetary constraints, the whole missionary enterprise would be threatened. Writing the FMB secretary R. J. Willingham in 1909, when the board contemplated just that, Entzminger warned:

> At this juncture it appears that the question is not whether to have or not to have a printing plant, but whether or not it is worthwhile to have publications. And it would be easy to decide this question by deciding whether or not it is important, whether or not it is worthwhile, to continue the work of evangelizing in Brazil. If we should close up the enterprise, the publication enterprise, it would be because we should abandon the whole evangelization enterprise.[44]

The publishing enterprise continued, and it allowed Baptist missionaries to tell a story, their story, about Antônio Teixeira.

The published story, however, could diverge from the way that Teixeira was portrayed in the correspondence of the missionaries he worked with, especially the Bagbys and the Taylors; their private communications reveal real tensions with him. Nor did Roman Catholic polemics about this ex-priest and his reasons for leaving the church make it into the Baptists' public accounts. Yet, these accounts never questioned the importance of Antônio Teixeira for the mission even when his leadership was downgraded to that of adjunct or assistant status. Already in the first decades of their work in Brazil, Baptists routinely mentioned Antônio Teixeira whenever the story of their missions was told. Antônia's father was a symbol of Baptist triumph and of ministerial collaboration between missionaries and locals, a vital token in the saga of one of the most successful mission fields Southern Baptists ever had.

The construction of his memory began in denominational magazines both in Brazil and in the United States. Already in 1880, E. H. Quillin cast him for an American audience as an example of Protestant triumph over Roman Catholic dominance.[45] This theme endured well after Antônio's death, even as William Bagby and Zachary C. Taylor reduced him to the role of their capable helper in

---

44. W. E. Entzminger to R. J. Willingham, November 2, 1909, IMB Archives.
45. E. H. Quillin, "A Roman Priest in Search of the Primitive Church," *FMJ* 7 (October 1880): 4.

language instruction, preaching, selling of Bibles, distribution of anti-Catholic tracts, and struggle against putative Roman Catholic oppression.[46] The same features show up much later in US missionary publications from the 1920s to the 1950s.[47] When Brazil got its first Baptist periodical, the *Jornal Batista*, in 1901, around fifteen years after Teixeira's death, it recalled him in much the same terms—unsurprisingly, as these memoirs might have been penned by Bagby and Taylor. The canonical memorialization probably came in a historic speech that Bagby delivered at the annual meeting of the Brazilian Baptist Convention in 1926, published in full by the *Jornal Batista*. The general profile was unchanged from decades before.[48]

As for books on Brazilian Baptist history, the first to be widely read on the national level appeared only in the 1930s, when A. R. Crabtree and Antônio Neves Mesquita published their two-volume work.[49] Translated into English, it remains one of the few English-language works on the topic. But local histories had emerged before that, of which John Mein's *A Causa Batista em Alagoas* is the most relevant to Antônio Teixeira's story. Mein published his account in 1929, during the period in which he pastored the church founded by Antônio Teixeira in Maceió, the capital city of Alagoas. His impression of Antônio Teixeira is consequential because Mein was already a crucial leader in Brazilian Baptist publishing by this time and would heavily influence Baptist educational efforts going forward.[50]

Mein's book curiously opines that Baptist work in Alagoas began when its native son Antônio Teixeira left the Catholic Church and converted to Protestantism. In fact, Teixeira did not become Protestant in Alagoas and

46. For a few examples, see William B. Bagby, "Change of Base," *FMJ* 14, no. 4 (November 1882): 3; William B. Bagby, "Further from Bahia," *FMJ* 15, no. 2 (September 1883): 4; Zachary C. Taylor, "Incidents in Bahia," *FMJ* 14, no. 10 (May 1883): 4; William B. Bagby, "Our Cause in Brazil," *FMJ* 15, no. 4 (November 1883): 4; and Zachary C. Taylor, "Bright Prospects," *FMJ* 16, no. 4 (November 1884): 3.

47. See Solomon L. Ginsburg, "Some Achievements and Prospects after Forty Years," *Home and Foreign Fields* 8, no. 5 (May 1924): 12–13; and Robert G. Bratcher, "A Well-Favored Land," *The Commission* 17, no. 8 (September 1954): 2–5.

48. See William B. Bagby, "Discurso Histórico," *Jornal Batista* 26, no. 12 (1926): 4.

49. See A. R. Crabtree, *História dos Baptistas do Brasil*, vol. 1 (Rio de Janeiro: Casa Publicadora Baptista, 1937); Mesquita, *História*, vol. 2.

50. Zaqueu Moreira de Oliveira, "Perfil Histórico da Educação Teológica Batista no Brasil" (paper delivered at the XIV Congress of the Associação Brasileira de Instituições Batistas de Educação Teológica, Fortaleza, 2000), 26–29.

would only return to Maceió seven years after his Presbyterian conversion elsewhere in 1878. In any case, Mein portrayed Antônio's religious journey as evidence of Baptist superiority not only to Catholicism but also to other Protestant denominations.[51] That is, having been converted amid Presbyterians and later joining the Methodists, Teixeira's eventual ordination as a Baptist minister gave proof positive of his high esteem for the Bible and his ever-progressive understanding of Scripture until he finally recognized the true New Testament church in Southern Baptist Confederate exiles.[52] Mein underscored the role played by Bagby and Taylor in recruiting Teixeira and in founding and building Teixeira's church in Maceió. In fact, Mein stipulated, "the direction of the activities" of Antônio's ministry "was given from Bahia," where Z. C. Taylor pastored.[53] Nonetheless, despite dying only five years after joining the Baptist cause, Teixeira was "full of activity, consecration and results," as evidenced in his contributions to church planting, church growth, and anti-Catholic polemics.[54]

More books on Antônio Teixeira started appearing regularly in Brazil after the 1930s, and they mostly took the public-facing accounts of the Bagbys and Taylors as reliable primary sources. Official Baptist history, in other words, long tended to follow the memories that the Bagbys and Taylors helped formalize. Crabtree's volume on Brazilian Baptist history—which remains influential nine decades after it was originally published—clearly uses William Bagby's 1880s accounts as well as his later writings in Portuguese as a foundation for his portrayal of Antônio Teixeira.[55] Once more, the first Brazilian Baptist pastor comes off largely as a skilled assistant to the missionaries. When authors from other denominations recognized his importance early in the twentieth century, they cast him in the same supporting role.[56] In sum, the standard portrait of Antônio Teixeira is that of a valued helper, a symbol of Protestant triumph, and a key companion to the pioneering Bagbys and Taylors.[57]

51. For more on the concept of "conversion journeys" as it relates to Brazilian Protestantism, see Helgen, *Religious Conflict in Brazil*, 20–21.

52. John Mein, *A Causa Baptista Em Alagôas* (Recife: STBNB, 1929), 9–10.

53. Mein, *A Causa Baptista*, 13.

54. Mein, *A Causa Baptista*, 12.

55. Crabtree, *História*, 1:70–71.

56. Erasmo Braga and Kenneth G. Grubb, *The Republic of Brazil: A Survey of the Religious Situation* (New York: World Dominion Press, 1932), 63.

57. For some examples, see Helen Bagby Harrison, *The Bagbys of Brazil* (Nashville: Broadman

All in all, Baptist literature in Brazil has exaggerated the role of the Bagbys and Taylors in the origins of the denomination and understated the role that Antônio Teixeira played both there and in Brazilian Protestantism as a whole.[58] In truth, he was much more than an assistant to Southern Baptist pioneers, more than a church planter and polemicist under SBC supervision. Antônia's father—and her whole family—has a rich story that is yet to be fully told. And not only a rich story but a strategic one. For in the traditional telling, his success ultimately meant missionary success, while any failure or tarnish would carry over in like manner.[59] Naturally, the sordid record of his daughter's assault would have to be covered up. But so would some key aspects of his own story. The next chapters reveal them in unprecedented ways.

Press, 1954); Marly Geralda Teixeira, *Os Batistas na Bahia: 1882–1925. Um Estudo de Histróia Social* (Salvador, Universidade Federal da Bahia, 1975); Betty Antunes de Oliveira, *Antônio Teixeira de Albuquerque: O Primeiro Pastor Batista Brasileiro* (Rio de Janeiro: self-published, 1982); Ebenézer Soares Ferreira, *História dos Batistas Fluminenses, 1891–1991* (Rio de Janeiro: JUERP, 1991); Daniel B. Lancaster, *The Bagbys of Brazil: The Life and Work of William Buck and Anne Luther Bagby* (Austin: Eakin Press, 1999); Oliveira, *Centelha em Restolho Seco*; Bianca Daéb's Seixas Almeida, *Uma História das Mulheres Batistas Soterapolitanas* (Salvador: Sagga Editora, 2017); Elizete Da Silva, *William Buck Bagby: Um Pioneiro Batista nas Terras do Cruzeiro do Sul* (Brasília: Novos Diálogos, 2011). J. Reis Pereira, in one of the most important books on the history of Baptists in Brazil, includes Antônio Teixeira in his chapter covering the pioneer Bagbys and Taylors. He does so, however, apologetically, having been unable to "find a better place" to include his brief treatment of Antônio Teixeira than in the chapter "dedicated to the pioneer missionaries who came from North America." Pereira also frames Antônio Teixeira mostly as a tool for the success of these Anglo pioneers. See J. Reis Pereira, *História dos Batistas no Brasil, 1882–1982* (Rio de Janeiro: JUERP, 1985), 19–20.

58. Several of the sources written by missionaries and FMB officials overlook Antônio Teixeira completely. For an early example, see T. B. Ray, *Brazilian Sketches* (Louisville: Baptist World Pub. Co., 1912), 111–13.

59. For examples, see Costa, *O Evangelho Chega*; Evilásio Rodrigues Prado, *Conquistando Alagoas para Cristo: Breve História dos Batistas de Alagoas* (Maceió: E. R. Prado, 2008).

2

The Rise of the (in)Famous Ex-Priest:
Catholic and Protestant Journeys

When Antônio Teixeira de Albuquerque converted to Protestantism, he brought along a controversial past. Six years before leaving the Catholic priesthood, this man who would become the pioneer Brazilian Baptist pastor had been thrust into the national spotlight due to his scandalous love affair with a teenaged girl. His life came into the public eye, and not just in the cities where he lived and worked; his was a national *cause célèbre*. Although Catholic priests who maintained intimate relationships with women were to some extent common in nineteenth-century Brazil, Antônio's case became a key token in the tension between Masonry and the Catholic Church, itself a symbol of the power struggle between church and state.[1] That struggle reached its peak at the moment when Antônio decided to take Senhorinha Francisca de Jesus from her parents' house.

The story of Antônio's bold move was picked up by pro-Masonry periodicals that used it as a weapon against Brazilian Catholic leadership. Catholic-friendly media, in turn, made clear that Antônio's actions were not Church sanctioned. The contretemps made Antônio a nationally known figure, a great

---

1. For works on the conjugal life of Brazilian priests, see P. Mendonça, "Sacrílegas Famílias: Conjugalidades Clericais no Bispado do Maranhão no Século XVIII" (master's thesis, Universidade Federal Fluminense, Niteroi, 2007); Edriana Nolasco, "Por Fragilidade Humana: Constituição Familiar do Clero, em Nome dos Padres e Filhos" (master's thesis, Universidade Federal de São João del-Rei, 2014); and Kelly Julio and Edriana Nolasco, "Entre Famílias: Alianças Matrimoniais Vinculadas a Relações de Poder—Padres e Filhos, Minas Gerais (Século XVIII e XIX)," *Notandum* 21, no. 47 (May–August 2018): 132–53.

advantage to the American missionaries when he eventually came over to their side. Antônio also brought considerable erudition to the Protestant cause, as we will detail in a moment, but by then he also had strategic experience in navigating controversy and maximizing media exposure. As a Protestant convert, Antônio used the very periodicals that had criticized him to frame his scandal with Senhorinha as a failure of Catholic doctrine, not of his personal morals.[2] This was central to the genius that made Teixeira so important to US missionaries, yet it has been largely overlooked. Paradoxically, then, the complexities of Antônio Teixeira's Catholic journey have kept his full story (like that of his daughter Antônia) out of most historical narratives—Catholic or Protestant, in Portuguese or English.

This chapter recovers the trail of Antônio's Catholic journey and conversion to Protestantism from the forces that have obscured it—the neglect sometimes of Protestant, sometimes of Catholic sources; sometimes of English, sometimes of Portuguese records; and of archives outside churches and theological schools. Moreover, both Catholics and Protestants have drenched their memories of the man in polemics. On the Catholic side, he is the "apostate and criminal Antônio," with no attention given to the institutional and personal complexities that pushed him to join the American missionary cause. Protestant sources, on the other hand, have never told Antônio's Catholic story even though it was as a Catholic that Antônio became nationally known well before he even considered leaving the priesthood. In short, it is precisely the Catholic aspects of Antônio's journey that account for his becoming one of the best-known Protestant figures of nineteenth-century Brazil. To understand Antônia Teixeira's predicament, we must first understand her father; and in order to understand him, we must navigate his Catholic journey.

Catholic Training and Ordination

Antônio Teixeira de Albuquerque was born on April 15, 1840, the only child of Felipe Ney de Albuquerque and Helena Maria da Conceição of Maceió, in the state of Alagoas.[3] Little is known about his early life, but a strong commit-

---

2. Because Brazilian Baptists know Senhorinha Francisca de Jesus Teixeira simply as Senhorinha, we have referred to her in this way throughout.

3. This is according to B. Oliveira, who admits that she was unable to find his birth in the

ment to the Catholic faith was central to his upbringing. The schools which he attended as well as some of his friendships suggest that his family was well-established financially. He studied first in the Lyceum of Maceió, a primary school, and later joined the Lyceum Alagoano, from which he graduated at the age of twenty-one.[4] It is unclear what happened in Antônio's life during the seven-year gap between his graduation from the Lyceum Alagoano and his matriculation to study for the Catholic ministry. But in 1868, Antônio entered the Catholic Seminary in Olinda, Pernambuco, to begin his training as a priest.[5]

The Catholic Seminary in Olinda—which remains in operation today—could number plenty of prestigious alumni and faculty by the time Antônio Teixeira enrolled there. With roots traceable back to the 1500s, the school was officially founded in 1800 by Dom José Joaquim da Cunha. It aimed to offer education according to the directives of the Council of Trent and prepare intellectual elites for service to church and state. From the start, the seminary propagated the influences of thinkers and movements seminal to the causes of political liberalism and secularization: Jean-Jacques Rousseau, Baron de Montesquieu, the American and French Revolutions.[6] During its first two decades—which some consider the Seminary's highest point of influence—the faculty pioneered the study of natural philosophy in Brazil with the explicit goal of forming "naturalists" or "philosopher priests."[7] Some of its students and faculty had been educated in prestigious European institutions, such as Coimbra and Montpellier. Figures celebrated in ecclesial and civil positions as well as in the humanities and sciences studied and taught there; graduates included college presidents, bishops, a master and preceptor of emperor D. Pedro II, and professors in military and ecclesial schools.[8] The Seminary in

---

baptismal records of the Catholic Church in Maceió (Oliveira, *Antônio Teixeira de Albuquerque*, 9). Nor was she able to locate any records of the father's ownership of land in Alagoas.

4. Costa, *O Evangelho Chega*, 51. Antônio's friendship with Mello Lins, who came from a wealthy family, also points to the social and economic status of the Teixeira de Albuquerque family.

5. Oliveira, *Antônio Teixeira de Albuquerque*, 2.

6. For a summary of the influences disseminated via seminary education in Olinda see Leandro Dantas, "Seminario de Olinda e a República," *Revista Algomais*, April 8, 2017.

7. Argus Vaconcelos de Almeida et al., "Pressupostos do Ensino da Filosofia Natural no Seminário de Olinda (1800–1817)," *Revista Eletrónica de Enseñanza de las Ciencias* 7, no. 2 (2008): 480–505.

8. Mons. Severino Leite Nogueira, *O Seminário de Olinda: E Seu Fundador o Bispo Azeredo Coutinho* (Recife: Governo de Pernambuco, 1985), 208–9.

Olinda also trained and employed priests who had taken leadership roles in two revolutions—one in 1817 and another in 1824.[9]

Thus, even though the Seminary in Olinda was not at the height of its influence when Antônio arrived there as a student, it was known as a national hub of liberal ideas, had formed several well-known leaders of nineteenth-century Brazil, and continued to provide a solid and prestigious education. By enrolling there, Antônio could start forming professional and intellectual networks with people from around the country. He could avail himself of a rich and rigorous curriculum—courses in both speculative and practical theology, philosophy, rhetoric, geography, universal history, Portuguese, Latin, French, English, and writing. All of it was informed by theological, philosophical, historical, and linguistic methods and assumptions drawn from the European Enlightenment with a Portuguese accent.[10]

Such a cosmopolitan, multilingual, and modern education put Antônio far ahead of most people in Brazil in terms of intellectual formation and career opportunities, as well as most Confederate exiles from the US South who had migrated to Brazil just a few years earlier. Southern Baptist institutions after the US Civil War were of modest distinction at best; compared to what was available to Antônio, whether in curriculum, pedagogy, or theological formation, the education provided to Southern Baptist ministers in the late nineteenth century was pitiful.[11]

Antônio's bishop in Olinda was Dom Francisco Cardoso Ayres, who had studied in Portugal, Italy, and England and participated in the First Vatican Council before his death in May 1870. His passing, however, meant that at the time of Antônio's ordination to the Catholic priesthood, on November 30, 1871, the Archdiocese of Olinda and Recife was without a presiding bishop, perhaps explaining why he was ordained in the city of Fortaleza, Ceará, 480

9. Rafael da Silva Virginio, "Seminário de Olinda: Entre o Discurso Religioso e o Liberal" (presentation delivered at the 25th National Symposium of History, Fortaleza, 2009).

10. The student documents between 1868 and 1871 (when Antônio Teixeira was enrolled in the seminary) were not found in the archives of the Catholic Seminary at Olinda. These courses, however, were listed as part of the curriculum as early as 1882. There is little indication that Antônio's curriculum was significantly different. Betty Antunes de Oliveira had access to the curriculum Antônio went through and the classes she lists are similar. For Oliveira's account of Antônio Teixeira's trajectory see Oliveira, *Antônio Teixeira de Albuquerque*.

11. For examples, see Gregory A. Willis, *Southern Baptist Theological Seminary, 1859–2009* (Oxford: Oxford University Press, 2009), 16–24.

miles away. The local periodical *A Constituição* recorded the event, in which Antônio was consecrated along with fifteen others in the chapel of *Nossa Senhora da Conceição da Prainha* (Our Lady of Conception of Prainha) by the diocesan bishop, Dom Luiz Antônio dos Santos (Dom Luiz).[12]

Antônio soon returned to Pernambuco on a boat that carried two other priests ordained in the same ceremony as well as two slaves.[13] But at Ceará, he had touched a notable current radically different from his eventual destiny. The Dom Luiz who ordained Antônio was already a renowned teacher, theologian, and church official, and the church where Antônio was ordained, founded in 1840, the year Antônio was born, remains in operation today, located on a street until recently named after Dom Luiz. In 1867, the year before Antônio started his studies in Olinda, Dom Luiz founded the Seminary of Prainha, whose faculty and alumni today include forty-eight bishops and two cardinals. Some of these are central to the history of Brazil, of the Roman Catholic Church, and of Latin American liberation theology, including Dom Helder Câmara—the famous archbishop of Olinda and Recife—and Dom Eugênio Cardeal Sales, who would become a personal friend of Pope John Paul II and one of the figures behind Brazil's famous base ecclesial communities.[14]

Dom Luiz would become archbishop of the state of Bahia just one year before the then-apostate Antônio arrived with Southern Baptist missionaries to plant a Baptist church in Salvador, the state's capital city. Thus, if the memory of Antônio was important for Southern Baptist missionaries, his leaving the Catholic priesthood despite his connection to such auspicious officials and institutions made it important for Catholics to deploy and sustain their own rememberings of him.

The Kidnapping Scandal

Antônio Teixeira entered the priesthood at a turbulent moment in the history of the Catholic Church in Brazil and did so as a graduate of an institution that had a reputation for forming rowdy priests. The *Questão Radical*—a contro-

---

12. "Ordenação," *A Constituição* 9, no. 174 (December 1, 1871): 2.

13. "Passageiros," *Diario de Pernambuco* 47, no. 281 (December 9, 1871): 3.

14. For a brief journalistic summary of Dom Helder Câmara, see Vinícius Sobreira, "Memórias da Resistência: A História de Dom Helder, o 'Arcebispo Vermelho' do Recife," *Brasil de Fato*, April 10, 2021.

versy between Masonry and the Roman Catholic Church in the 1860s and 1870s—was especially important in this connection. The Brazilian press was closely engaged in the matter, and some of Antônio's decisions made him a national figure around whom the character of the whole Catholic Church would be judged in various corners of the Brazilian intelligentsia. In the 1870s, the growing rift between the Catholic Church and the state involved leading bishops' resistance to Masonic lodges. Antônio's new bishop in Olinda and Recife, Dom Vital Maria Gonçalves de Oliveira (Dom Vital), was one of the most important figures in this fray and was eventually arrested by Brazilian authorities for his views.[15] Antônio intentionally entered the controversy by publicly supporting Dom Vital. Before that, however, his personal life was thrust into national discussions about the trustworthiness of the Catholic Church.

The scandal hit newspapers around the country: a thirty-two-year-old priest, Antônio Teixeira de Albuquerque—educated in the Seminary in Olinda, ordained by Dom Luiz Antônio dos Santos, and a strong supporter of bishop Dom Vital—had kidnapped a seventeen-year-old girl from her parents' house to satisfy his sexual lust. Major periodicals in Maceió, Alagoas, and Recife, Pernambuco, made the event public and expectably so, these being the places, respectively, from which Antônio originally hailed and to which the couple fled. But the story circulated well beyond these locales to reach the states of Pernambuco, Alagoas, Minas Gerais, Espirito Santo, Rio de Janeiro, and Pará.[16] Antônio was indeed a national sensation.

The story of Antônio's scandal developed into a war of words in which Masonic and Catholic periodicals alike used Antônio as fodder for their own political and ideological purposes. The harsh version went like this: On November 17, 1872, Antônio Teixeira carried out an orchestrated plan to kidnap seventeen-year-old Senhorinha Francisca de Jesus, the daughter of Manoel Quirino dos Santos and Generosa Maria da Gloria, pious Catholic parents who

15. Lilia M. Schwarcz and Heloisa M. Starling, *Brazil: A Biography* (New York: Farrar, Straus and Giroux, 2015), 351.

16. Periodicals that printed the story included *Jornal de Alagôas* (in the state of Alagoas), *Jornal do Recife* (in the state of Pernambuco), *Diario de Pernambuco* (in the state of Pernambuco), *A Família* (in the state of Rio de Janeiro), *Correio do Brasil* (in the state of Rio de Janeiro), *O Apóstolo* (in the state of Rio de Janeiro), *O Santo Officio* (in the state of Pará), *O Liberal do Pará* (in the state of Pará), *Noticiador de Minas* (in the state of Minas Gerais), and *O Espirito-Santense* (in the state of Espírito Santo). Many stories by periodicals in Recife (in the state of Pernambuco) and Maceió (in the state of Alagoas) brought the scandal to national attention initially.

lived in Maceió.[17] Less than a month after the incident, the Masonic periodical *A Família*, in Rio de Janeiro, then the country's capital city, added pejorative detail: "The Mr. Father Antônio Teixeira de Albuquerque, before going up the altar and celebrating the holy sacrifice of the Sunday Mass of Sunday, November 17th, made preparations to take power over the young Senhorinha de Jesus, a 17-year-old daughter of poor but honorable parents, after the religious service."[18] The thirty-two-year-old priest, the article emphasized, had frequented the house of Senhorinha's parents and seduced her, then used the Mass to distract the parents while his cousin waited outside of the church in a horse-drawn carriage, ready to take her away. Afterwards, Antônio met her at a previously designated place, and the couple fled to Pernambuco by boat.

Independent sources confirmed that Antônio lived on the same street as Senhorinha's family, adding plausibility to the charges that he was a common visitor to her family's home.[19] In addition, some periodicals added information from the police report filed by Senhorinha's parents and identified several people connected to the plan. These included the name and address of Antônio's cousin who helped execute the plan, the name of the business from where the horse-drawn cart was rented, and the name of the owner of the boat Antônio used to make the trip to Pernambuco with Senhorinha.[20] The periodical *Correio do Brasil*, which circulated in the country's capital and focused on news related to commerce, agriculture, and industry, reprinted Antônio's story from the *Jornal do Recife* but added cheeky pictures of Antônio's post-abduction honeymoon: "One must confess that he [Antônio] could not have chosen a more pleasant place to make nest. He is eating fresh fish, drinking coconut water, laid down under the shadows of the palm trees, listening to the birds sing, and breathing the fresh breezes of the ocean. The master father must have composed many poems."[21]

A few periodicals admitted that, even though the scandal remained shocking, no official crime had been committed. After all, Senhorinha was seventeen years

17. "Alagôas," *Diario de Pernambuco* 48, no. 273 (November 27, 1872): 3.

18. "Chronica," *A Família* 1, no. 15 (December 12, 1872): 4.

19. City records from 1873 show that Antônio lived on "Rua do Livramento." A number of periodicals that printed the story of the incident with Senhorinha placed the family's house on the same street. For Antônio's address, see *Almanak da Provincia das Alagoas para o Anno de 1873, Anno II* (Maceió: Typ. Social de Amintas & Soares, 1873), 157.

20. "Rapto," *O Espirito-Santense* 3, no. 161 (January 10, 1973): 3.

21. "Onde Foram se Animar," *Correio do Brasil* 1, no. 387 (December 8, 1872): 2.

old and thus could provide legal consent; the assumption, which was sometimes mentioned but never emphasized, was that she most likely agreed to or was even an accomplice in Antônio's plan.[22] Indeed, the two would marry in a Presbyterian church after he left the priesthood six years later. Nonetheless, the scandal was typically framed as a kidnapping and allowed Masons—many of whom were Catholic themselves—to turn the table on their Catholic critics. Antônio was displaying "the character of the men who every day criticize Masonry vociferously, attributing to Masonry the growth in immorality and crime."[23]

Several other periodicals added irony, indignation, or both. A periodical from the state of Pará, *O Liberal do Pará*, majored in indignation: "Whoever hears of such monstrosity may think that we live among savages; and that the propagation of vices is so strong that even a priest, the same who should give the example of morality, is the same who seduces single women and snatches them from their parents' home to prostitute them! And he did that after celebrating the Holy Sacrifice of Mass! It is terrible, but it is true."[24]

If Brazilian elites who opposed the Catholic Church's power weaponized the story, Church supporters felt forced to criticize Antônio to let people know that his behavior violated Catholic rules and custom. For example, the Catholic periodical *O Santo Officio*, printed in the state of Pará, acknowledged: "Here and there, bad priests exist."[25] Baptist renditions of his life, by contrast, would largely overlook the episode—in fact, would bypass Antônio's entire Catholic past except, recently, for a few footnotes. When forced to deal with them, Baptist accounts implausibly dismiss the controversial reports about Antônio's life as mere Catholic polemics meant to avenge his eventually leaving the priesthood. Even something that might seem to serve the Baptist cause— for example, Antônio's notoriety around Brazil as a priest whose behavior exemplified Roman Catholic corruption—is completely bypassed by Teixeira's biographer Betty Antunes de Oliveira. For his part, Antônio would weather the storm. Whatever the scandal's role in and after his eventual conversion to Protestantism, for now he remained committed to his Catholic calling.

The scandal of Antônio's kidnapping of Senhorinha eventually died down, only to see his name reappear in Brazilian newspapers for other reasons. He

22. "Rapto," 3.
23. "Chronica," 4.
24. "Um Santo Exemplo," *O Liberal do Pará* 5, no. 6 (January 9, 1873): 1.
25. "Rapto por um Padre," *O Santo Officio* 3, no. 1 (January 6, 1873): 3.

not only remained committed to the priesthood and various Catholic institutions and initiatives but supported the church's most conservative elements. In 1874, for example, Antônio signed a document defending his bishop, the controversial Dom Vital, in the latter's showdown with the Brazilian state. As one of the most iconic defenders of ultramontanism in Brazil, Dom Vital's defense of the Catholic Church's superiority to the Brazilian state led to his imprisonment in 1875. The issue at hand involved his longstanding fight against Masonry and therefore against Brazilian imperial law which, contradicting the Vatican, allowed Masons to be part of the Catholic Church.[26] Eventually, Dom Vital extended this war to Protestantism too, regarding US missionaries as part of a Masonic-Protestant coalition aimed at weakening the influence of the Catholic Church in Brazil.[27] For now, Antônio's name appeared with those of several other priests in the *O Apóstolo*, a periodical that circulated in Brazil's capital, lauding Dom Vital as a hero of the Catholic faith: "Only you, glorious successor of the Apostles, we will recognize as our only legitimate Bishop in communion with the Holy Apostolic Faith and with the Vicar of Jesus Christ on earth. These are the sincere and ardent votes of the cosigners below, who hope that these are also the votes of all clergy in this diocese."[28] In short, just a few years before being ordained a Baptist minister in a Masonic lodge named after George Washington, Antônio stood boldly on the ultramontane side of Catholic theo-politics.

Antônio was also involved in national politics by virtue of his involvement in institutions that promoted education and culture in the state of Pernambuco. He was listed in the 1876 board of directors of the *Instituto Litterario Olindense* (Literary Institute of Olinda), for which he also served as official orator.[29] The Literary Institute of Olinda was an academic organization with strong Catholic roots, a rich multilingual library, and a prestigious standing among intellectuals in the state of Pernambuco.[30] In December 1876 alone, reads its official record, 182 people visited the institute's library and consulted 124 works dealing with different topics: "58 of literature, 3 of politics, 8 of religion, 11 of biography, 4 of philosophy, 6 of legislation, 8 of medicine, 3 of geography, 8 encyclopedias, 9 of

26. For a brief assessment see Helgen, *Religious Conflict in Brazil*, 10–11, 166–67.

27. Helgen, *Religious Conflict in Brazil*, 10–11, 166–67.

28. "Protestos," *O Apóstolo* 9, no. 9 (January 22, 1874): 4.

29. "Instituto Litterario Olindense," *Diario de Pernambuco* 52, no. 283 (December 12, 1876): 1.

30. Alfredo de Carvalho, *Recife: Cultura Academica* (Recife: Imprensa Industrial, 1907), 77.

history, and 179 periodicals."[31] The same record lists the books donated to the library, written in multiple languages, especially French and English. Antônio Teixeira donated one book authored by the French secular Catholic priest and historian Henri Congnet, entitled *Soldat et Prêtre* (Soldier and Priest).[32] Newspapers recommended the library of the Literary Institute of Olinda to the public alongside those of the city's law school (the oldest in the country) and university.[33] Antônio continued on as an advisor to the institute even after he left the Catholic priesthood, illustrating his connections and commitment to broader academic endeavors and networks.[34]

In short, when thirty-eight-year-old Antônio decided to turn Protestant, he was a highly educated, multilingual, well-connected, and nationally known leader who had learned to navigate his way around controversy. He had rubbed shoulders with colleagues and mentors educated in some of the most prestigious institutions in the world, and he journeyed alongside some of the country's foremost religious and academic minds. He left the Catholic Church while tension between the church and the Brazilian empire was still a palpable reality. His encounter a few years later with two Southern Baptist Americans marked, by these measures, a significant step down. William Buck Bagby and Zachary C. Taylor were young, inexperienced, unsophisticated, monolingual, and undereducated. Yet Antônio's fate became tied to theirs. So was that of his daughter.

The Conversion Controversy

Antônio Teixeira was back in the national spotlight again in 1878 as periodicals all around the country gave prime coverage to his conversion to Protestantism.[35] Most simply reprinted the original account that appeared on the front

---

31. "Instituto Litterario Olindense," *Diario de Pernambuco* 53, no. 10 (January 13, 1877): 2.

32. "Instituto Litterario Olindense," 2.

33. "Sociedade Propagadora da Instrução Publica," *Diario de Pernambuco* 54, no. 55 (March 7, 1878): 3.

34. "Instituto Litterario Olindense," *Diario de Pernambuco* 55, no. 160 (July 15, 1879): 2.

35. Some of the newspapers that printed the story of Antônio's conversion to Protestantism included *A Regeneração* (in the state of Santa Catarina), *Gazeta de Joinville* (in the state of Santa Catarina), *Jornal do Recife* (in the state of Pernambuco), *Monitor Campista* (in the state of Rio de Janeiro), *Diario de Pernambuco* (in the state of Pernambuco), *Diario de São Paulo* (in the state of São Paulo), and *Gazeta de Notícias* (in the state of Rio de Janeiro).

page of the May 4 issue of *Jornal do Recife*: "Changed cults—We inform you that the Rev. Sr. Antônio Teixeira de Albuquerque left the Roman Catholic Church and embraced the cult of the evangelical church, of which he is now a minister. They tell us that he will briefly publish an exposition of the motives that pushed him to take this step."[36] Contrary to the report, he was not yet a Protestant minister, though he would soon become one.

The anti-Protestant bias of the nineteenth-century Brazilian press is well-documented, and Antônio certainly faced sharp criticism from around the country for this move.[37] But the news was also publicized in English by the *The British and American Mail*, based in Rio, and, given the intra-Catholic disputes of the *Questão Religiosa*, Protestant-friendly voices also gave him room. Five days after news of Antônio's conversion broke, the *Jornal do Recife* printed a congratulatory note from the Protestant A. L. Barros. After praising Antônio's willingness to follow the guidance of the Holy Spirit and the Bible, Barros concluded: "Courage, brother! If you indeed find yourself with the same resolution of Saint Paul when he found himself going from Damascus to Jerusalem, may the grace of our Lord Jesus Christ, the beloved Father, and the communion of the Holy Spirit be with you, and all the faithful servants of the Lord, now and forever, amen."[38] In short, Antônio certainly had detractors in the national media, but he also had fans.

In the eyes of most Brazilians, Antônio, a former priest, had joined a new heretical sect.[39] His Catholic detractors tried to add to his disrepute by revisiting the story of his alleged kidnapping of Senhorinha Francisca de Jesus, now six years in the past and faded from public view. Antônio fought back with his own allegations about the perversion of the Catholic Church. Published originally in the *Jornal do Recife* but reprinted more broadly in different versions around the country, this controversy sheds light on the complex relationship between Antônio and the Catholic Church, which had ordained him a priest but now considered him an apostate.

Antônio publicly poked the Catholic bear for the first time in the May 7, 1878, edition of the *Jornal do Recife*. He began with a bold introduction:

36. "Mudou de Culto," *Jornal do Recife* 21, no. 102 (May 4, 1878): 1.

37. César Leandro Santos Gomes, "O Veneno da Heresia deve ser queimado: O Antiprotestantismo Católico da Imprensa Pernambucana (1895–1910)," *PLURA—Revista de Estudoes de Religião* 11, no. 2 (2020): 90–124.

38. A. L. Barros, "Parabens ao Padre," *Jornal do Recife* 21, no. 106 (May 9, 1878): 2.

39. "Brazilian Notes," *The British and American Mail* 5, no. 10 (May 24, 1878): 4.

"I, Antônio Teixeira de Albuquerque, ex-presbyter of the roman church, renounce the same church and its dogmas, introduced *ex-abrupto* into the church of Our Lord Jesus Christ; I also abjure all its ordinances, apostolic letters, bulls, encyclicals, and all that goes against the Sacred Scriptures."[40] Antônio denied that he as yet had been ordained a Protestant minister, contrary to some reports, but his next article, on May 10, fulfilled the promise that had circulated with the initial news of his conversion: he outlined the reasons why he had left. Over time he produced different versions of these complaints in various Brazilian periodicals and eventually published a consolidated account as a separate tract.

Antônio's allegations would change in emphasis for practical purposes. Originally, he stated that the basic reason for leaving the church was "the salvation of my soul, the tranquility of my spirit, and the regimen of my life according to the Gospel of Jesus Christ."[41] But he moved on to a frontal attack against the whole Roman Catholic apparatus with an evangelistic call based on Protestant understandings of the Bible. He wrote: "Oh! Unfortunate Rome! Turn your eyes to the Gospel of Jesus Christ, contemplate and follow the truth; purify your heart. It is enough, leave your worldly desires behind, confess to God and not to your gods, because these cannot hear you. Math. 7:7–9."[42] Antônio was asking for a fight, and his former colleagues obliged. The Brazilian press welcomed the dispute, which was great for business.

The Catholic opposition, however, did not initially take up theological concerns as Antônio wished. They focused instead on Antônio's character. If Antônio appealed to his studies of the Bible, his anonymous detractors directed their readers to the quality of the student: "Those who don't know Mr. Teixeira may believe him, but it is imperative that you know his whole character so that it can be seen that Catholicism doesn't lose with the rebellion of a minister without faith, without conscience, and without character; to the contrary, Catholicism wins [with Antônio's departure]."[43] This piece went on with one of the most detailed accounts of Antônio's kidnapping of Senhorinha de Jesus, their honeymoon, and the tensions that the scandal created between Antônio and his superiors. But it also provided an interesting flashback that

40. Antônio Teixeira de Albuquerque, "Abjuração," *Jornal do Recife* 21, no. 104 (May 7, 1878): 2.
41. Teixeira de Albuquerque, "Abjuração," 2.
42. Antônio Teixeira de Albuquerque, "Abjuração," *Jornal do Recife* 21, no. 107 (May 10, 1878): 2.
43. "Ao Publico," *Jornal do Recife* 21, no. 112 (May 16, 1878): 2.

revealed how the diocesan bishops, back at the moment of the scandal, had been under intense public pressure to address it.

An article from 1873 in *O Pelicano*, in the state of Pará, shows how the scandal was used to attack Antônio's bishop, Dom Vital, directly. After repeating the story of the kidnapping and enumerating how Antônio's behavior violated the criminal code, the anonymous article went on: "In the midst of this whole scandalized world, only one conscience, very cold, was not impressed with the stupendous crime—the conscience of Mr. bishop friar Vital Maria, the very one who, for individual honor, if not for the rigorous obligation of his public office, should have demonstrated signs of life in this atrocious event." The prelate seemed to be as bad as the priest:

> The bishop remains impartial even when the public cries are universal, even when the scandal agitates the most phlegmatic personalities. It is known that the criminal was, a few days ago, in the S. Frei Pedro Gonçalves neighborhood, in Recife. Since there is no episcopal order against him, he could even have celebrated (Mass) in that parish without being questioned. What does Mr. Fr. Vital want his *ex-informata* conscience for? To threaten the cowards, and to fight with the Masons.[44]

Thus, as a result of public pressure, years before Antônio's conversion Dom Vital did suspend Antônio's exercise of the priestly office.[45] Antônio's opponents now pointed out that his subsequent defense of Dom Vital had not been sincere. Rather, he was a hypocrite, maneuvering to get his own suspension lifted.[46] His bishop had been firm with Antônio but, his critics argued, also kind and extremely patient. Furthermore, several "companion priests" had tried to intervene in Antônio's scandalous love life in order to get him reinstated, going so far as taking Senhorinha from his house and helping to support her financially. In short, Antônio's detractors deliberately refused to enter theological debates with him because they didn't believe his reasons for

---

44. "Que Bello Exemplo!," *O Pelicano* 1, no. 56 (January 2, 1873): 2.

45. "Ao Publico," 2.

46. "Ao Publico," 2. All of the references provided in the piece were accurate. The note of appreciation to Dom Vital signed by Antônio when he was invited to the spiritual retreat by Dom Vital was printed by the *Diario de Pernambuco* on December 10, 1873. See "Um Voto Eterno de Agradecimento," *Diario de Pernambuco* 49, no. 283 (December 10, 1873): 3.

conversion were theological. Rather, he saw in the decadent religion of the Protestants the possibility of reaching his ultimate goal: to fulfill his sexual lust in an environment that sanctioned rather than punished his behavior. They concluded by simply citing Prov. 11:19 in Latin: "Truly the righteous attain life, but whoever pursues evil finds death."[47]

In reply, Antônio never denied—in fact, quite often admitted—that he had indeed taken Senhorinha from her parents' house. He also never qualified the detailed story his detractors had articulated; that, for Antônio, was beside the point.[48] The point was the Bible, he insisted, and he put it center stage in his narrative and held it there. As for his sexual desire and practices, Antônio figured that the best defense was offense. He repeatedly promised that he would not scandalize the public by revealing (even as he broadly hinted about!) "the most shameful facts that exist, not only in this capital and province, but in many others; facts that are the rule among the roman priests, not an exception; horrors . . . [that] are not punished by the *justa curia*, and shall not be punished, so that they can perform their false mission well."[49] Given his opponents' principal charge, Antônio decided that henceforth he would make Catholic celibacy a central point of his critique. The alleged horrors practiced by his former companions he would never detail, but in reminding his audience that he knew them well, he implicitly warned former friends and colleagues that he could reveal their dirty secrets whenever he pleased. Implied here as well was his conviction that celibacy was indefensible on both practical and theological grounds. In all this controversy, surprisingly, Antônio's children with Senhorinha never came up, even though several of them were born before he left the priesthood. Were Antônio's veiled threats to those once closest to him part of an unspoken agreement not to involve the children of priests in their polemics? Whatever the case, no details involving Antônia or any of her siblings made the pages of the newspapers in stories about Antônio's scandalous public persona.

It is also apparent that the public nature of Antônio's relationship with Senhorinha forced his superiors to punish him in ways that they did not punish others with similar proclivities. That inconsistency and perceived unfairness

47. "Ao Publico," 2.
48. Antônio Teixeira de Albuquerque, "Ao Publico," *Jornal do Recife* 21, no. 114 (May 18, 1878): 2.
49. Antônio Teixeira de Albuquerque, "Ao Publico," 2.

angered Antônio. It was undeniable that he had never been able to work undeterred as a priest and maintain his relationship with Senhorinha, whereas in less public cases that arrangement was quite possible in nineteenth-century Brazil. Thus, bitterness against the church to which Antônio had committed his life was an element of his hermeneutical turn that he was reluctant to bring to the surface. His inability to exercise both conjugal love and priestly vocation as a Catholic, as he clearly tried to do for years, preceded what both Antônio and Southern Baptist missionaries would frame as his pure, exclusively spiritual enlightenment issuing from a self-evident reading of the Bible.

Antônio's controversy with the Catholic Church would continue along these two divergent though not incompatible paths for some time. The official story Protestants chose to tell was perpetuated by Antônio and his supporters: he had simply read the Bible and come to the truth. In more detail, this narrative recounted that Antônio, while a seminary student, came upon an Italian Bible and in reading it discovered that much of his seminary training was not in accord with Holy Writ. Antônio then secretly consulted his friend Mello Lins, who had converted to Protestantism and had an even more unsettling story.[50] Nonetheless, Antônio completed his theological course of study, was ordained, and returned to Alagoas. Still perturbed, the young priest decided to engage in a detailed comparison of the Greek New Testament with different versions of the Bible. He concluded that those used by Protestants were not "false Bibles" as he had been led to believe by his teachers.[51] In this official version, Antônio's decision to take Senhorinha as a wife played no role in his decision. His Catholic opponents, on the other hand, made it the pivot point: Antônio's disaffection for the Catholic Church had sexual, not theological, roots.

Although Protestant retellings of Antônio's story deliberately glanced over his controversial past, they did give a glimpse of it occasionally. J. Reis Pereira's recounting of Antônio's conversion (which otherwise conforms to that of Oliveira and Crabtree) mentions in passing that a young female friend assisted Antônio in leaving Maceió and fleeing to Recife.[52] E. H. Quillin, associated with

---

50. Oliveira, *Antônio Teixeira de Albuquerque*, 3.

51. Antônio writes about these experiences in his pamphlet, *Three Reasons Why I Left the Church of Rome* (*Três Razões por que deixei a Igreja Romana*). Versions of this document are repeated in several publications, including Crabtree, *História*, 1:41–42; and Pereira, *História dos Batistas no Brasil*, 19–20.

52. Pereira, *História dos Batistas no Brasil*, 20.

the Santa Bárbara Mission in Brazil, wrote a long entry on Antônio for the Baptist *Foreign Mission Journal* entitled, "A Roman Priest in Search of the Primitive Church."[53] He, too, recounted the struggle of conscience Antônio experienced in trying to reconcile his reading of the Bible with Catholic doctrine. Quillin turned scandal on its head by claiming divine intervention: "Providence intervened ... by throwing a motive upon his heart to play with the tender sympathies of his nature, and nerve him for the daring deed of tearing loose from the Church at Rome." That motive took the form of "an intelligent and lovely female—a friend of early youth—[who] strangely laid hold upon his vision—singularly played upon the tendrils of his heart—while she threw around his mind the enchantment of her virtue."[54] Even such suggestions, however, mentioned nothing of an abduction or the age difference between Antônio and Senhorinha.

Quillin went on to contend that Teixeira was first induced to remain a cleric with promises of promotion and honor; that failing, he spent six months in prison and then was publicly excommunicated. None of that happened in real life according to many of the sources to which Quillin's English-only audience in the United States had no access, including Antônio himself. It is very difficult to know when missionaries tell the whole truth to their US audiences or to adjudicate when their skewing of fact are intentional and when it is driven by their lack of capacity to understand local languages and cultural codes.[55] Quillin mentioned as well that Antônio lost friends and was shunned by his parents—maybe that happened.[56] In short, in Quillin's account Antônio was "abandoned by the church—disgraced by popular sentiment, and forsaken by his friends. Without means of support, or friends to comfort, Antônio Teixeira de Albuquerque and his wife were thrown upon the theatre of life, to struggle with its stern realities."[57] Yet in 1880, when Quillin wrote his account, Antônio had already publicly denied that he had been excommunicated. In addition, although he never emphasized the more scandalous aspects of his story, he

53. Quillin, "Roman Priest," 4.

54. Quillin, "Roman Priest," 4. The sources also refer to E. H. Quillin as E. H. Quillen. All mentions in the text will refer to him as "Quillin" for consistency.

55. For a few more examples of how Southern Baptist missionaries in Brazil often misrepresented local issues to the FMB, see Chaves, *Global Mission*.

56. Crabtree, *História*, 70–71.

57. Quillin, "Roman Priest," 4. The editors of the *Foreign Mission Journal* note that at the time of printing (1880), Antônio had become a Baptist.

never shied away from admitting that his relationship with Senhorinha Francisca de Jesus played a role in his disappointment with the Catholic Church. Such inconvenient details mattered little for Southern Baptist missionaries, however; they told the most useful story they could tell without mentioning details that might jeopardize their objectives. For his part, Antônio did what he could to turn the Catholic infamy that had thrust him into the national spotlight into Protestant fame.

Conclusion

When Antônio Teixeira de Albuquerque announced his departure from the Catholic Church in the *Jornal do Recife*, the thirty-eight-year-old was no naïve Brazilian who would be easily controlled by religious organizations. Rather, he was a highly educated, well-connected former priest who was willing to bring his fight against the Catholic Church into the public square. The Protestant missionaries with whom Antônio would join forces benefited from his rich Catholic past. Missionaries would also witness aspects of Antônio's dispositions that some of them would not always appreciate. He brought to their camp sophisticated academic preparation, a broad cultural repertoire, substantial experience in navigating public controversy, access to media outlets, local and national exposure, and a willingness to disagree publicly with one of his country's most powerful institutions. He also brought a level of independence and autonomy that Southern Baptists were seldom willing to grant local workers. Nevertheless, US missionaries recognized the practical value of having Antônio join their enterprise, not to mention the symbolic value of recruiting a former priest. Protestants deployed the image of Antônio's conversion as a symbol of Catholic decadence, and they did so in the pages of the many periodicals that showed themselves ready to sell the story of an apostate priest who had kidnapped a teenager in Maceió.

For Antônio, the shift to the Protestant religion represented the possibility of reimagining an infamous past in ways that might provide some theological legitimacy to his questionable behavior. Antônio turned his Catholic detractors' insistence in pointing out the moral issues in his kidnapping of Senhorinha back against them. If they made sexual lust the centerpiece of their attempts to delegitimize his Protestant ministry, Antônio argued that Catholic celibacy was unbiblical and that priestly violation of celibacy vows was the rule in Brazil, not the exception. Even though Protestants in general and Southern Baptists in particular benefited from the national exposure made possible by Antônio's scandalous relationship with Senhorinha, they chose not to tell that story. Brazilian Protestants, similarly, ignored the broadly known details of Antônio's scandalous past and simply repeated the story Antônio told: his conversion was a result of his reading of the Bible and nothing but the Bible.

Thus, the Baptist protection of Antônio's legacy—which became inseparable from the Southern Baptist missionary legacy in Brazil—did not begin with the concealment of the rape of his teenaged daughter Antônia in Texas. It began with the concealment of Antônio's own lust for and abduction of the teenaged Senhorinha. Antônio's biographer—a careful historian who cited, for other purposes, some of the periodicals that mentioned the kidnapping scandal that Antônio never denied—thus chose to date Senhorinha's birthday according to the memory of her granddaughter. Despite abundant proof to the contrary, different editions of this biography state that Senhorinha was born in 1842, which would have put her at age thirty when she left Maceió with Antônio instead of the well-documented seventeen.[58] It is very difficult to know when denominational historians tell the whole truth to their local audiences and whether their narratives are intentionally misleading or simply marred by a lack of capacity to go beyond the romanticized, the convenient, and the hagiographic. In any case, before Antônia arrived in Texas, her own father's sexual scandal was kept from his Protestant record. The forgetting of Antônia would be another brick in the wall of Southern Baptist legacy building, and it would include powerbrokers in the state of Texas. It was Antônio's short Baptist ministry that introduced Antônia and her family to the missionaries who would deliver her to these parties. We turn to that aspect of the story next.

58. Oliveira, *Centelha em Restolho Seco*, 202.

3

The Making of a Baptist Celebrity: Antônio Teixeira in Public Imagination

A mid national controversy caused by his public conversion, Antônio Teixeira married Senhorinha Francisca de Jesus on September 7, 1878, in Recife, Pernambuco. A Presbyterian minister, Rev. John Rockwall Smith, performed the ceremony in a church that had been formed just a month before on the first floor of a building.[1] Antônio began to learn more about Protestant theology from Smith. Soon after the wedding, however, the couple left Recife for Rio de Janeiro, where, on March 9, 1879, they were received as members of the Catete Methodist Church by baptism and profession of faith.[2] The church was led by the missionary John James Ranson, who immediately recognized the benefit of Antônio's education and cultural competencies. No sooner was he received as a Methodist than he was featured in an open debate regarding the question, Should the cult of the images be allowed? The periodicals *Gazeta de Notícias* and *O Reporter* reported that the debate—which included Antônio, local professors, foreign missionaries, and other locals who held doctorates—

---

1. Oliveira, *Antônio Teixeira de Albuquerque*, 3, citing Teixeira de Albuquerque, "Three Reasons Why I Left the Church of Rome," 20; Oliveira, *Centelha em Restolho Seco*, 179. The document of the marriage could not be found in the archives of the church in Recife. The original church split and the documents were presumably lost in the process of moving them from one church building to another.

2. See the first book of minutes of the Igreja Metodista do Catete, in Rio de Janeiro. Antônio was the third member received by that church. Although some secondary sources state that their Catholic baptism was accepted, their acceptance by "baptism and profession of faith" means that their Baptist baptism would be their third.

was very well attended.[3] Antônio, as expected, defended the opinion that the Catholic "cult of images" was not allowed in the Bible.

The next month, Antônio was granted certification to teach all subjects in primary and secondary education.[4] Soon afterwards he moved to Piracicaba in the State of São Paulo, supposedly having been summoned to help Rev. Junius E. Newman, whose family had started a school in that region.[5] Antônio was among the better prepared and credentialed teachers in and around Piracicaba and is said to have taught not only students in the Newman School but also private students, like the children of Prudente de Moraes, a future president of Brazil.[6] It was in Piracicaba that Antônio made contact with the Baptists, particularly the Southern Baptists living in the Confederate colony in Santa Bárbara D'Oeste.

In June 1880 Teixeira presented himself to two Baptist churches in Brazil, one in Station and one in Santa Bárbara, both attended mostly by US citizens, as a candidate for baptism *and* ordination. The latter rite took place in a Masonic lodge named after George Washington, frequented by Southern men of both churches.[7] E. H. Quillin described the event:

> He [Antônio] was received into the Church by request of the pastor, was baptized by Elder R. P. Thomas in the midst of a large congregation of Americans and Brazilians. After Baptism the Council met in conference and unanimously called for his immediate ordination, which was performed in order. Elder Thomas officiating with the pastor in the ordination. After which the Council unanimously passed the following resolutions.
>
> That we earnestly request the Foreign Mission Board of the Southern Convention to appoint and sustain him to the amount of 600 dollars per anno . . . that they make this appointment at its earliest convenience.[8]

3. See *Gazeta de Notícias* 5, no. 79 (March 21, 1879): 2; and *O Reporter* 1, no. 74 (March 21, 1879): 1.

4. *Gazeta de Notícias* 5, no. 113 (April 25, 1879): 1.

5. Costa, *O Evangelho Chega*, 53.

6. Costa, *O Evangelho Chega*, 53.

7. Oliveira, *Centelha em Restolho Seco*, 183. Oliveira reproduced the original document in the same manuscript, 703–4.

8. The letter, dated June 1880, was forwarded on July 12, 1880, by the clerk of the Baptist Church in Santa Barbara to Dr. Henry Tupper, Executive Secretary of the Foreign Mission Board. The original letter is reproduced in Oliveira, *Antônio Teixeira de Albuquerque*, 77, appendix 2.

His ordination was meant to place Antônio as a minister in the Station church, which was not far from Santa Bárbara. But Quillin and other Baptists in the region may have had additional reasons for this step, for soon after Antônio joined the Baptists, he and Quillin went into the education business together, perhaps as part of a broader church-planting strategy.

Only days after Antônio's ordination, the two men announced in the local newspaper that they were starting a new business venture in the city—a school called Collegio Nacional. Scheduled to begin classes on July 5, 1880, the Collegio Nacional listed Quillin as the director and Antônio as an adjunct, though the vast majority of the courses fell well within Antônio's seminary training. They would teach Portuguese, English, French, Latin, philosophy, mathematics, arithmetic, geography, astronomy, rhetoric, and music.[9] The school featured an emphatically secular stance: "We want the public to know that we do not teach religion in the college."[10] Simultaneously, the Collegio Newman that Antônio had come to Piracicaba to help went temporarily defunct. Although Antônio is not commonly given credit for its fleeting success, Collegio Newman operated from the beginning of 1879 to June 1880, the exact period of his Methodist phase.[11] Once the Collegio Nacional was underway, Antônio published a series of articles about the importance of education in a local newspaper. This too gave no hint of Protestantism; Quillin and Antônio knew that if the venture were to succeed, they needed to recruit mostly Catholic students. In fact, some of Antônio's articles were packaged well within the contours of the Catholic natural theology he had learned at the Seminary in Olinda.[12]

But Quillin's and Antônio's partnership did not last long either. Within four months, Antônio let the public know that he was starting the Collegio Albuquerque, teaching almost all the same subjects as at the Collegio Nacional: "Antônio Teixeira de Albuquerque declares to the respectable public of this city that he dissolved completely the partnership he had with Mr. E. H. Quillin, in relation to the College and religious matters. He also declares that he has his own College at Alferes José Caetano Street, corner with Pescadores

---

9. "Collegio Nacional," *A Alvorada* 1, no. 3 (June 23, 1880): 3.

10. "Collegio Nacional," 3.

11. *O Apostolo* 18, no. 24 (March 2, 1883): 1.

12. For example, see A. Teixeira de Albuquerque, "A Educação," *A Alvorada* 1, no. 7 (July 23, 1880): 2; Teixeira de Albuquerque, "A Educação," *A Alvorada* 1, no. 11 (August 25, 1880): 3; and Teixeira de Albuquerque, "A Educação," *A Alvorada* 1, no. 12 (August 31, 1880): 2–3.

#30—where he teaches Portuguese, French, Latin, Arithmetic, Linear Draw-
ing, Architectonic Drawing, and vocal and instrumental Music."[13] Antônio, an
experienced and educated local, might well have realized that he was better
equipped to lead a school than to play a subordinate role. For his part, Quillin was nowhere to be found in local periodicals after the separation, likely
meaning that he, like the American Methodists before him, struggled to run a
school without Antônio. But the next March, the SBC missionary William B.
Bagby suggested that Quillin never preached to the Brazilians, that he was
contemplating withdrawing his name as a missionary, and that his school was
"purely secular," which suggests that he continued as a competitor of Antônio
in the local education market.[14]

Tension between Quillin and Antônio emerges in the documents of the
Foreign Mission Board as well as in missionary correspondence. Although it is
unclear if the failed partnership was a cause or a result of the tension, it certainly
factored into Quillin's—and consequentially the FMB's—perception of Antônio.
At their meeting on November 1, 1880, in Richmond, Virginia, FMB administrators felt compelled to investigate Antônio's fitness as a fellow Baptist worker:

> Whereas the churches of our Mission in Santa Barbara have united in the
> ordination to the gospel ministry of Sig. Antônio Teixeira (pronounced Ta-
> sha-rah), a recent convert to Baptist principles and practice from the Romish
> priesthood, and have committed him to our Board for missionary appoint-
> ment as a Christian minister of great power among the Brazilians, Resolved
> that the Board rejoice with our brethren in Brazil at the accession to their
> number of one who seems to promise so much strength to their cause among
> his fellow countrymen as Sig. Antônio Teixeira and that the Corresponding
> Secretary be instructed to make such inquiries with regard to their brother
> as shall give the fullest practicable assurance as to his fitness for the position
> to which the mission at Santa Barbara would have him called by our Board.[15]

At that same meeting, the board passed a resolution to examine Rev. W. B.
Bagby "as a candidate for missionary work and that should that examination

---

13. "Collegio Albuquerque," *A Alvorada* 1, no. 22 (November 28, 1880): 4.
14. Bagby, "Brother Bagby on Brazil," 2–3.
15. "Foreign Mission Board Minutes," November 1, 1880, accession number 1213, IMB archives.

be satisfactory, Mr. and Mrs. Bagby be sent to our mission in Santa Barbara at a salary of $1200 per annum as soon as the funds shall have been raised."[16] While the board's initial excitement about Antônio eventually morphed into suspicion, the young Bagby would later intervene in favor of the Brazilian— and of what the Brazilian could do for the FMB.

The FMB Secretary who had been instructed to make "inquiries" regarding Teixeira's "fitness" for appointment and support by the board found "the brother" wanting. A brief report to the February 1881 meeting of the Administrative Council noted cryptically that "the information which he had received with reference to Sig. Teixeira of Brazil was not of a favorable character." The minutes contain no further explanation, though it is conceivable that the unfavorable information included news of Antônio's scandalous past. But there were other possibilities as well—Antônio's background as a Catholic priest or his abduction of a teenaged girl. Perhaps Quillin and other White Baptists were suspicious of Antônio's potential insubordination or perhaps reports regarding Antônio's children had surfaced. After all, some of Antônio's children, including Antônia, were born before he and Senhorinha were married in 1878, which would pose a challenge for the FMB. At any rate, the FMB took no action at the time to affiliate with Antônio. That would soon change.

The Bagbys, Taylors, and Teixeiras: Necessity and Suspicion

In March 1881, William and Anne Bagby arrived in Brazil as newly appointed Baptist missionaries.[17] A year later, Z. C. and Kate Taylor joined them in Campinas, just a few miles away from Antônio. Still monolingual and under-

---

16. "Foreign Mission Board Minutes." Bagby's proposed salary was double that requested for Teixeira, though the FMB minutes report that much of the Bagbys' support was coming from churches, district associations, and the State Convention of Texas. It should also be pointed out that at this time, examination for missionary appointment would not have been perfunctory. Given C. H. Toy's forced resignation from Southern Seminary in June 1880, the Foreign Mission Board was hyper-sensitive to charges that "heterodox" candidates were being appointed as foreign missionaries. For example, John Stout and T. P. Bell were denied appointments as missionaries to China by the FMB in June 1881. See Parsons, *Crawford Howell Toy*, 96–99.

17. After a nearly two-month voyage aboard a cargo ship (to save funds), Anne Bagby wrote in her diary entry on March 1, 1881, about sighting land on the southeast Atlantic coast of Brazil near the city of Rio de Janeiro: "Land! Land! Cape Frio is in sight" (Anne Bagby diary, March 1, 1881).

prepared, W. B. Bagby and Z. C. Taylor went to recruit Antônio as a language instructor.[18] Bagby wrote to Superintendent Henry Tupper regarding the

> anxiety of Senhor Teixeira to be recognized by our Board and his sadness at being so long allowed to rest under the cloud of the charges brought against him while Bro. Quillin was teaching school at Piracicaba. Satisfied from all I could learn of him when at P. some months ago. That Bro. Teixeira was living quietly and inoffensively and ought to be assisted and encouraged as well as made use of by us. I promised to communicate with the Board on the Subject and to consult with Bro. Taylor as soon as he arrived as to what we ought to do in the case. He also told us of Bro. Teixeira's secret removal to Capivary where he has a small school. We went down the next morning to Capivary and called to see Senhor T. at his house. We found him teaching school in a small room in the house where he lives. He received us very cordially and we talked with him several hours during the day.[19]

Teixeira, Bagby continued, was "very anxious to be vindicated from the suspicions against his character and to be enabled to assist us in our work." There was pressing need on his side as "his school is very small, it being well known that he is a Protestant and he is barely able to provide bread for his family." But Bagby and Taylor felt pressed too: "We will need a teacher wherever we are and will also need someone who is to assist us in our first experiences in preaching sermons and to assist us in the Portuguese of our sermons." Moreover, it was an immediate "necessity" that "we commence a school" for which "it will be very advantageous to have a finely educated man with us, such as Senhor Teixeira is—to teach." Given all this "and in the hope that Senhor T. may prove worthy of the ministry (he is anxious to preach) we decided to employ him to teach us, and to such other work at any time as we may have him to do." On the material side, "a present salary of one hundred milreis per month (at the present low rate of exchange equal to about $42)" would do, although "it will very probably [be] necessary to increase" that soon. For his part, Teixeira

18. Bagby and Taylor to H. A. Tupper, March 27, 1882, IMB Archives; Kate Taylor diary, March 22, 1882. Bagby penned the section regarding Teixeira.

19. Within two months, Taylor would report that Teixeira's school had increased to twenty-seven students, "but he still signifies his willingness to go with us as teacher." Z. C. Taylor, editorial journal, May 29, 1882, IMB Archives.

agreed to give us his whole time and be governed by the same rules as to life and deportment that we are governed by. Finding that he and family were in need of clothing and bedding, we found it necessary to advance him a hundred milreis on his salary. We were reluctant in taking this step, but found his needs were pressing and his school bringing in very little. We hope to find a location and be prepared to move to our new house by June, but of course we cannot tell exactly.[20]

As a Roman Catholic priest, Antônio would have been part of the Brazilian middle-class in the 1870s and '80s, with a potential average salary of 130,000 milreis per month.[21] In addition, he could benefit from other privileges afforded to clergy, such as subsidized housing and reduced food costs. The average salary of a successful professor was comparable but slightly lower than that of a priest. That Teixeira seemed to have been open to accepting an even lower salary from missionaries could indeed mean that his school had yet to become established. All in all, it seems that Antônio had misjudged how successful his schools would be, or his Protestant commitments affected his venture in ways he didn't predict. One thing was clear: Quillin was a strong antagonist to Antônio, while in subsequent reports to the FMB, Taylor and Bagby continued to extol Antônio's gifts for ministry.

In his report for the quarter ending May 31, 1882, Taylor reiterated the need for a salary for Teixeira, praising him as "talented, cultivated and of admirable disposition. He is just the man our mission needs—a special favor of God to the Baptist mission here."[22] In September of the same year, Taylor wrote Tupper that those who had heard Teixeira preach "say he is an attractive speaker."[23] Taylor rec-

20. Bagby and Taylor to H. A. Tupper, March 27, 1882. Toward the end of the letter, Taylor presents a proposed budget for the Foreign Mission Board's consideration, including a salary of $600 per annum for Teixeira "as teacher and assistant in our work." Concern over the financial straits of the Teixeira family continued. In May 31, 1882, Taylor indicated the Bagbys and Taylors had "been aiding our bro. Teixeira from private means—some given; some loaned to be paid back later." Z. C. Taylor to H. A. Tupper, May 31, 1882, IMB Archives.

21. Rodrigo Goyena Soares, "Estratificação Profissional, Desigualdade Econômica e classes sociais na crise do império. Notas Preliminares Sobre as Classes Imperiais," *Revista Topoi* 20, no. 41 (May/August 2019): 446–89. Soares outlines the general incomes of different classes and activities based on information drawn from the states of Minas Gerais, Rio de Janeiro, and São Paulo.

22. Z. C. Taylor, Quarterly Report to the Board (ending May 31, 1882), IMB Archives.

23. Z. C. Taylor to H. A. Tupper, September 7, 1882, IMB Archives.

ognized that Teixeira was much more than a language teacher. Teixeira "showed a readiness to join us in our mission, acting as our teacher and preaching as well. The hand of the Lord was again visible in this provision of a native brother, teacher, and preacher, all in one and he on the ground ready and waiting for us."[24]

In August 1882, the three families—the Teixeiras, Bagbys, and Taylors—moved to Bahia, where they established a mission station and eventually organized the first native Brazilian Baptist Church.[25] W. B. Bagby indicated the present and promised importance of Teixeira's role in the new venture: "Brother Teixeira and family are with us. He goes as our teacher, and will help us in many ways. He will probably be able to get a school in Bahia, or some private pupils that will enable him to get a living. We want him with us, and hope he will eventually prove of great service in our work."[26] By the following March, Teixeira had joined Taylor in "selling Bibles and religious books and distributing tracts."[27] In June 1883 Senhorinha Francisca, Antônio's wife, was baptized along with two others, bringing the total membership of the Bahia church to eight.[28] Soon, Antônio was leading evening services: "Our Brazilian brother has been leading in the Wednesday night services, and attracts the people. He lately commenced a series of discussions of the leading doctrines of Rome, and giving his experiences as a priest." These activities gained the attention of some of the leading citizens: "A gentleman of some influence here, an officer of the government . . . has offered to publish these lectures of Senor Teixeira's in one of the city papers."[29] Antônio's thoughts, of course, had been publicized years before, but he continued conducting a form of what would today be called public theology and engaged the media frequently. By June 1883, he was preaching every Sunday.[30]

24. Taylor, "Rise and Progress," 20.

25. Bagby, *Brazil and the Brazilians*, 12. On the date of departure, see Kate Taylor diary, August 24, 1882. Taylor indicated that the missionaries "brought our native brother Teixeira and family with us at our own expense" and agreed to pay him forty dollars per month; Z. C. Taylor, Remarks, Quarterly Report to the Board (ending August 31, 1882), IMB Archives. Later Taylor would remark that although "our native bro. Teixeira deports himself well, the greatest weakness we see is his lack of knowing the worth of a dollar. However, we hope to correct this by our own example and complete control of his monied affairs. So far he shows a docile spirit." Z. C. Taylor to H. A. Tupper, September 7, 1882, IMB Archives.

26. Bagby, "Change of Base," 3.

27. Z. C. Taylor, "From Brazil," *FMJ* 14 (June 1883): 3.

28. Z. C. Taylor, Quarterly Report, June 12, 1883, IMB Archives.

29. W. G. Bagby, "From Brother Bagby," *FMJ* 14 (July 1883): 2. The letter was dated April 30, 1883.

30. Bagby, "Further from Bahia," 4.

Nonetheless the Brazilian's rise among his younger companions was not without obstacles. Before Antônio became the de facto preacher of the Bahia church, Taylor privately communicated his suspicions about Antônio to Superintendent Tupper. "Our native brother while he does not fall below our expectations still does not give undoubted evidence of genuineness and usefulness. We have not given him our consent to preach yet nor will until doubts are cleared away." The problem seemed to be that Teixeira did not meet US evangelical standards for true faith:

> In relating his experience to me I failed to see where a heart change took place even after interrogation. He says he has no doubts as to his conversion. His moral life is good, except in a want of economy and a lack of a sense of honor in borrowing—dependence. Is it right to license a man to preach, whose conversion we doubt although the candidate says he has no doubt? He has talked with some persons about the externals of religion but nothing to any of us about experimental religion.

One wonders what precisely the Rev. Taylor needed to hear. Antônio's own published testimony was simply eloquent and passed the most exacting test of evangelical experience:

> Happy day! When I was able to say: my soul rests in Jesus, and he in me. Oh! dear reader, I do not have expressions that are clear enough to signify the joy that my soul has found itself possessed by since the moment I accepted my Savior, Jesus Christ: when I opened the doors of my heart for him to come in, and for the Holy Spirit to do the great work of regeneration of my soul.... This is the new birth, not of the flesh, but of the Spirit—a new nature—that it takes to save our souls, filled with sin by our old nature, inherited from our parents.
>
> From the happy moment I left the burden, not only of Rome, but of sin, having cast myself upon the mercy of God, that "my spirit rejoiced in God my Saviour." My soul felt peace and joy, and shadows and darkness vanished forever.[31]

---

31. See appendix 1, below: Antônio Teixeira de Albuquerque, *Three Reasons Why I Left the Church of Rome.*

Perhaps he had not passed through the prescribed steps of soul experience in just the right Southern Baptist sort of way. Yet in light of so clear a testimony, which can be multiplied several times over from his tract, we need to wonder to what extent theology and to what extent ethnic pride produced the mixture of condescension and control with which Taylor went on to assure Tupper: "he is only our teacher and a private member of our church, though was ordained by Baptists at Sta. Barbara. When he shows evidence of conversion and openness to teach people the way of life, we shall be happy to give him full opportunity, until then we do not feel safe in trusting our cause into his hands."[32]

Taylor might defend himself by appeal to other missionaries' reports of Antônio's controversial past. In February 1883, when Antônio's role in the Bahia church was already growing, Taylor updated Tupper:

> I wrote you some time since respecting our native bro. Teixeira saying we thought so & so, i.e., that he was not really converted. I have found since that bro. & sister Bagby think differently, which I state as a correction. My mind is the same as when I wrote. The missionaries who knew him and his reasons for changing doubt his conversion. He has shown a fair moral life with us but in all our conversations and studies with him, and his talks at prayer-meetings I have not seen evidence that satisfies me.

Yet, Taylor had to admit, "I cannot say that he is not converted. It is a special object of prayer that God will direct us in this matter. Pray for us. Rev Mr. Smith of Pernambuco knows his history."[33]

That summer, when Antônio was already the lead preacher at the Bahia church, Taylor continued to vacillate. Although he recognized he needed Antônio, he was not ready to recommend his promotion to missionary: "Our native teacher is yet a problem. I still have doubts as to his conversion, although I am not without a little satisfaction. I cannot recommend his appointment. We shall need his services yet awhile; at least one fourth of his time. When he is thrown more on his own resources, we may be better able to judge of his qualifications."[34]

Taylor's doubts about Teixeira never made it into denominational renditions of Antônio's story.

---

32. Z. C. Taylor to H. A. Tupper, December 11, 1882, IMB Archives.
33. Z. C. Taylor to H. A. Tupper, February 3, 1883, IMB Archives.
34. Z. C. Taylor to H. A. Tupper, August 11, 1883, IMB Archives.

Bagby, however, was not so suspicious of his Brazilian companion. Contrary to Taylor, by September 1883, Bagby had publicly appealed for the Foreign Mission Board to extend a missionary appointment to Antônio:

> We wrote last week recommending the establishing of a new mission in the Empire and the appointment of Senhor Teixeira as our assistant here. . . . as to Senhor Teixeira, let me say that we only recommend him for appointment after abundant opportunities for testing his character and abilities. He has now worked with us a year and has shown ability as a teacher and preacher of the gospel. He has been a great service to the mission as a teacher, Bible-seller, preacher, Sunday-school superintendent and general assistant and counselor, and I consider his appointment a necessity; as he will continue to be of great service to the cause, I do not really see how we could do without him now (humanly speaking) and therefore, urge his appointment on the salary mentioned.[35]

The next May, however, the Bagbys moved to Rio to begin a new work, leaving the Taylors and Teixeiras to continue on in the Bahia church, whose numbers now exceeded thirty.[36] Teixeiras's capacities, paired with the missionaries' needs, would gradually open more space for his independent action.

Antônio Teixeira as FMB Missionary

Bagby's plea for a board appointment for Antônio was finally realized in September 1884. For the first time the *Foreign Mission Journal* listed "Sen. Teixeira" with Z. C. and Kate Taylor as among "our missionaries."[37] Taylor even complimented Teixeira for carrying on the work of the mission while Taylor was away visiting the work in another city.[38] That same month Antônio journeyed to Alagoas—whence he had taken Senhorinha—with two colporteurs or salesmen.

---

35. Bagby, "Our Cause in Brazil," 4.

36. Z. C. Taylor, "Persecution and Progress (May 24, 1884)," *FMJ* 15 (July 1884): 2.

37. "Our Missionaries," *FMJ* 16 (September 1884): 2. In each issue, SBC missionaries are listed along with the country of their mission.

38. Z. C. Taylor, "Quarterly Report (12 July 1884)," *FMJ* 16 (October 1884): 3. Apparently Senhorinha had made application for baptism a month earlier but was delayed by Taylor. "One of the applicants spoken of is our teacher's wife; but we are not satisfied as to her experience." Z. C. Taylor to H. A. Tupper, May 19, 1883, IMB Archives. Taylor's suspicions of Teixeira now extended to his wife.

They sold one hundred Bibles and four hundred tracts, and Teixeira preached to a crowd of some two hundred in a physician's home, where his audience showed "real interest."[39] For Christmas 1884, the mission gave Antônio a study gown and a "Popular Commentary on the New Testament," published by the Baptist Publication Society in Philadelphia.[40]

Antônio's passage in Alagoas, however, did not go unnoticed by local Catholic observers. In November 1884, a local newspaper from Maceió announced Antônio's return to his hometown with biting hostility: "Coming from Bahia, the apostate priest Antônio Teixeira de Albuquerque arrived in this capital. He would drag from here, after Mass, a girl, with whom he would marry, joining the Presbyterian church. It is known that this sad minister, planning to open here in the capital some conferences of his sect, was stopped by the authorities, who should not allow him to pour into the sincere and God-fearing hearts the germ of apostasy."[41]

A week later, in an article entitled "Refutation Against the Lectures of the Apostate Priest Antônio Teixeira de Albuquerque," it specified that Antônio's beliefs and the Protestant Bible translations that he and his companions sold were fulfilling that warning: "It is presumed by sincere Catholics that this hungry wolf plans to attack your orthodoxy, and we make a vow to God wishing that this quitting priest, distancing himself from error, converts to the faith that he professed when he was ordained."[42]

The piece was likely written by a local priest given its portions in Latin and its express resentment against Antônio for having left the Catholic Church and tainting the legacy of Dom Luiz, who had ordained him. After revealing Antônio's alleged personal and theological shortcomings, the author concluded with a declaration of open resistance to the infamous ex-priest: "here we are with pen in

---

39. Z. C. Taylor, "Bright Prospects," 3. In that same column, Taylor reported that Teixeira had received an invitation from "an old friend in Maceió" to establish a church. In the next issue of FMJ, Taylor reported that Teixeira had indeed traveled to Maceió, "the capital of the Province of Alagoas, the home of Sr. Teixeira" with the prospects of planting a church there. Z. C. Taylor, "Quarterly Report (31 October 1884)," *FMJ* 16 (January 1885): 3.

40. W. B. Bagby, "Christmas at Bahia (26 December 1884)," *FMJ* 16 (March 1885): 2. Presumably, this is a reference to the first releases of *An American Commentary on the New Testament* (Philadelphia: American Baptist Publication Society, 1881).

41. *O Orbe* 6, no. 130 (November 9, 1884): 2.

42. "Refutação as Conferencias do Sacerdote Apostata, Antonio Teixeira de Albuquerque," *O Orbe* 6, no. 134 (November 19, 1884): 2.

hand for a debate, so that we can see how you would present yourself in the light of truth."[43] Antônio evidently had value for Catholics as well as Protestants.

Antônio as Church Planter and Polemicist in Maceió

In January 1885, Antônio was in Bahia, where he baptized three converts who joined the Baptist church there.[44] Later that month, he and his family went back to Maceió, a testament to his willingness to face danger, controversy, and violence. In May, Antônio, Senhorinha, and their oldest son, Antônio Jr., formally requested a transfer of church membership from Bahia to the newly founded church in Maceió.[45] The next month Antônio Teixeira submitted his first report as a missionary there. He had preached sixteen sermons, paid twenty-two pastoral visits, and conducted eight baptisms. Ironically, in the same issue of the *Foreign Missionary Journal* carrying his report, Antônio was no longer listed alongside the Bagbys and Taylors as a missionary to Brazil but rather as a "native preacher." The title looks like a demotion at the same time that Teixeira's responsibilities on the field had increased.[46]

Antônio would die less than two years after the Maceió church's founding, leaving it with dozens of members and another congregation in the nearby town of Rio Claro.[47] In many ways, Antônio was a White, privileged man. His whole ministry took place before slavery was abolished in Brazil, and he ministered and transited freely in and between Salvador and Maceió, two cities with large numbers of enslaved Blacks.[48] As a matter of fact, the *Jornal do Recife* reported that a Senhorinha Francisca de Jesus freed three slaves in the Piracicaba region the same year that Antônio died.[49] Although it is impossible to ascertain definitely that these slaves belonged to the first Brazilian Baptist couple, it is not in-

43. "Refutação as Conferencias," 2.
44. Z. C. Taylor, "Later," *FMJ* 16 (March 1885): 2.
45. Z. C. Taylor, "Quarterly Report," *FMJ* 17 (August 1885): 2.
46. "Our Missionaries," *FMJ* 17 (October 1885): 2. In addition to the changes listed above, this issue now lists another missionary, Senhor Mesquita, alongside the Bagbys and Taylors as FMB appointees.
47. Costa, *O Evangelho Chega*, 69.
48. Danilo Luiz Marques, "Um Covil de Escravos Fugidos: A Cidade de Maceió na Década da Abolição" (paper delivered at História e Democracia, UNIFESP/Campus Guarulhos, September 3–6, 2018).
49. "Revista do Interior," *Jornal do Recife* 30, no. 251 (November 4, 1887): 2.

conceivable—Antônio was White and from a rich family. Yet it is also important to note that he came back to his hometown, Maceió, as a religious minority with a scandalous past and a history of directly challenging the Catholic Church. That posed real physical danger to him and his family.[50] The distribution of his tract titled "Three Reasons" was certainly a cause for much ideological and physical persecution as well as a demonstration of Antônio's marketing genius.[51]

Antônio had already published an independent "pamphlet" version of "Three Reasons" (see appendix 1) by the time he arrived in Maceió, synthesizing the various iterations of the anti-Catholic argument he had made from the time he announced his conversion to Protestantism and before he became Baptist. The full-fledged pamphlet version was never his sole way of evangelizing, nor did it remain an exclusively Baptist resource. Copies of the tract were sent to several newspapers around the country, and the piece was published in part or in full several times over.[52] It made its way into various local libraries and circulated in several metropolitan areas as a pamphlet or via reproduction in periodicals.[53] For example, almost six hundred miles north of Maceió, in the city of Fortaleza, the periodical *O Libertador* told its readers where they could find copies of the pamphlet and emphasized Antônio's prestigious education: "This priest was educated in the Seminary in Olinda and, it is said, was ordained here in this city. These books can be found in Deposit of Bibles and Religious Books, at Flores Street #6."[54] Thus, Southern Baptist missionaries, while presumably in authority over Antônio, benefited from his exposure in many areas of the country. The same was true for anti-Catholic voices of other stripes.

In light of Antônio's multichannel marketing strategy, the Catholic opposition stepped up its activity from periodicals to book-length refutations. The local periodical *O Orbe*, for example, made sure to let the Maceió population know that they "received the volume containing the refutation of father Antô-

---

50. On Catholic-Protestant violence in Brazil, see Helgen, *Religious Conflict in Brazil*.

51. Z. C. Taylor reported from Bahia in October 1885 that Antônio's tract (which Taylor, in his autobiography, took credit for aiding Antônio to write) "has been a bomb in their [Catholic] camp." See Z. C. Taylor, "A Stir in Brazil," *FMJ* 17, no. 5 (December 1885): 2. Several reports from missionaries emphasized the extent of anti-Protestant persecution.

52. See "Imprensa," *Jornal de Recife* 29, no. 228 (October 5, 1886): 1.

53. For examples see "Bibliotheca de Goyanna," *Jornal do Recife* 30, no. 253 (November 6, 1887): 2; "Gabinete de Leitura Instructiva e Recreativa Gamelleirense," *Diario de Pernambuco* 62, no. 2 (January 4, 1887): 3.

54. "Notas Religiosas," *O Libertador* 6, no. 85 (April 17, 1886): 3.

nio Teixeira's apostate doctrine. The text of this work provides clear evidence of the baselessness of those who, abandoning the religion that keeps without defect the tradition of Christ's doctrines, will look for the bosom of a sect that was the product of revolted pride against the authority of the Church."[55] Periodicals in other regions of the country trumpeted similar news.[56] In the process, Antônio's opponents pivoted from an exclusive focus on his character toward theological refutation. Apparently, his substance was selling in the Brazilian religious market.

The most powerful presentation was a 103-page book entitled *O Padre Antô-nio Teixeira de Albuquerque e as Razões de Sua Apostasia* (*The Priest Antônio Teixeira de Albuquerque and the Reasons for His Apostasy*). Printed in Recife in 1886 and distributed broadly, the anonymous book—signed "THE CATHO-LIC CHURCH"—is a direct refutation of Antônio's pamphlet, presenting solid theological argumentation sandwiched with attacks on his character.[57] The book does not lack epithets to describe Antônio—heretic, viper, apostate, dirty mouth, etc.—but tries to refute all of Antônio's major theological points via citations from the Bible and tradition. It translates scriptural passages from Latin to Portuguese and calls on Augustine, Aquinas, Justin Martyr, Tertullian, Cyprian of Carthage, and even Luther and Melanchthon, to name a few. The book also cites Brazilian legislation to prove that because Antônio was still a priest, his marriage had no legal validity, leaving the couple in "pure concubinage."[58] The volume was certainly written by a Catholic priest; Antônio had attained such a magnitude in the country's religious disputes that some priests came to be known for their opposition to his ideas. For example, when Rev. Fr. Luiz Ignacio de Moura of the Archdiocese of Olinda visited the capital of the state of Sergipe, 340 miles south, he was praised by the local newspaper for having "combatted, via the Pernambuco printing press, the heresy of the priest Antô-nio Teixeira de Albuquerque, making the latter move from Pernambuco."[59] By that date the Baptist pastor had been dead for over eighteen months.

---

55. "Recebemos," *O Orbe* 8, no. 146 (October 29, 1886): 1.

56. "Imprensa," *Gazeta do Norte* 7, no. 236 (October 18, 1886): 1.

57. *O Padre Antonio Teixeira de Albuquerque e as Razões de Sua Apostasia* (Recife: Typographia Industrial, 1886). The manuscript was distributed in at least five states: Pernambuco, Alagoas, Ceará, Rio de Janeiro, and São Paulo.

58. *O Padre Antonio*, 65.

59. *A Reforma* 2, no. 95 (November 4, 1888): 3.

Antônio exceeded expectations as a Baptist leader in the region despite the challenges and opportunities entailed by his public persona. In their reports to the *Foreign Mission Journal*, Southern Baptist missionaries—especially Z. C. Taylor—praised Antônio's efforts and celebrated his accomplishments. Taylor wrote in 1885 that Antônio's anti-Catholic pamphlet "has been a bomb in their [Catholic] camp."[60] A few months later, Taylor reported that Teixeira received so many calls—presumably to preach and write—that he could not meet the demand.[61] The paper that Southern Baptists began in the northern region, *Echoes of Truth*, was quickly gaining subscribers, as were published sermons, both certainly benefiting from Antônio's popularity.[62]

His health, however, limited Antônio's contribution to the Southern Baptist cause in Brazil. His declining condition was broadly known among SBC missionaries, so it was no surprise when he died in April 1887, just forty-seven years old. The missionary C. D. Daniel, who would later return to work among Mexicans in Texas—and also translate Ku Klux Klan material into Spanish to help Southern Baptist evangelization efforts there—stepped in temporarily to lead the Maceió field.[63] Some, like Taylor, hoped Antônio's oldest son would pick up his mantle, but he did not.[64] Yet the work in Maceió did go on successfully; and with it, the impact of Antônio and his work.

Memory and Postmortem Impact of Antônio Teixeira

Before news of Antônio's death arrived at the FMB headquarters in Richmond, Virginia, it had already circulated around Brazil in several periodicals.[65] His example and work remained significant for the Protestant causes that directly followed from him as well as for the missionary memory of his Brazilian journey. Two years after his death, the *Diario de Pernambuco*, based in Re-

---

60. Taylor, "A Stir in Brazil," 2.

61. Z. C. Taylor, "Quarterly Report of Bro. Z. C. Taylor," *FMJ* 18, no. 3 (October 1886): 3.

62. Z. C. Taylor, "Letter from Z. C. Taylor," *FMJ* 18, no. 4 (November 1886): 3.

63. For more on C. D. Daniel's KKK affiliation, see David J. Cameron, "Race and Religion in the Bayou City: Latino/a, African-American, and Anglo Baptists in Houston's Long Civil Rights Movement" (PhD diss., College Station, Texas A&M University, 2017), 84–91. For one announcement that Daniel would replace Antônio temporarily, see E. H. Soper, "Rio De Janeiro-Brazil," *FMJ* 18, no. 12 (July 1887): 2.

64. Z. C. Taylor, "One Hundred Baptized into the Church at Bahia," *FMJ* 19, no. 2 (September 1887): 2.

65. *Gazeta de Noticias* 13, no. 111 (April 27, 1887): 1; "Falleceu," *Gutenberg* 6, no. 77 (April 12, 1887): 3.

cife, published an article about a trip from the cities of Escada, in the state of Pernambuco, to the city of Pilar, in Alagoas. When the writer described the major sites in Alagoas, he wrote: "Beyond the stations I mentioned, there are the following stopping points: Nicho, between Branquinha and Muricy; Gitiranda, between Itamaracá and Bom Jardim; Rio Largo, between Utinga and Fernão Velho; and still the point in Agua Clara where one can see erected a catacomb in which was buried the sad priest Antônio Teixeira de Albuquerque, who became an apostate of the Catholic faith so that he could marry and move to Protestantism."[66] Even after death, Antônio kept on giving. When Protestants of different persuasions wanted to attack the Catholic Church, they often enlisted Antônio's example and writings. Antônio's popularity opened space for evangelistic initiatives and may have even inspired a broadly Protestant ex-priest movement in Brazil. At the very least, Masons, Methodists, Presbyterians, and Brazilian secularists were not shy about using him for their respective purposes.

The ecumenical use of the *Diario de Minas*, based in Juiz de Fora, is a case in point. In 1888, Methodists printed a five-part series that reproduced in full Antônio's *Three Reasons* tract. The first article in the series included an articulation of why Methodists practiced a "good religion" and defended their right to distribute religious books, especially Antônio's tracts, which served their own evangelistic polemics. The Methodists used the local authorities' attempt to criminalize their distribution of Antônio's tract to publicize their religion broadly via Antônio's words.[67] Earlier that February, over 1700 miles north, in São Luiz, Maranhão, the *Pacotinlha* reproduced Antônio's tract in full in a three-part series. The series concluded with a question that went beyond Antônio's tract: "p.s.—Innocent Question: Why is it that the priests label 'libidinous' those who abandon them and marry legitimately according to imperial law and live honestly from God—while the priests themselves live in concubinage and adultery under the condemnation of God and men?"[68]

66. "Um passeio por Terra até a Cidade do Pillar da Provincia de Alagoas Partindo-se da Cidade da Escada em Pernambuco," *Diario de Pernambuco* 65, no. 99 (May 3, 1889): 3. This account contradicts Betty Oliveira's mentioning that Antônio was buried in Rio Largo.

67. For the first article, see "A Lei," *Diario de Minas* 1, no. 62 (August 31, 1888): 2. The other articles appear in issues 1, no. 63 (September 1); 1, no. 64 (September 2); 1, no. 67 (September 5); and 1, no. 68 (September 6)—all in 1888.

68. "O Protestantismo," *Pacotinlha* 8, no. 54 (February 24, 1888): 2. For the other articles in the series, see issues 1, no. 41 (February 11); 1, no. 47 (February 17)—all in 1888.

Antônio's Catholic weakness had turned into a Protestant strength, and not only for him and the Baptists but for all who had practical uses for the Protestant version of his story. In terms of United States–controlled Protestant denominations, Methodists and Baptists were joined in 1889 by the Presbyterian-led periodical *Imprensa Evangélica*. Its list of "reformed priests" included Antônio as an Anabaptist preacher who had died two years before. Of the many other priests listed who had renounced their Catholic ministry, some were then preparing for the Protestant ministry. Antônio was the first Brazilian to have married and become a Protestant minister.[69]

Antônio's story remained a prominent feature in denominational publications and reports both in English and Portuguese. The ex-priest kept on appearing in the *Jornal Batista*—the major Baptist denominational publication in Brazil—as an important local co-founder of SBC work in the country alongside the Taylors and the Bagbys. However, none of these accounts mentioned the potentially damning aspects of his Catholic past or acknowledged his importance to Brazilian Protestantism beyond the missionary work of Southern Baptists.[70] Publications in the United States remembered Antônio in various ways. Celebrating Antônio's legacy became commonplace in SBC annual reports, FMB reports, articles in missionary journals, and histories of SBC missions in Latin America.[71] Thus, Antônio's legacy has been constructed and preserved in ways that presented him as a type of a local saint. Pioneer missionaries praised his success as their own; their legacies became inseparable, so that anything that tainted Antônio's would also shame theirs. Perhaps this is why, even in the midst of so much detail on Antônio's adult life and ministry, there is no mention of Antônia in denominational publications before or after

69. "Padres Reformados," *Diario de Minas* 1, no. 250 (March 3, 1889): 2. For a study of the Imprensa Evangélica, see Silas Daniel dos Santos, *O Jornal Imprensa Evangélica e as Origens do Protestantismo Brasileiro no Século XIX* (PhD diss., Universidade Mackenzie, São Paulo, 2018).

70. C. C. Duclerk, "O Evangelho em Alagoas," *Jornal Batista* 27, no. 32 (August 11, 1927): 13–14; Mario Ribeiro, "Rio Largo: Berço e Túmulo de dois pioneiros Batistas (Mello Lins e Teixeira de Albuquerque)," *Jornal Batista* 75, no. 6 (February 9, 1975): 4–5; and Betty Antunes de Oliveira, "Antônio Teixeira de Albuquerque," *Jornal Batista* 77, no. 26 (June 26, 1977): 7.

71. For examples, see William Buck Bagby, "The Death of Antonio Teixeira d'Albuquerque," *FMJ* 18, no. 17 (June 1887): 1; Z. C. Taylor, "One Hundred Baptized into the Church at Bahia," 2; SBC Annual Report, 11 May 1888, appendix B, IMB Archives; Ginsburg, "Some Achievements," 12–13; Ninety-Fifth Annual Report of the SBC, 12 June 1940, IMB Archives; Ninety-Sixth Annual Report of the SBC, 14 May 1941, IMB Archives; Bratcher, "Well-Favored Land," 2–3; and Roberta Hampton, "American Settlers in Brazil," *The Commission* 30, no. 4 (April 1967): 8.

his death. She is a mystery of whom even the great majority of those who claim to be specialists on the life of Antônio Teixeira never heard.

Where Is Antônia in Her Father's Story? A Conclusion

William Buck Bagby claimed that Antônio and Senhorinha already had many children by the time he met them. Yet, little is known about any of them. Antônio's biographer, Betty Antunes de Oliveira, made some progress collecting a few details about their six children. Birth records of 1800s Brazil are not always easy to come by, so Oliveira tracked down descendants and interviewed them to get most of her information. She then cross-referenced that information as best she could with the sparse documentation to be found. When Oliveira published the first version of Antônio's biography, she knew he had an older daughter but did not know her name; she only bore the label "firstborn." In her second edition, Oliveira had discovered in the archives of Baylor University that one Antônia Teixeira had been there. Although at some places in her book Oliveira seemed uncertain that Baylor's Antônia was indeed Antônio's "firstborn," she did mention that Taylor brought her to Baylor and placed her under the care of Rufus Burleson and his wife.[72] Not once does Oliveira mention the sordid details that followed, which seems intentional given Oliveira's otherwise copious information and detective-like documentation of primary-source material. In the whole literature on Brazilian Baptist history, Antônia is mentioned on two cryptic pages—in the two versions of her father's biography.

Adding to the mystery, there is some conflict in the historical record regarding the number of Teixeira children who made the trip from São Paulo to Bahia. W. B. Bagby reported that there were a total of twelve persons in the entourage: the Bagbys and their daughter, the Taylors and their maid, and the Teixeiras and their four children.[73] Oliveira, on the other hand, suggested that the Teixeira family had five children with them when they arrived in Bahia on August 31, 1882.[74] Likewise, when Bagby reported Antônio's death to the *Foreign Mission Journal*, he mentioned that Antônio was survived by five children and

---

72. Oliveira, *Centelha em Restolho Seco*, 216.

73. William B. Bagby, *"O Gigante que Dome"* (Rio de Janeiro: Casa Publicadora, 1947), 9. Taylor states Teixeira's "4 children are bright and promising"; Z. C. Taylor to H. A. Tupper, September 7, 1882, IMB Archives. So also Pereira, *História dos Batistas no Brasil*, 22.

74. Oliveira, *Antônio Teixeira de Albuquerque*, xx.

a devoted wife.[75] One of Teixeira's children died soon after birth and may have been dead before Antônio became Baptist, leaving a total of five living children.[76] If we are to take Oliveira's account of the Teixeira children's birth order, it is conceivable that Antônia could have been born in 1872, when Antônio kidnapped Senhorinha from her parents' home. According to Oliveira, Antônio's youngest son, Pedro, was born in 1881, and there is documentation that Antônio Filho—the third oldest child and oldest son—was born in 1873 or 1874.[77] That means that the two oldest daughters, Antônia and Madá, had to have been born by 1872, when Senhorinha left Maceió with Antônio. That would explain why Antônio and Senhorinha would have engaged in what seemed like a desperate escape from Maceió; Senhorinha might have been pregnant with Antônia. It is also possible that Antônia was the daughter of another woman, although this hypothesis seems less likely in light of the evidence at hand.

If indeed Antônia was born in 1872—a rather conservative assumption given that her brother Antônio Filho was born no later than 1874 and that Madá had been born before him—she was in her early twenties when she was raped in Waco, Texas. Yet, she passed as a fourteen-year-old, and she boarded the *Alliança* steamboat toward the United States as a young teenager. Did the Taylors lie about her age to make it easier to bring Antônia to the United States as their dependent? Was the change in age a strategy to conceal the fact that Antônia was born before Antônio and Senhorinha were married? Were missionaries bringing Antônia to the States to help protect the legacy of Antônio Teixeira, whose pre-Protestant story had been concealed by Baptists? Despite looking for documents across several states in two countries, no absolute answers to these questions were found. Undeniably, however, Antônia did arrive in Waco, was brutally raped, and was the root of yet another sexual scandal involving towering denominational figures.

75. Bagby, "Death of Antonio Teixeira," 1.
76. Oliveira, *Centelha em Restolho Seco*, 214–17.
77. Oliveira, *Centelha em Restolho Seco*, 214.

4

Voyage to Waco: Crossing Borders

A fter the death of Antônio Teixeira de Albuquerque in April 1887, the economic status of his family, vulnerable even while he was alive, took a sharp
turn for the worse. In a letter dated July 18, 1887, Zachary Taylor appealed to
Henry Tupper of the Foreign Mission Board for financial aid for the family.
He suggested paying Teixeira's replacement 75 percent of what Teixeira had
received (about forty dollars per month), apportioning the remaining ten dollars per month for Teixeira's widow and children. His appeal was not without
some barb and urgency: "The widow is helpless, was for several years insane,
and really merits such appropriation *for remainder of this con[vention] year.*"[1]
Tupper's response is not extant, so it is unclear how the Teixeira family survived over the next several years.

In the meantime, Kate Taylor's health deteriorated.[2] Both Taylors had suffered various maladies since their arrival in Brazil, forcing them to take extended

---

1. Z. C. Taylor to Henry Tupper, July 18, 1887, Southern Baptist Convention Library and Archives, Nashville, TN (emphasis original).

2. Kate Taylor (born Crawford) was from Belton, Texas, and the niece of T. P. Crawford, a
famous (if not notorious) missionary to China who served with Charlotte "Lottie" Moon. The
Taylors married on Christmas Day 1881 and were appointed missionaries to Brazil the following
January. They arrived there in February 1882 and joined W. B. and Anne Bagby in establishing the
Baptist mission in Brazil.

sabbaticals to regain their health.[3] In 1891, Kate became very ill with smallpox.[4] Soon after, a tumor was discovered on her thigh. Kate was prescribed to take up residence by the sea, but the tumor continued to grow.[5] Kate traveled to Rio de Janeiro, where it was determined that the tumor was malignant and "advancing to an alarming extent." A consultation with the family physician confirmed the diagnosis and the need for her leg to be amputated.[6] Taylor detailed the problem in a letter to Henry Tupper, secretary of the Foreign Mission Board:

3. In fact, Taylor's appeal to Tupper on behalf of the Teixeiras was sent from Houston, where Taylor had been recuperating from some undefined health issue. Z. C. Taylor was finally forced to leave the mission field because of neuritis or Reynaud's disease, which rendered him unable to return despite his desire to do so. Taylor retired to Corpus Christi in 1909. In September 1919 Taylor and his second wife, Laura Barton Taylor, drowned in a hurricane that swept their beach house off its foundations; cf. S. P. Brooks, "A Story of the Corpus Christi Storm," *Baptist Standard*, October 16, 1919.

4. Zachary Taylor described the episode in his autobiography:

She [Kate] had a severe spell of sickness. The doctor was treating her one morning, when he discovered she had small pox. He left saying, "she needs a nurse," and returned no more. I got Dona Eduviges, a good sister and efficient nurse. This disease and some others do not need a doctor, only a good nurse to keep the patient in a normal state, while the disease runs its course. . . . We sent our two children, Tarleton and Mabel, off to the care of friends. Wife passed through the three stages of the disease and recovered rapidly no one else catching it. (Taylor, "Rise and Progress," 62)

The manuscript is undated but was probably composed between 1917 and 1919 (the summer before Taylor's death). See Glendon Donal Grober, "An Introduction to and Critical Reproduction of the Z. C. Taylor Manuscript: The Rise and Progress of Baptist Missions in Brazil" (master's thesis, Ouachita Baptist University, 1969), 34. The thesis includes a critical edition of the "Cowsert text" (so called because it was typed by George Cowsert); the original document is lost. Page references are to the Cowsert text, though one is encouraged also to consult the Grober text for places in the Cowsert text that are difficult to decipher.

5. Taylor reported that the tumor grew into a "kind of ball, four inches in diameter" ("Rise and Progress," 62). Bagby was also aware of Kate's illness, which he described as "being very serious if no remedy is found." W. B. Bagby to H. A. Tupper, August 25, 1891, FMB Archives.

6. Curiously, Taylor did not accompany his wife to Rio for the tests; rather, he "left North for the interior," returning only after receiving letters from W. B. Bagby that indicated the seriousness of her illness (Taylor, "Rise and Progress," 62). One of the consulting physicians shared his evaluation with the family:

"I have examined Mrs. Kate Taylor and find her very anemic and in such a reduced condition, considering the climate here and the serious operations necessary for her re-establishment to health, I judge it best for her to go to North America *as soon as possible*, as I have hopes that the voyage will be an advantageous addition to the means adopted to improve her health." R. Cleary, M. D. [P. S.] "She is suffering with a large, as large as a coconut, tumour, which occupies the lower inner side of the left thigh . . . it is of eighteen months growth." RC. (Dr. R. C.

It is with a sad heart that I write you this letter. Mrs. Taylor's ailment became so bad that at the urgent request of friends she came here for treatment on the 10th of Sept. After examination, the Dr. pronounced it a tumor which should be cut out immediately. She called one from Bahia for consultation. After I arrived here we then had it examined by 2 of the best physicians and surgeons of Rio. They all pronounce it a dangerous growing tumor on the order of a cancer. All of them advise an operation to cut it out, but agreeing she is too weak to stand it and that it will be a risk of her life at any time.[7]

In the same letter, Taylor both cast his burden on the Lord and sought the wisdom of the Foreign Mission Board as to what they should do:

We know not what to do but submit to the wisdom of our Heavenly Father, hoping yet preparing for the worst. The doctors say that delay is dangerous. If it is a question of suffering here or in the States we (Mrs. Taylor and I) prefer that it be here. If it is a question of time only to develop and finally take away her life, we prefer it be here. Still we are willing (if God wills) to leave our work and make the sacrifice necessary for her restoration. While it is our desire and pleasure to work on for God among these people however God does not need us. He can do without us, but we cannot do without Him. . . . In this dangerous condition, we ask the counsel of the Board. Advise us what to do. An operation in this country could be perhaps more expensive than expenses of trip and operation in the States would cost besides the danger in this warm climate especially now as we are at the beginning of summer.[8]

Cleary, Physician's Consult, October 10, 1891 [emphasis original], included in Z. C. Taylor to Henry Tupper, October 10, 1891, FMB Archives)

Dr. Cleary added that his opinion was confirmed by two of the best Brazilian surgeons in the country. Bagby commented on Kate's condition to Tupper: "We feel very sad over Sister T.'s condition. There seems no reason to hope for a cure. The doctors here all say that nothing but a surgical operation could affect anything at all and that in all probability this in itself would be fatal as she is very weak." William Bagby to Henry Tupper, October 23, 1891, FMB Archives.

7. Z. C. Taylor to Henry Tupper, October 10, 1891.

8. Z. C. Taylor to Henry Tupper, October 10, 1891. Taylor and Tupper exchanged several letters over the next several weeks, but apparently the Board had come to no decision regarding the Taylors' return to the United States. Finally, on December 10, 1891, Taylor wrote:

We have worked on with the hope of being able to find a cure for Mrs. Taylor's ailment here. . . . that hope seems to have fled. I called in the best surgeons of Bahia a few days ago to examine

With no decision from the board forthcoming, the Taylors determined to return to the States for the surgery on the steamer *Alliança* in late December 1891 or early January 1892. It was not certain whether the surgery should take place in New York, Philadelphia, or Richmond.[9] Henry Tupper of the FMB arranged through C. R. Blackall, an editor at the American Baptist Publication Society, to have the surgery performed by Dr. W. W. Keen at the Jefferson College Hospital in Philadelphia free of charge.[10] The *Alliança* arrived at New York on January 26, 1892.[11] In his autobiography, Taylor reflected on what came next:

> Landing at five we cleared the Custom House by six and were in Philadelphia at eleven; an ambulance bore away the sick one to the hospital. A boarding house for myself and three children was arranged three blocks away. For three days the patient was in preparation for the operation. Then [on February 13] Dr. W. W. Keen, the Baptist deacon, and dean of the Hospital, in the presence of 300 students, Dr. Wyatt of New York, author of the process . . . amputated that limb above the knee, taking out the bone at the hip-joint. The operation was most successful.[12]

---

and cut out the tumour. . . . our English physician says amputation of thigh joint is necessary but advises not to have it done here, as the skill and appliances are insufficient for so dangerous an operation here. Without having heard from the Board it seems we shall be obliged to return to the States for her treatment in hospital. (H. A. Taylor to Henry Tupper, December 10, 1891, FMB Archives)

Bagby was much more pessimistic regarding Kate's prospects: "We are very much grieved at the state of health of Mrs. Z. C. Taylor. She was with us a month. The drs gave no hope of her recovery." William Bagby to Miss Tharnie(?), November 14, 1891, FMB Archives. After the decision to return to the States for surgery, he wrote Tupper: "She has shown wonderful fortitude and trust in God. May her precious life be spared though we are very much afraid she will never be able to return to Brazil." William Bagby to Z. C. Tupper, December 22, 1891, FMB archives.

9. Kate Taylor's mother wrote Tupper offering to nurse her daughter and care for the couple's three small children even if she did not have the money necessary to travel to New York to meet them: "The children are too small to be sent to us without someone to care for them. If the board must employ someone to make the trip with them, I am at its service and will be ready to undertake the journey at a moment's warning if the board will furnish the means." Mrs. E. C. Crawford to Henry Tupper, January 24, 1892, FMB Archives.

10. C. R. Blackall to Henry Tupper, January 20, 1892, FMB Archives.

11. "Allianca, List of Passengers, January 26, 1892," accessed October 23, 2021, https://www.statueofliberty.org/discover/passenger-ship-search/.

12. Taylor, "Rise and Progress," 63.

Dr. Keen explained to his audience, to whom he lectured both before and after the surgery, that amputation was necessary because of the probability that the sarcoma was in the bone (osteosarcoma) so that leaving any part of the infected bone would cause the disease to return. The surgery took an hour. It was also rare enough to prompt Keen to publish a pamphlet describing and analyzing the event, along with tips for modifying certain aspects of the procedure were he ever to perform it again.[13]

Kate Taylor developed a low-grade fever but had no general infection. She did suffer from traumatic delirium and severe phantom pain in the amputated leg.[14] The most life-threatening moment for her, however, came two months after the surgery when, while still convalescing in the hospital, she fell from her wheel chair and landed on her "unhealthy stump." The attending physician, Dr. Lipscomb, described it as "almost a fatal collapse."[15] Meanwhile, Zachary Taylor had his hands full with his three children:

13. Keen said that a hip-joint amputation had only been previously performed five times at the Jefferson Medical College. He measured both the patient, Kate Taylor (five feet two inches tall, 101 pounds in weight, thirty years of age), and the tumor: "The tumor measures twelve and five-tenths inches in length, and the circumference of the lower part of the thigh is twenty-three inches. The lymphatics in the groin are not enlarged. The pains are now dull in character and not as severe as they have been. Her digestion is good. She is, unfortunately, five months pregnant." W. W. Keen, MD, "Amputation at the Hip-Joint by Wyeth's Method. A Clinical Lecture Delivered at the Jefferson Medical College Hospital, February 1892," in "The Medical News," 26 March 1892, p. 3, Zachary Taylor Papers, Texas Collection, Baylor University. The pamphlet consisted of thirteen pages of text to which were added three pages of clinical notes.

Keen detailed the enormous risks of such a surgery. The mortality rate of hip-joint amputations ranged from 90 percent among military surgeries to 40–60 percent among civilians. Mrs. Taylor's pregnancy increased the danger of losing one or both lives. The pamphlet also provides an interesting look at the state of medicine at a most advanced clinic in the late nineteenth-century. There were three acute dangers involved in the operation, Keen explained: hemorrhage, shock, and sepsis. To prevent the risk of hemorrhaging, Keen employed the Wyeth method, which involved inserting metal pins in the upper thigh and winding pure rubber tubing above them to constrict the blood vessels without damaging them or the nerves. Shock was treated by wrapping the body with a thick layer of raw cotton and administering "an ounce of brandy and 1/20 of a grain of strychnine." Sepsis required thorough cleansing of the leg, buttocks, abdomen, and bowels. Still, the risks of such a surgery were enormous (Keen, "Amputation," 6–9). As Taylor notes, Dr. Wyeth was present at the surgery, and Dr. Keen acknowledged his presence and praised his method to limit hemorrhaging.

14. Keen, "Amputation," 12.

15. This incident was recorded in hand-written script at the end of Keen's pamphlet and signed by J. S. Lipscomb, MD. The fall was attributed to "overbalance" of the wheel chair.

One day I returned to the boarding house to hear that my oldest boy of six had been walking on a parapet of the roof, seven stories high. Another night they blew out the gas instead of turning it off, and came [near] being asphyxiated. My experience with children for a few days showed it was more trouble to care for them than all of the churches. So about the twentieth day [in March] I started to Texas with them to the home of relatives.[16]

Three months after the surgery, Kate delivered her fourth child, Marquis, on May 8. By August, the Taylors had returned to their work in Brazil. With donations from family and friends, Taylor bought Kate a small house by a bay, and with the assistance of a streetcar and crutches, she continued her work with Brazilian women and supervising a school for children. Unfortunately, another tumor soon developed, and Kate died in August 1894, just short of two years after returning to Brazil.[17]

Given all this trauma, it is perhaps understandable that Antônia is missing from these accounts. Missing she nonetheless is, obscuring the background of her own trauma to come. We know from other reports that Antônia Teixeira accompanied the Taylor family on this trip. Given the scandal that lay ahead, it stands to reason that Taylor would not record the fact in his autobiography, written some thirty years later. Neither did he mention Antônia in his letters to Henry Tupper that outlined his plans to bring his whole family to the States for Kate's surgery. We know from Rufus Burleson, however, that Taylor contacted him about bringing Antônia to Waco in order for her to attend school at Baylor. When Burleson replied that he and Mrs. Burleson would provide board, tuition, books, and clothing in return for her domestic service, Taylor responded, according to Burleson: "No arrangement on Earth could please

---

16. Taylor, "Rise and Progress," 63–64.

17. Taylor, "Rise and Progress," 64–65. In a letter to his parents, Taylor expressed his bereavement and determination to continue in his ministry: "It has pleased the Lord to take away my companion and helper for her good and mine, no doubt. Now my faith may have to pass a second proof and trial. My heart's desire was always to teach and preach the gospel." He worried also about what to do with his children, whether to send them back to the States or keep them in Brazil with him. He also told his parents that he was sending them part of the windfall from selling Kate's house for $2500 (after reimbursing $1000 to the FMB) but cautioned them to "keep this to yourselves dear parents for others will not understand." The balance, he said, was for his children. Zachary Taylor to Archibald and Sarah Taylor, November 17, 1894, Zachary Taylor Papers, Texas Collection, Baylor University.

me better, and I will bring her . . . with me when I bring my wife for medical treatment to the United States."[18]

Antônia is, in fact, listed in the ship's manifest of passengers along with Zachary and Kate Taylor and their three children. However, the Taylor family is listed first—he as a minister and Kate and the children as "tourists," lodged in the cabin aft, along with fourteen other passengers. Antônia and the remaining eighteen passengers were listed as "second class" and staying in the second cabin; Antônia was identified as a fourteen-year-old servant whose native country was Brazil.[19] Again, while Taylor does not mention it, Antônia must have been with the children in the hotel (apparently, she didn't prove to be a very good sitter!) while he was at the hospital with Kate. Antônia then traveled with Taylor and the children when he took them to Belton, Texas, to be with the children's grandparents, presumably in March 1892.[20] Taylor then returned to Philadelphia, returning to Belton after the baby was born in May.[21] Shortly before the Taylors left Belton on August 1 to return to Brazil, Antônia Teixeira arrived in Waco to begin her studies at Baylor University.[22]

18. Rufus Burleson, "The Brazilian Girl and Baylor University," box 2, folder 7, William Cowper Brann Collection, Texas Collection, Baylor University. Burleson stated that Taylor wrote him in 1892, which would mean Antônia was already in the United States, but one should not give that statement more weight than is necessary. It is certainly conceivable that Taylor's correspondence was in late 1891, when he was making arrangements for the transatlantic voyage, a point confirmed by Taylor's reported response, cited above. Burleson also reported that Taylor intended to bring a "young Brazilian preacher" with him and later in the pamphlet mentioned "the young preacher, Geronymo Souza," who, with Antônia, repeated the Lord's Prayer in Portuguese at the Texas Baptist Convention in Waco. One might draw the conclusion that the young preacher was Souza, but Souza was already enrolled as a student at Baylor and was not listed in the *Aliança*'s manifest of passengers. So apparently, that part of Taylor's plan did not materialize.

19. "Allianca, List of Passengers."

20. This fact is confirmed by Antônia in her interview in the *Waco Morning News*, June 16, 1895.

21. By May 26, 1892, the Taylors were back in Belton, from where Taylor wrote Tupper to report that "Mrs. Taylor will be fully able to travel by July. Her wound has closed up and only a small surface at orifice lacks healing." Z. C. Taylor to H. A. Tupper, May 26, 1892, FMB Archives. From Belton, Kate also wrote a note of gratitude to Tupper: "I can never express my appreciation of the kindness the Board has shown me and trust the Lord will enable me to so live and work that they will never regret the expense and care I have had to them. . . . I shall be able to accomplish some good for the Master's cause in Brazil." Kate Taylor to Henry Tupper, July 26, 1892, FMB Archives. It is our sense that Kate was the driving force behind bringing Antônia to Waco for education, and her death just before the assaults would deprive Antônia of her closest ally among the Baptist missionaries in Brazil.

22. *Waco Morning News*, June 16, 1895; Taylor expressed his desire to Tupper "to take passage

Besides providing Antônia room, board, and clothing, Rufus and Georgia Burleson, the president and first lady of Baylor University, promised to "teach her housekeeping as requested, on Saturdays, mornings, evenings when not conflicting with her studies."[23] The sacred return on this investment, Burleson hoped, would be "that the girl would become . . . useful in the cause of religion and education in Brazil."[24]

Baylor University in the 1890s little resembled the university of today, functioning more like a Christian academy with three levels of education: primary, preparatory (equivalent to modern-day middle and high school), and collegiate. In its 1893–94 catalogue, Antônia is listed as a student in the primary division (which consisted of five grades) along with 29 males and 32 other females.[25] The preparatory division enrolled 180 men and 75 women; the Collegiate, 168 and 88, respectively. Along with 35 "special" students, there were 608 students attending Baylor during the 1893–94 academic year.[26] The school was racially segregated and would remain so for more than seven more decades. Thus Antônia occupied a space of racial liminality at Baylor—not discriminated against as other non-White persons but also not considered an equal to her Southern White peers. Her precarious status would become

---

on the Vigilancia that leaves NY Aug 10th . . . we wish to leave Belton about the first of August." Z. C. Taylor to H. A. Tupper, June 28, 1892, IMB Archives.

23. Burleson, "Brazilian Girl." There are conflicting reports as to where Antônia lived her first year. Burleson said she lived with them from the outset, but Charles Wellborn (probably drawing on the claims of W. C. Brann—see below) claimed she was a boarding student on campus, only later to be taken in the Burleson home. Charles Wellborn, "Brann vs the Baptists—Violence in Southern Religion," *Christian Ethics Today* 72, no. 33 (2001): 14–18. The Baylor Board of Trustees in their report to the Baptist General Convention of Texas, however, denied that Antônia ever resided in Georgia Burleson Hall. "Proceedings of the Forty-Seventh Annual Session of the Baptist General Convention of Texas," p. 50, Baptist General Convention of Texas Annuals, Religious Collections, Baylor University Digital Collections, https://digitalcollections-baylor.quartexcollections.com/Documents/Detail/proceedings-of-the-47th-annual-session-10th-since-consolidation-of-the-baptist-general-convention-of-texas-held-with-the-first-baptist-church-of-belton-texas-october-11-14-1895/1070073?item=1070080.

24. Burleson, "Brazilian Girl."

25. "Catalogue of Baylor University, Waco, Texas, 1893–94," University Catalogues, Baylor University Archives, Baylor University Digital Collections, https://digitalcollections-baylor.quartexcollections.com/Documents/Detail/catalogue-of-baylor-university-at-waco-texas-1893-1894/843719?item=843731. Apparently, the 1892–93 catalogue is not extant in this collection.

26. "Catalogue of Baylor University," 25.

evident in the ways in which she would be treated when she most needed institutional support.

In her first term at Baylor in 1893, Antônia received passing marks in reading (80) and penmanship (78) but "deficient" grades in arithmetic (70) and orthography (70).[27] Her grades were understandably marginal given that she was a young female adjusting to a foreign land and language without the support of her birth family. Still, Antônia's conduct was graded "100" without any "Demerits" for the term. At the least, she began to fulfill part of Baylor's goal for female education, which was "to encourage character, piety, and the thirst for education in the female students of Baylor."[28]

As time went on, Antônia spent less time in the classroom and more time in the Burlesons' kitchen. There Antônia's place in her new world took a sharp and devastating turn.

27. Report card for Antônia Teixeira, Baylor University, spring term, 1893, box 2, folder 7, William Cowper Brann Collection, Texas Collection, Baylor University. The report card explains the grading system: "The above grades are upon a basis of 100 for perfection in recitation and deportment, regardless of time. If less than 75, he is Deficient; if less than 60, Bad. A Student who receives 20 Demerits in a term of five months is publicly notified his standing is bad, and when his Demerits amount to 50, he is sent home or otherwise severely punished. Rufus C. Burleson, D.D., L.L.D., President."

28. Quoted from the historical marker Georgia Burleson and Early Female Education at Baylor, on Baylor's campus.

Part 2

The Rape of Antônia Teixeira

5

Case 1165: The State of Texas v. Steen Morris Examining Trial

On June 15, 1895, Antônia Teixeira appeared before Justice of the Peace Bayliss Earle and swore an affidavit in which she accused H. Steen Morris of having committed a sexual assault on her in November 1894. Under oath, as reported in the *Galveston Daily News*, Teixeira claimed that Morris forced her to drink something that deprived "her of her power of resistance." This early newspaper report of what would become a much-bruited episode contained some misleading or otherwise uncorroborated information concerning her family: "Her parents, who are Portuguese people, have been advised of the condition of their daughter. . . . The young lady has brothers in Brazil, one of whom, it is said, will come to Waco to look after his sister."[1] Of course, Teixeira's family was Brazilian, not Portuguese, and there is no indication in any subsequent primary documents that Antônia's brother (presumably her oldest brother, Antônio) came to her assistance.

Steen Morris was arrested on a capias warrant and jailed on a charge of rape. Bail was set at $3,000 (c. $100,000 in today's currency). The bond was paid by F. B. Williams, J. T. Battle, O. I. Halbert, Bart Moore, and E. E. Easterling, men who represented a coalition of leading citizens and/or supporters of Baylor University.[2] Williams and Battle were Waco real estate agents.[3] Battle was an active member of Waco's First Baptist Church and also served at various times

1. *Galveston Daily News*, June 16, 1895.
2. *Waco Morning News*, June 16, 1895.
3. "Morrison & Fourmy's General Directory of the City of Waco, 1894–95," Waco City Directories, Texas Collection, Baylor University Digital Collections, accessed August 24, 2021, https:// digitalcollections-baylor.quartexcollections.com/Documents/Detail/morrison-fourmys-general

as both secretary of the Baylor Board of Trustees and secretary and treasurer of the Texas Baptist Convention.[4] Halbert was a local physician who would later testify on behalf of the defendant at trial. Bart Moore was the vice president of the Waco Railway and Light Company, which in 1891 had begun modernizing Waco's public transportation by replacing mule-drawn cars with electric cars.[5] E. E. Easterling was a twenty-seven-year-old attorney who had been admitted to the Texas bar in 1890 and would assist veteran attorney Captain Tom Blair as lawyers for the defendant.[6] Already, some news accounts were giving a positive portrayal of Morris as "favorably known in Waco from boyhood."[7] The *Galveston Daily News* eagerly anticipated "a highly sensational preliminary hearing."[8]

For his part, Morris, no doubt with the help of these friends of his extended family, enlisted forty-six-year-old Captain Thomas Alexander Blair as lead attorney in his defense.[9] Like Burleson, Blair was a Confederate veteran. He studied law in Mississippi and practiced there and in Tennessee before moving to Texas in 1877. He was an attorney in Waco and McLennan County for several years before going into private practice.[10] Blair was celebrated as a "great trial lawyer" and was, no doubt, among the best money could buy.[11] For their part, sympathizers of Antônia had pooled resources to hire the attorney John L. Dyer to assist the prosecutor, L. T. Williams, and to defray her other expenses.[12]

Examining Trial

The "examining trial," or preliminary hearing, took place on July 24 and 25, 1895. Its purpose was to determine if there was probable cause to carry the case

-Directory-of-the-City-of-waco-1894-95/166209. Fenny Williams was partner with James Horne in the real estate business.

4. Frank E. Burkhalter, *A World-Visioned Church: The Story of the First Baptist Church Waco, Texas* (Nashville: Broadman, 1946), 135.

5. *Waco Tribune-Herald*, April 24, 1912.

6. Betty Ann McCartney McSwain, ed., *The Bench and Bar of Waco and McLennan County 1849–1976* (Waco, TX: Texian Press, 1976), 211.

7. *Galveston Daily News*, June 16, 1895.

8. *Galveston Daily News*, June 17, 1895; cf. *Waco Morning News*, June 16, 1895.

9. *Dallas Morning News*, July 9, 1895.

10. Dayton Kelley, ed., *The Handbook of Waco and McLennan County* (Waco, TX: Texian Press, 1972), 29.

11. McSwain, *Bench and Bar*, 53.

12. *Galveston Daily News*, June 17, 1895; *Dallas Morning News*, July 9, 1895.

to a jury trial.[13] The State of Texas v. H. S. Morris was assigned the case number 1165. The *Galveston Daily News* reported that by 9:30 a.m. on July 24, when the court was called to order, "the 250 seats on the floor were all filled and the gallery, which holds 200, was crowded."[14] A reporter described what followed:

> H. Steen Morris appeared, promptly, accompanied by his wife and Rev. S. L. Morris, his brother. Shortly after the defendant entered, Miss Antônio [sic] Teixeira came down the aisle, followed by her friend, Mrs. Ollie Jenkins, who carried the baby in her arms. . . . Miss Teixeira is a modest appearing girl. . . . She has been pallid since the birth of her child. Today the pallor was a little relieved by sunburn, the result of camping on the Bosque.[15]

The presence of an infant, presumably the result of Antônia's assault, certainly added to the sensationalism around the case. Its provenance would figure as a major piece of evidence. (See pp. 96–97 below.)

Presiding over the hearing was a twenty-nine-year-old justice of peace, Bayliss Earle.[16] Though it was more typical for a district judge to conduct an examining

13. *Galveston Daily News*, July 25, 1895. According to the retired Baylor University law professor Gerald Powell, "probable cause" is a lower standard than "beyond a shadow of doubt." The examining trial was typically at the defendant's request and the purpose was to prevent "trial by ambush" by discovering the prosecutor's evidence and to question the credibility of the primary witness. Gerald Powell, Baylor professor of law emeritus, oral interview with author, August 19, 2021.

14. *Galveston Daily News*, July 25, 1895. Apparently, the trial took place in the courthouse on Second and Franklin. This courthouse, the third in McLennan County's history, had been completed in 1877 and was designed by the architect W. C. Dodson in the Second Empire architectural style for about $25,000. (Dodson designed a number of Texas courthouses in the late nineteenth century, including those in Coryell, Hill, and Lampasas Counties.) By the 1890s it was already too small to accommodate the steady stream of legal proceedings, so many criminal cases were moved temporarily to the basement of the massive Provident Bank Building, which stood at the corner of Fourth and Franklin Avenues. The Provident Bank Building was completed in 1890 at a cost of $438,000 and was "regarded as the biggest and finest office building in the Southwest." Geof Hunt, "Texas over Time: Waco's Provident Building—Once the Biggest Office Building in Central Texas and Beyond," *The Texas Collections* (blog), Baylor University, June 19, 2019, https://blogs.baylor.edu/texascollection/2019/06/19/wacos-provident-building/. W. C. Brann, editor of the *Iconoclast* and a major combatant in the controversy over the Morris-Teixeira case, was counted as one of its tenants in 1895. Newspaper references to the gallery suggest that the courthouse, and not the Provident Bank, was the venue for the trial; its two-story courtroom could have accommodated the large crowd anticipated far better than the bank's basement.

15. *Galveston Daily News*, July 25, 1895. The *Galveston Daily News*, July 26, 1895, reported that Antônia and Mrs. Jenkins had encamped on the Bosque River for the infant's health.

16. Earle (1866–1930), named for his grandfather who served as a US congressman from South

trial, this move was not unheard of, and Earle had due authority as a magistrate of the court.[17] Both the state and the defense listed their witnesses and announced they were ready for trial.[18] After Morris waived his right to make a voluntary statement, the morning was taken up with testimony from Antônia. Accounts reported that her testimony "did not vary in any material respect from her original statement [on June 15] when she first accused Morris of criminally assaulting her."[19] Fortunately, the testimony of Teixeira and others has been preserved in the McLennan County Archives, it being common for trials in McLennan County in the nineteenth and early twentieth centuries to be missing written testimony.[20]

Antônia's testimony under examination of the prosecution took most of the morning session, and the crowded court room latched onto it: "There was much eagerness displayed to hear the testimony of the complainant and many of the spectators were standing on the benches craning their necks in an endeavor to see the girl and hear what she had to say. She spoke in a low voice and could not be heard but a few feet distant."[21]

Carolina, was a young man who earned his law degree in 1890 and began practicing law in Waco in 1893. After a brief stint as justice of the peace, he soon abandoned the field of law and made his fortune by founding and operating an independent telephone system in Waco and surrounding cities in competition with the Bell Telephone System. His success was recognized by his peers in his selection as vice president and director of the United States Independent Telephone Association. Earle's father, Baylis Wood Earle (1801–1859), was a physician who moved to Waco in the mid-1850s and built a Greek Revival–style home, known today as the Earle-Harrison House (completed 1858).

17. McLennan County Archivist Kerry McGuire has indicated that his research of nineteenth-century trial records disclosed many trials presided over by justices of the peace in McLennan County (McGuire, interview with author, August 19, 2021). It could be that the Fifty-Fourth District Court judge, Sam Scott, was unavailable, which might also explain why it was Nineteenth District Court Judge L. W. Goodrich (rather than Scott) who subsequently filed the writ of habeas corpus on behalf of the defendant after the examining trial concluded.

18. One witness for the defense, Mrs. Samuel Johnson, did not appear in court that day, and the defense attorneys asked for an "attachment" (a writ issued by a court clerk authorizing an officer of the court to bring the witness before the court at an appointed time). The trial records in the McLennan County Archives preserve several such attachments issued for the May 1896 jury trial.

19. *Galveston Daily News*, July 25, 1895.

20. McGuire, interview. The record of the preliminary hearing runs to twenty pages, some hand-written, some typed. Unfortunately, the record of the jury trial held the next year, May 18–20, 1896, is not extant. For that reason, the facts of the case are presented here from the examining trial with a summary and recap of the jury trial in the next chapter.

21. *Galveston Daily News*, July 25, 1895; quotation from the *Fort Worth Gazette*, July 25, 1895. As was the custom of the day, a court stenographer did not provide a verbatim transcript of the court proceedings but rather a narrative summary, which witnesses signed to attest to the accuracy of

Antônia began by stating her name and giving her age (which she said was fifteen). She then described her routine at the Burlesons' and meeting Steen Morris:[22]

> I know the defendant H. S. Morris. I first met him at Mrs. Burleson's three years ago. I lived there at that time. He also lived there at that time and until about a year ago, I lived there. I helped work in the house and went to school at Baylor University. The first year I went six months all day and after that I just work in the morning for the rest of the year. The next year I work half of the session in the morning and the balance of the year I worked around the house. Last year I lived at the place and went to school when I had spare time.

She then recounted the first assault by Morris:

> Mr. Morris did not live at Mrs. Burleson's but lived at his brother's just across the street. I saw Mr. Morris in November of last year. It was about 9 o'clock p.m. I was in the kitchen at Mrs. Burleson's washing the dishes. No one was

---

their testimony. Thus, the nature of some of the responses (especially during cross-examination) make clear that the witness is responding to specific queries. This observation is confirmed by newspaper accounts, which occasionally interject an additional point or question in their summaries of the trial. For example, see the *Fort Worth Gazette*, July 25, 1895, which reported that "after one or two other further statements the witness [Antônia] said she could not explain further, and a leading question brought an objection from the defense. The justice told her to proceed and explain the best she could."

22. All quotations are taken from the court record of case 1165, The State of Texas v. Steen Morris, Fifty-Fourth District Court in McLennan County, McLennan County Archives. The twenty pages of signed, written testimony given on July 24 and 25 were certified by Justice J. B. Earle on September 2, 1895. Our appreciation to the archivist Kerry McGuire for providing copies of this testimony and other court records associated with this case. This chapter contains several large block quotations from the court stenographer's narrative summary that are attributed to Antônia Teixeira since this is the closest we can come to hearing her authentic voice. Given that so many had so much to say about her, it is important to give Antônia the opportunity to "speak" for herself insofar as that is possible now, 125 years later. Of course, even this stenographer's report does not give unmediated access to Antônia's point of view, so we have compared that record with the version in the *Fort Worth Gazette*, July 25, 1895, and with her interview with the *Waco Morning News*, June 16, 1895 (see appendix 2: Synopsis of Antônia Teixeira's Testimony). As with all witnesses in a court case, Antônia had been "prepped" by her attorneys; she admitted in re-direct examination that there were terms and concepts she did not know before the assault: "At that time all this come up I did not know what the term illicit intercourse or connection meant. I did not know what was to be pregnant or what pregnancy was until the doctor informed me."

at the house except Grandma Jenkins who is 85 years old and she was in the front room of the house. There are three rooms between the front room and the kitchen where I was.

Antônia continued:

> At about 9 o'clock the defendant came to the kitchen door which was shut. I heard someone walking around outside and opened the door to see who it was and saw it was the defendant. He was about six feet from the door and asked me to come out then which I refused to do. He then took me by the arm and pulled me out there. He then threw me down on the ground and got on top of me. He said when he dragged me out there he was not going to hurt me. He just got on top of me[,] pulled my clothes up and stayed on me about 10 minutes and when he quit I was all bleeding in my privates. He entered my private organ with his male member. He penetrated me.[23]

Obviously, and as was routine, Antônia had been coached by the prosecutor to use particular terminology that was not part of her normal parlance ("my private organ," "his male member"). But her next words, in their specificity and nuance, testify to authenticity on her part:

> He hurt me but did not hurt me very bad. It made me bleed, not a great deal. I had on a pair of drawers open at the side; he tore those open. I tried to get away from him but I couldn't because he was holding me so tight. I tried to holler, but could not because he was holding me so tight. I could holler a little but not loud which I did. He kept telling me not to holler that he was not going to hurt me.

When her assailant was finished, "I went in the house and did not say anything that night. There was no one there but Mrs. Jenkins. She was in bed and I think she was asleep. The next morning I told Mrs. Burleson." Then the crucial legal point: "I did not consent but resisted."

---

23. In the interview in the *Waco Morning News* (June 16, 1895) Antônia said that Morris let her go after a few moments "without fully accomplishing his purpose." The medical testimony, however, suggests that it was more likely that this first assault in early November and not the third in early December that resulted in her pregnancy.

Then Antônia described a second attempted assault by Morris, this time about two weeks later. The circumstances were similar to the first. She was washing dishes when Morris pulled her out of the house and threw her to the ground. Although she herself did not see or hear anything, something or someone startled Morris, and this time he ran away. Then came the third attack, the most brutal:

> I next saw the defendant about the first of December 1894 which was about 2 weeks after he had run away. I saw him at the same place and about the same hour. I was again washing dishes. I did not see him at all until he opened the door and pulled me out. He threw me down on the ground [and] pulled up my clothes. [He] got on top of me and that hurt me. He kept me down about 10 minutes. He penetrated me and it hurt my private organ.

Again, Antônia was specific and had a clear consciousness of degree: "It lacerated me and made me bleed more than it did the first time. I could not hardly walk and couldn't go to school the next day. No one was at home but Grandma Jenkins."[24]

And again, "I complained next morning to Mrs. Burleson. I did not know what it was called or really was. I did not see him anymore. There was a great deal of soreness and laceration produced from each time and I did not recover from it until about a month ago."[25] As for her apparent naivete about sexual matters, it was understandable given that "I first had my monthly sickness about several months before the first assault." As for Morris's culpability:

---

24. In her review of Antônia's testimony, Dr. Ann Sims assesses that "Antônia's description of the degree of injury ('he did not hurt me bad' after the first assault and 'made me bleed more than the first time' and 'I could hardly walk' after the third assault) again add to the detail that makes Antônia's testimony so credible" (see appendix 3: Medical Comments).

25. In the interview in the *Waco Morning News* (June 16, 1895), Antônia asserted, "I said nothing of this last assault to anyone, as before my statements were denied by Morris and disbelieved by others." In this interview Antônia (according to the reporter) maintained that she reported the attack to Mrs. Burleson who then talked to Mrs. S. L. Morris (her daughter) who in turn "spoke to Steen Morris about and he denied having seen" Antônia at all. This account is not recorded in the court testimony, probably because it constituted hearsay and would not be accepted as evidence. At stake here would be whether Antônia told Mrs. Burleson twice or three times about the assaults. It is certainly understandable if Antônia did not tell Mrs. Burleson after the third assault since no action had resulted from her previous disclosures.

The first time he came he gave me something in a little glass and told me to drink it, that it was good. This was before he had dragged me out. I was on the inside and he on the outside. He got the glass and bottle out of his pocket. It was a little flat vial. It was white fluid. The only effect I noticed was it made me dizzy. It made me sleepy. I went to bed and was still dizzy when I went to sleep.[26]

So much for the assaults themselves. Antônia next testified to an encounter with the defendant, his brother S. L. Morris, and Rufus Burleson in April 1895, after a medical examination determined she was pregnant. This time the abuse was verbal:

The defendant was on the front porch. At first, Dr. Burleson asked me if I would swear it before the defendant. I said yes and he went after him. And his brother said he was on the front porch already. The defendant came right in with Dr. Burleson and Dr. Burleson asked me would I say before the defendant what he had done to me. I then accused him to his face of it. He looked pale and excited and trembled. He just looked at me. He said he didn't do it.

Meanwhile, "the defendant's brother kept asking me questions and I told him all about it. When the defendant denied it there in my presence, I said to him, 'You did it. You know you did it, and if you didn't what are you so pale and trembling for.'" Then Dr. Burleson intervened to give the defendant a turn.

He said yes and asked me what kind of drug that was he had given me. I told him he had it and gave it to me and he ought to know himself. The defendant then said he wasn't there at all and I then asked him why he was so pale and trembling if he was innocent. I did not say so very much because everything I would say S. L. Morris would call me a liar and tell Dr. Burleson that I was lying and that his brother had never told a lie.

There followed a typical ploy of the day: "Mr. S. L. Morris asked me in that conversation if it wasn't a little Negro boy around the house that did it and asked

26. It is possible the drug/alcohol that Morris forced Antônia to drink dulled the pain of this first attack, compared especially to the third assault.

me if I didn't know it was. I said no. He then asked me if it wasn't a school boy named Ola Leesburg. It was then known that I was pregnant."

Some telling details emerge from this story—above all, attempts at intimidation. That Burleson would confront Antônia in the presence of two other grown men, one of whom was her accused assailant, was, in the most charitable interpretation, a regrettable misjudgment. More realistically, it was a reprehensible attempt to force Antônia to change her story. Perhaps Burleson thought Antônia did not have the nerve to accuse Steen Morris of rape to his face. If so, he was wrong; she was remarkably brave and blessedly point-blank: "You did it. You know you did it, and if you didn't what are you so pale and trembling for."[27]

Furthermore, S. L. Morris's behavior, as described by Antônia, was despicable, especially for an ordained minister of the gospel. He constantly interrupted her, accusing her of lying and making the outlandish claim that his brother "never told a lie." He then accused Antônia of consorting with a "little Negro boy." When Antônia denied that accusation, Morris then named Ola Leesburg, a schoolmate of Antônia, as the guilty party. That name (though not Leesburg himself) would recur in the saga.

When Burleson asked Steen Morris if he had any questions for his accuser, he posed an odd line of inquiry, asking what kind of drug he had given Antônia. Morris seemed to be attempting to deflect Antônia from the real topic at hand—his brutal assaults. Antônia's response was brilliant: "I told him he had it and gave it to me and he ought to know himself." She refused to be derailed despite the difficult circumstance of being alone before her accused assailant on his home ground and in the company of his imposing allies. Morris's denials, at least in Antônia's version of events, seem weak and unconvincing. Why did he not rise more ably to his own defense?

Back to her court testimony. Antônia ended with these assertions: "My home is Bahia, Brazil. I have been in Texas about three years. I gave birth to a girl June the 18th. It is white. The laceration and wounds caused from the assaults continued until about the time I was confined. The Defendant Steen Morris is the father of my child."

27. Dr. Ann Sims suggested that Antônia's boldness might support the view that Antônia was an older adolescent or young woman (eighteen to twenty-two) rather than a younger adolescent of twelve to fifteen. Sims, oral interview with the author, July 29, 2021.

After the noon recess, Antônia was cross-examined by T. A. Blair, lead at-torney for the defense. Blair attempted to expose inconsistencies in her story, for instance, asking which arm Morris had grasped ("I can't say which one").[28] Despite these efforts, the *Fort Worth Gazette* reporter found that her "testi-mony was substantially the same as the direct evidence."[29] Antônia did give more detail regarding her relationship with Morris prior to the attacks:

> I used to go over to Mrs. Morris' and would see him but never talked to him. From the time he left up to the time of this first assault he never spoke to me and I never to him. During the two years he lived there he never said anything to me where any one was but always did when there was no one present. He never said anything to me but called me to go out with him. He was always calling me to go out with him.

This was "about six months" after she had first met him. "He called me to come to him late in the evening. He would call me and tell me to come out there and did so every time he had a chance to." The whole time "he was living at the same place with me he never took hold of me . . . there had been no trouble up to that time and he had not hurt my feelings up to that time."[30] It was when he moved out of the house that things changed.

Antônia also expanded on the nature and extent of her injuries following the first assault: "I was bloody but can't say just how much. I saw the blood on my clothes. It hurt me and as soon as I got in the house I examined myself and found blood on my clothes. I don't know what became of the defendant. I had said nothing to him." She also commented on the drug that Morris forced her to drink:

28. Cross-examination of Antônia Teixeira, case 1165, The State of Texas v. Steen Morris, Fifty-Fourth District Court in McLennan County, McLennan County Archives. In her review of the testimonies of the case, Dr. Sims observed that "the childlike detail and consistency remained the same, without an attempt to add information that she wasn't sure about (i.e., she said didn't know which arm he grabbed, and she was not sure how much she bled). These are very important things to notice when attempting to get medical information from a child without asking leading questions, and attempting to assure as much as possible that the child is being truthful and has not been coached ahead of time" (see appendix 3).

29. *Fort Worth Gazette*, July 25, 1895.

30. Antônia made a similar observation about previous unwanted advances.

It was the first time he came that he gave me the drug and before he pulled me out that he gave me the drug. He gave me the drug when he was pulling me out. He pulled me and told me that there was something to drink from a glass he took out from his pocket. . . . He had hold of me with one hand and the glass in the other. I told him I didn't want it and he said it was good and to drink it. And I did so and it made me dizzy by the time I got back in the house and not before.[31]

She also clarified what she had told Mrs. Burleson after the first assault: "The next morning, I told Mrs. Burleson that Steen Morris was bothering me. I didn't tell her that he threw me down and had connection with me—she never asked and I didn't know how to tell her." Mrs. Burleson replied that "she was going to ask him about it. That is all that I did tell her. It was before breakfast out in the kitchen that I told her about it." Little good that did; nonetheless, "I told Mrs. Burleson the second time he came in the same way that I told of the first."

The attorney Blair also pressed Antônia on how Morris might have known that there was no one at home with her besides the elderly Mrs. Jenkins. She confessed that she did not know. Later, during the redirect examination of Mrs. Burleson, it was established that the first alleged assault occurred on the night that the Waco Cotton Palace opened.[32] Mrs. Burleson claimed that she rarely left her mother at home in the evening but one exception was to attend the wedding of a Miss Pruitt, which occurred on the evening of the Cotton Palace's grand opening.

Attendance at the Cotton Palace grand opening played a significant role in Steen Morris's testimony: "I was not there on the night of Nov. 6 the night she alleges that I raped her. On that night I was at the Cotton Palace." As a

---

31. Dr. Sims observed: "'Drugging' a child or adult prior to sexual assault/abuse, as happened in the first encounter, is common today and used by perpetrators of both children and adults" (see appendix 3).

32. This part of the testimony is recorded in type. Beneath the redirect examination of Mrs. Burleson is this handwritten note: "It is agreed by both parties that the Cotton Palace opened on Nov. 6, 1894." Other historical records place the date on November 8, 1894. The confusion over the date is evident in the cross-examination of Steen Morris, who remarked: "If the Cotton Palace opened on the 6th I don't know where I was on the night of the 8th. If it opened on the 8th I don't know where I was on the 6th." It was the event and not the date that was important for the parties to agree to as marking the alleged first sexual assault on Antônia Teixeira.

member of the Waco city fire department, he had been "with the Baylor Hose company all that day when they were having parade. I was with them from the time they met through the parade. That night I had supper about 6 o'clock and went back to the Cotton Palace and remained there until it closed about 11 o'clock that night."

Morris's alibi, however, was soon undermined by G. A. Waddell, ironically a witness for the defense: "I am a member of the Baylor Hose company and this company was on parade on the day the Cotton Palace opened. I know the defendant in this case. On the day of the opening of the Cotton Palace we tramped around through the street on parade and the defendant was with me." Yet Waddell did not know "whether the company went to the opening that night or not." In any case, "I didn't see Steen Morris there that night. I left there at about 12 o'clock." When pressed in cross-examination, Waddell clarified: "I don't know where the defendant was about nine o'clock that night."

As for the assault that occurred in early December, Morris had only a denial and no alibi: "I heard her [Antônia] testify that about the first of December I was there and raped her. I was not there at that time. I never did have connection with this girl at any time. I state that I never did at any time have connection with this girl and that during the months of November and December I never gave her any fluid." As for his whereabouts on the nights of the other alleged incidents, he simply said: "I could not state where I was on the night of the 12th of November. I can't tell where I was on the night of December 1st."

Steen Morris also disputed Antônia's report of the conversation between herself and Burleson, S. L. Morris, and the defendant. Under direct examination by the defense attorney, he simply said: "I have heard her . . . [say] she asked me if I was not guilty why I trembled and looked pale. I heard no such statement there and didn't tremble for I was not afraid." Under cross examination, Morris was forced to clarify his comments:

I do admit that I was present at the time of this conversation mentioned. I heard my brother make the statement there addressing himself to Dr. Burleson that she was lying. I don't know what it was she said that caused him to make that statement, he had asked her some question but I can't remember what all of them were. I don't know any one question the answer to which he said was a lie.

He did remember Antônia accusing him "before Dr. Burleson of having had connection with her" but not his brother's suggestion "if it was not a little negro boy there on the place or a school boy who had had connection with her." Quite simply, "I can't tell what the prosecuting witness said that they accused her of lying about but it was the whole thing, just all the way through." And no, he replied to the state's attorney, his sketchy memory had nothing to do with his state of mind at the time: "I don't think I fail to remember the things that were said on account of the agitation I was laboring under." Nor was anything wrong with his brother's approach: "I wouldn't pronounce the conduct of my brother on that occasion as very overbearing or oppressive." Finally, Morris made it a point to remind all present that he was "a married man and have been married since January." Indeed, reporters noted that his "wife was present by her husband's side throughout the entire examination."[33]

The defense called other witnesses to challenge Antônia's testimony. One of the chief rebuttal witnesses was Mrs. Georgia Burleson; in fact, the headlines shouted: "Plaintiff's Testimony: The Wife of the President of Baylor University Denies the Testimony in Part."[34] Mrs. Burleson's main purpose was to deny any knowledge of Steen Morris's alleged attacks on Antônia: "This girl never on or about the 6th of November or any other time made any complaint to me about the conduct of Steen Morris. I never noticed anything peculiar about her or her condition about that time, that is November or December." She repeated her assertion under cross examination: "This girl never complained to me that this defendant had been bothering her and never mentioned his name to me." Then, sorting out bloodlines, she stipulated: "Steen Morris is not related to me by blood or marriage, his brother married my daughter."[35]

A secondary purpose was to deny Antônia's claim about being home alone with Mrs. Jenkins on the night(s) of the assault(s). Mrs. Burleson countered:

33. *Fort Worth Gazette*, July 25, 1895.

34. *Fort Worth Gazette*, July 25, 1895.

35. At some point, Mrs. Burleson apparently claimed Antônia said she would swear on a Bible that no man had ever had intercourse with her (the stenographer's report appears garbled at this point) because Antônia was recalled to the stand to make one statement: "I didn't tell Mrs. Burleson that I never had connection with Steen Morris and that I would put my hand on the Bible and swear it." Rufus Burleson will later attribute these words to Antônia in the pamphlet, "The Brazilian Girl and Baylor University" (see chapter 6).

"I know Mrs. Jenkins who lives at my house. She is my mother and is 85 years old. I never left her with the girl at night during these months. I never did leave her at home at night in my life." *Never?* pressed the state's attorney. No, never, she responded: "My son-in-law and daughter lived just across the street but I never went across to visit them at night. I was not in the habit of going to church with my husband at night and have not been since I have been living here. I rarely left home and when I did I left someone with my mother." Well, mostly never: "I don't remember leaving but twice and I left someone there on each occasion. Once when my niece was married and again when I went to Miss Pruitt's wedding and when I got Mrs. Blunt to remain there. I can't tell what I didn't see as to the parties staying there while I was away, but found them there when I returned." Again, the wedding of Miss Pruitt was on the night the Cotton Palace was opened, the very night the first assault occurred. Nor was Mrs. Blunt called as a witness to corroborate Mrs. Burleson's claim about that evening.

Mrs. Burleson also testified that Antônia had menstrual periods before she arrived in Waco and had them regularly since that time.[36] It may seem a strange line of inquiry, but presumably the defense was trying to establish that Antônia was older than fourteen when these incidents occurred. Upon cross examination, Mrs. Burleson stated: "I knew about the periods of menstruation of this girl and that her sickness came on her before she came to this country and stated it from the information I got from Mr. Taylor."[37] Although it is not reported in the court stenographer's records, apparently Mrs. Lena K. Daniel, who met the Teixeira family for about a week when she and her husband briefly served in the Baptist mission in 1885, was called to verify that Antônia was older than claimed.[38]

36. Antônia had claimed her periods began only months before the first assault occurred.

37. This is an interesting claim because, as we discovered in the previous chapter, it was likely Taylor who maintained Antônia's younger age.

38. Mrs. Burleson also attempted to challenge the details of Antônia's account of the assault, claiming the arrangement of the kitchen and back door would not allow someone to reach through the door and drag out another person. She also stated that "during the months of December and November, I never have the dishes washed as late as nine o'clock. I superintend the washing of the dishes myself. I state that in the months of November and December I saw the washing of the dishes completed." Of course, this statement does not account for the evening(s), such as the night of the Cotton Palace, when Mrs. Burleson was not at home.

A witness for the defense, Mr. Ed Norris, who boarded in the home of Mrs. Powers across the

Most of the testimony taken on the next day, July 25, 1895, was offered by medical personnel. Dr. C. T. Young, called to testify on behalf of the state, indicated he had been a practicing physician for six years, had first examined Antônia Teixeira in May 1895, and had visited her frequently since then:

> The first time I visited her I made an examination. I found her pregnant with labor setting in or labor threatened. I examined her to see if she was threatened with labor. About two days afterwards I made an examination of her minutely and carefully. There was an ulceration in the lower part of the vulva. It was an old ulcer due to laceration. There had been an abrasion there and it had not been attended to and it had ulcerated. That is the only ulceration that I found.

What might have caused the laceration? Through the Victorian verbal screen, the answer is painfully evident: "It might have been produced by the insertion of the male member of a man. It was a tear of the lower portion or back portion of the vulva. I could not tell just how long it had been there, but could tell that it had been there for several months. It was the result of laceration." Young further explained that if a laceration "heals promptly it does not ulcerate, but if it does not heal rapidly it does ulcerate. I did not find that to be the result of any venereal trouble. In making a digital examination for pregnancy with the finger I would not notice the laceration unless it was very extensive."[39]

Dr. Young added one more important point: "I did not discover the evidence of any Ethiopian blood in the child." That is, in Dr. Young's opinion and despite S. L. Morris's accusations, the child could not be the product of intercourse between Antônia and a "black servant." All in all, Dr. Young's medical

---

street from the Burlesons was called to clarify a claim (passed on by an acquaintance, Will Bailey, to John Dyer, Antônia's attorney) that he had seen Steen Morris in the Burleson backyard. He denied seeing Morris there and asking him what he was doing there. Norris did admit to seeing Morris at the Burleson home in November or December but did not speak to him. "I said I had seen him there one time at night and frequently about the house, but didn't say that it was at night." On cross examination, Norris clarified that he saw Morris in the Burleson backyard around 6:00 p.m. and that darkness falls about that time in December, but he claimed Morris "didn't seem to be hiding, was standing up near the hydrant" near the back barn.

39. Dr. Young also was of the opinion based on her development that Antônia was about fourteen or fifteen years old.

opinion was consistent with Antônia Teixeira's claim of being the victim of a brutal sexual assault.[40]

On cross examination, Young conceded that the laceration and ulcer might have been only a month old but that it was "hardly probable that it was there for as much as a year." He also admitted that he could not tell exactly what had caused it: "Anything to tear the parts would have caused it, instruments or anything else." Dr. Young indicated he had been called to see Antônia by the family of Mrs. Ollie Jenkins and before any complaint was filed against Steen Morris. He also "took it for granted that she knew she was pregnant" but that "she didn't say how she became pregnant."

The physician called as a witness for the defense was Dr. O. I. Halbert, the Burlesons' family doctor and a practitioner in Waco for about twenty years. He had examined Antônia in April 1895: "I made a digital examination and I discovered that she was pregnant and supposed her to be so for about four and a half months. I did not discover an abrasion or tear in her parts. The hymen was not there which would have necessarily been so. She complained of no soreness at the time that I remember. She was a little nervous and excited. I discovered no abscesses, the parts felt natural." Dr. Halbert was not so delicate about Antônia's character: "From my examination my impression was that the parts had been used more than once, it didn't make the impression on my mind that they had been just occasionally used. It made the impression on my mind that the parts had been used a great deal." True, "that feeling might be fallacious and it does not follow that they had been but that was my impression. The parts were relaxed and it follows from use in sexual intercourse." After all, "usually rape on a small girl leaves the parts abraded and very sore, that occurs in the first sexual act with all women, and it is more likely to be more so where there has been rape than otherwise."

In her review of Halbert's testimony, Dr. Ann Sims concluded: "The hormones of pregnancy make the genital organs relaxed, especially the vagina, so the relaxation described by Dr. Halbert reflects the hormonal state of Antônia, not her sexual activity."[41] Dr. Craig Keathley also questioned Halbert's conclusion:

40. See also the conclusion of Drs. Sims and Keathley in appendix 3.
41. Dr. Ann Sims's medical review; see appendix 3.

Dr. Halbert describes a digital vaginal exam with a finding of "laxity" and the impression that "the parts had been used a great deal," suggesting sexual promiscuity. This is an unsupported inference on his part and is just as easily explained by the more detailed findings of Dr. Young, who describes a visual inspection with a finding of an "ulcer due to laceration." A laceration that is left untended will heal by a process called second intention with formation of granulation tissue that would have a similar appearance to an ulcer. The lack of a primary repair and approximation of the edges of the laceration would also contribute to an enlargement of the opening that Dr. Halbert would perceive on digital examination as laxity.[42]

Halbert also stated that when he informed Antônia that she was pregnant, she stated "that Steen Morris had something to do with her. . . . I don't know whether she stated anything about being raped or not. I don't remember what she said about it. From the conversation I judge she knew what had been done to her. . . . I had no difficulty in making her understand her condition."[43] This last statement, of course, contradicted Antônia's earlier claim that she did not understand what pregnancy meant until the doctor explained it to her.

On cross examination, Dr. Halbert was pressed regarding the statement that he observed no vaginal laceration. He admitted,

> I only made a finger examination of this girl. In making that kind of an examination it would depend on where the laceration was as to the ability to detect it. I did not make an ocular examination of the parts. . . . Assuming that there was laceration in the lower or backward portion of the vulva I would not discover it unless my attention was called to it by her flinching from the soreness.

Halbert then seemed to respond to the previous testimony of Dr. Young: "A physician making an ocular examination in May would be more likely to discover the laceration if there was any than I would have been in April. If I had

---

42. Dr. Craig Keathley's medical review; see appendix 3.

43. Halbert concluded this part of his statement with the condescending comment: "She seemed to be a girl of ordinary intelligence."

made an ocular examination of the vulva, I could have determined whether there had been laceration or not."

Both doctors were questioned closely about the gestational period of the infant. They agreed that the child had not gone to full term when born on June 18, 1895.[44] Halbert, who had not examined the child, based his opinion on his view that Antônia was four-and-a-half months pregnant when he examined her in April. Young, who had examined the child, observed that the child "had fingernails and a little hair, had film over the eyes and the external genitals were not fully developed and the bones of the head were very soft. I don't think it was a nine months child." But Young also observed: "I never heard of a child to live at six months and a half." On redirect, Young clarified: "A child might be born a little before the expiration of the seven months and live. Seven-month-old children do frequently live." In any case, it was established that the child had not been conceived nine months prior to its birth date. The gestational stage fit the general parameters of a sexual encounter in either early November (more likely from Young's point of view) or early December.

Analysis of Medical Testimony

Two questions emerged from the medical testimony by Drs. Halbert and Young. Did the age of Antônia Teixeira's child establish conception to have occurred within the timeframe of assaults described by the victim? And could it be established that Antônia Teixeira was the victim of rape?

As to the child's gestation, Dr. Keathley commented:

> The description in the testimony suggests a preterm delivery that would support a conception date about November 1894. A conception occurring late November or early December would have put the gestational age at delivery [6/18/1895] at approximately thirty weeks. . . . A baby born at thirty weeks in the late nineteenth century would most likely not survive and die shortly after birth. The fact that this child did survive until spring of 1896 would suggest a somewhat later gestational age consistent with a conception in the early part of November. This would correlate with a gestational age closer to thirty-four weeks. A child born at this gestational age in the late nineteenth

---

44. The *Waco Morning News* (June 18, 1895) placed the birth on June 17. The preliminary hearing was postponed until July to allow Antônia to recover.

century would still be considered significantly premature but would be much more likely than a thirty-week delivery to survive for the several months that this child apparently survived.

But didn't trial testimony mention Antônia having a menstrual period on or about November 12, almost a week after the alleged rape on November 6? "An episode of vaginal bleeding (whether it was truly a menstrual period is unknown) following a sexual encounter does not necessarily eliminate that encounter as a potential conception date," Dr. Keathley explains. Dr. Halbert's suggestion that this was improbable though not unknown "lacks support . . . [for] certainly any woman or young girl that ovulates can conceive during any sexual encounter as was pointed out by Dr. Young in his testimony." In sum, "the baby was clearly premature based on the testimony, and survival of the child beyond the immediate neonatal period suggests a date of conception earlier in the sequence of events rather than later."[45]

There is, therefore, no reason to think Antônia's pregnancy occurred outside the November 6–December 1, 1894, timeframe within which the assaults occurred.

As to the second question, whether or not the evidence points to Antônia Teixeira having been the victim of rape, Dr. Ann Sims concluded:

> The findings testified to by these doctors, especially Dr. Young, are very consistent with the history that Antônia gave. The pain and bleeding created by the events Antônia described are consistent with forceful entry of some object into the female genital organ (which by definition is all the genital organs proximal to or closer to the body than the plane formed by the outmost surface of the labia majora). Together, Antônia's description and the physicians' findings are consistent with sexual abuse/sexual assault.[46]

Similarly, Dr. Craig Keathley also reviewed the medical testimony from the preliminary hearing and concluded: "In reviewing the medical testimony of Drs. Halbert and Young, there are consistencies in both testimonies that support physical-exam evidence of vaginal injury consistent with rape."[47]

45. Appendix 3.
46. Appendix 3.
47. Appendix 3.

Conclusion

The examining trial concluded on July 26, 1895. The evidence presented there seemed to have exceeded the relatively low bar of probable cause necessary to proceed to a jury trial.[48] The defense attorneys, however, filed a writ of habeas corpus, demanding that the prosecution show it had valid reasons for detaining the accused. The next day, Morris appeared before Judge L. W. Goodrich of the Nineteenth District Court.[49] Judge Goodrich had several options before him. He could have retained the case for trial, ordered the defendant released from custody without dismissing the case, or, failing to find probable cause, dismissed the case altogether. After reviewing the transcript of the preliminary hearing and having Georgia Burleson and S. L. Morris repeat their testimony under oath, Goodrich released the defendant from custody. The *Galveston Daily News* reported, "There was something of a scene in the court room when the defendant found himself restored to freedom and back among his friends."[50]

Goodrich might have chosen the second option, to release Morris from custody, since the case would retain the same number. On the other hand, another indictment for Morris's arrest was issued in the following September, suggesting that the case may have been dismissed altogether.[51] In either scenario, this particular battle was over. The war had just begun.

48. This conclusion is supported by the assessment of the testimonies by Drs. Sims and Keathley (see appendix 3) and the oral interview with the law professor Gerald Powell.

49. Judge Goodrich (1836–1911) was admitted to the bar in 1866; in 1890 he was appointed Nineteenth District Court judge. The Nineteenth District Court met in both McLennan and Falls Counties; later the jurisdiction included only McLennan County. Goodrich retired from the bench in 1898 and moved to a farm in Marlin, TX. McSwain, *Bench and Bar*, 101–2.

50. *Galveston Daily News*, July 27, 1895. What written evidence did Judge Goodrich consider? Professor Gerald Powell suggested that Blair had everything except Antônia's initial testimony typed for presentation to Judge Goodrich. Powell, interview with author, August 19, 2021.

51. It should be noted that both W. C. Brann and Rufus Burleson understood that Goodrich had dismissed the case altogether.

6

The War of Words:
W. C. Brann v. Rufus Burleson

The *Waco Morning News*'s exposé of the sexual assault and pregnancy of Antônia Teixeira, published on June 16, 1895, included an interview with Dr. Rufus Burleson, the president of Baylor University.[1] After recounting the circumstances in which he had agreed to Z. C. Taylor's proposal that the Burlesons provide board and schooling for Antônia Teixeira, he found that he now had to "reflect on the character of this most unfortunate girl." To be sure, he did so "with exceeding great reluctance," yet forged bravely on because "the sternest necessity of justice demands it at my hands."[2]

In his interview Burleson first denied that Antônia "was treated as a servant and not given money compensation." She was rather "treated as my granddaughter"; indeed, he "gave her board, tuition and clothes or more than double the worth of her help" around the house. Burleson next attacked Antônia's character, claiming that despite "her genial nature and pleasing disposition, the girl was utterly untrustworthy." Mrs. Burleson had to keep her expense money locked away; more to the point, Burleson insisted, "the girl was crazy

---

1. The June 16 article was the first time Antônia's pregnancy had been publicly revealed. In an earlier article, there was a vague reference to "a most deplorable affair . . . in which a young and thoughtless girl is the victim of her own indiscretion and man's criminality" ("Deplorable Indeed," *Waco Morning News*, June 6, 1895). Apparently, this "teaser" was the first, albeit opaque, reference to her condition, a supposition supported by the repetition of the word "deplorable" in the June 16 article.

2. *Waco Morning News*, June 16, 1895. All quotations in this section are taken from this newspaper article.

after the boys. . . . On account of these faults," the president confessed, the Burlesons had "admonished her, prayed for her and wept over her." Despite these interventions, he further rued, Antônia was "powerless to resist these inherent passions and vices."

Nonetheless, the Burlesons "kept her" on, being unable to return her to Brazil. Never, however, had "the girl ever informed Mrs. Burleson of an assault on her by Stein [sic] Morris or any other person," Burleson insisted. Any statement to that effect was "wholly false." He added an unnamed amour to the mix, "a young student at the University" who "pleaded that she forced herself upon him." Burleson concluded the interview with his unwavering summary on the matter: "I think the idea of rape in this case simply preposterous."

W. C. Brann's *Iconoclast*

William Cowper Brann was a keenly interested reader of Burleson's interview. A talented journalist who had settled in Waco in 1894, his journal, the *Iconoclast*, would eventually reach a circulation of 100,000.[3] Brann was a controversialist who took great pleasure in criticizing what he perceived to be the hypocrisy of the local religious establishment—Methodists, Episcopalians, and especially the Baptists and their educational crown jewel, Baylor University. Antônia's story was tailor-made for him, and in the July 1895 issue of the *Iconoclast* he issued a scathing rebuke of Baylor and Burleson.[4] It was not his custom to deal with the "sexual crimes of professing Christians," he opined, as they took up too much space and were not profitable. Yet, "once or twice in a decade a case arises so horrible in conception, so iniquitous in outline, so damnable in detail

---

3. For more on Brann, see Charles Carver, *Brann and the Iconoclast* (London: T. Nelson, 1958); and more recently, Eric S. Ames, *Hidden History of Waco* (Charleston, SC: The History Press, 2020).

4. Jerry Flemmons has speculated about Brann's obsession with the Teixeira incident:

> An earlier tragedy could explain his dogged, angry pursuit of the Waco controversy that ultimately took his life. At age 13, his daughter Inez committed suicide. Blaming himself for her death, he wrote of her passing and locked away the words until he died. They had argued over a boy who wanted to court Inez, and as a proper Victorian father, Brann had forbidden his daughter to see him. She left a note: "Tomorrow I will be dead. I took all the morphine. I don't want to live. I could never be as good as you want me to. You would be ashamed of me. I hope God will take me to Heaven." He wrote, "The most perfect life is not worth the living for itself alone. There's still more shadow than sunshine, less pleasure than pain . . . my ignorance and anger killed Inez." Small wonder that he came to champion the plight of young Antonia Teixeira. (Flemmons, "Truth: The Life and Death of the Iconoclast, W. C. Brann," *Heritage* 3 [1999]: 14–16)

that it were impossible to altogether ignore it. Such a case has just come to light, involving Baylor University, that Bulwark of the Baptist church."[5]

Brann claimed the reprehensible event to be nearly indescribable, so he would have to press hard to capture its enormity: "As there is a depth of the sea to which the plummet will not descend, so are there depths of human depravity which mind cannot measure. Language hath its limits, and even a Dante could only liken the horrors of Hell to earthly symbols. It were as impossible to describe in print the case of Antônia Teixeira as to etch a discord or paint a stench."[6] He began by recalling Antônia's arrival in Waco:

> We all remember the coming to Texas of Antônia Teixeira, the dove-eyed heteroscian, and the brass-band display of the modest little thing by the Baptist brethren, whose long years of missionary labor in Brazil had snatched her from the Papal power—a veritable brand from the burning. . . . The child was to be given five years' schooling, then returned to her native land to point out to her benighted Catholic countrymen the water route to the Celestial City.

He then unleashed his considerable capacity for satire: "To be educated, and useful and honored both in the world and the world to come, instead of an ignorant little beggar about the streets of Bahia. Bearded men prayed over her and sentimental women wept to know that she was saved—saved from the purgatorium of Popery! And then she was 'consecrated' and began her studies at Baylor, the duly ordained 'ward of the Baptist church.'" Brann could only imagine: "How the poor little heart must have swelled with gratitude to the good Baptist brethren, and how she must have loved everything, animate and inanimate, that the good God had made." But exploitation soon set in: "ere long she found herself in Dr. Burleson's kitchen instead of the class-room. Instead of digging Greek roots she was studying the esculent tuber. Instead of being prepared for missionary work, this 'ward of the Baptist church' was learning the duties of the scullion."[7] While "Dr. Burleson has informed the world through the public prints that as a servant she was not worth her board and clothes,"

---

5. William Cowper Brann, *The Complete Works of Brann, The Iconoclast,* 12 vols. (Brann Publishers, 1919), 2:286. *The Complete Works* do not identify the issue or date of the material cited; they have been determined here by comparison with quotations in Carver's *Brann and the Iconoclast.* Carver identifies the material cited here as coming from the July 1895 issue of the *Iconoclast.*

6. Brann, *Complete Works,* 2:287.

7. Brann, *Complete Works,* 2:288.

Brann retorted, "she was not brought hither to sling pots, but to prepare for the saving of souls."[8]

There followed a rehearsal of what had transpired after Antônia's assault: "it was discovered that the 'ward of the Baptist church' was about to give birth to a babe. . . . She was sneaked off to a private house and nothing said about her condition to the secular authorities—no steps taken to bring the destroyer of the child in short dresses to justice."[9] Then the editor turned Burleson's own words in the *Waco Morning News* against him:

> What did the aged president of Baylor, that *sanctum sanctorum* of the Baptist church, do about it? Did he assist in bringing to justice the man who had dared invade the sanctity of his household and despoiled the duly ordained "ward of the Baptist church?" Not exactly. He rushed into print with a statement to the effect that child was a thief and "crazy after the boys"—that he had "prayed and wept over her" without avail.[10]

Brann next cited a medical examination, reported in the papers, which found Antônia to be the victim of a savage attack, countering Burleson's allegation that the idea was "preposterous." He also answered Burleson's claim that Antônia was boy crazy by citing (unnamed) Baylor students who judged her to be "particularly modest and womanly."[11]

Brann next went after S. L. Morris, brother of the accused assailant and Burleson's son-in-law. Morris had "tried to make it appear that the father of her unborn child was a negro servant and her accepted paramour," Brann observed, but "Antônia replied to this insult added to injury by putting a white child in evidence—a child with the pale blue eyes and wooden face characteristic of those who defamed her."[12] Brann was careful not to venture into libel, repeatedly asserting that he did not know whether or not Morris was

8. Brann, *Complete Works*, 2:288–89.

9. Brann, *Complete Works*, 2:289. Referring to Antônia as the "ward of the Baptist Church" was a recurring refrain in Brann's critique over the next year or so.

10. Brann, *Complete Works*, 2:289–90.

11. Brann, *Complete Works*, 2:290.

12. Brann, *Complete Works*, 2:291. Later (June 1896), Brann will go so far as to say that the child resembles Steen Morris himself; here he only alludes a general "family resemblance." Brann's hyperbolic rhetoric, here and elsewhere, made it easier for Burleson and his Baylor allies to dismiss Brann's critique (much of which is insightful and convincing) as "vile slander" (Brann, 5:87).

guilty of the crime of which he was accused.[13] Brann did, however, criticize the "Baptist brethren" who refused to provide material support to Teixeira and chose rather "to blacken her name, to forestall pity, prevent charity and make an impartial trial of the case impossible." Instead, it was folk "who never professed religion, who never expect to wear feathers and fly through Elysian fields" who collected "a handsome purse" to provide for Antônia and "the young Baptist she was about to bring into the world."[14] He closed with real rhetorical flourish: Because of the religionists' neglect of duty toward Antônia Teixeira in her hour of need, it would have been "better a thousand times that she should have remained in Brazil to say her pater nosters in the Portuguese tongue; better that she should have wedded a water-carrier in her native land and reared up sturdy sons and daughters of the Church of Rome, than to have been transported to Texas to breed illegitimate Baptists."[15]

While critical of the perceived hypocrisy of Baylor's leaders and allies, Brann himself was certainly no progressive in our sense of that word, especially regarding matters of race. He used racial slurs with abandon and constantly condescended toward Antônia, referring to her as "ignorant," a "child in short dresses," "uneducated," etc.[16] There is a certain callousness in Brann's writing about Antônia's predicament; he seemed more than content to sit in his second-floor *Iconoclast* office at the corner of Fourth and Franklin Streets firing off missives apparently more intent on scoring rhetorical points than in understanding the reality of Antônia's isolation and suffering. Had she known it, Antônia may have repeated the adage "with friends like this, who needs enemies?" Still, with all his shortcomings, Brann was one of the few allies that she had and was certainly the most eloquent and powerful among them.

With the preliminary hearing over, Brann's ire shot around from Burleson and his allies to his university and back. The August 1895 issue of the *Iconoclast*

13. Though admittedly, this apparent objectivity looks like a very thin veneer in some of Brann's more pointed posts.

14. Brann, *Complete Works*, 2:291.

15. Brann, *Complete Works*, 2:292.

16. Part of the issue, at least in regard to Antônia, is that Brann, like most of the residents of Waco at the time, believed that Antônia was between thirteen and fourteen years old at the time of her assault. As discussed in previous chapters, it seems much more likely that she was in her late teens when she arrived in Waco. Legally, as Brann will point out, it would make no difference if she were older since the age of consent in Texas at the time of the assault was twelve. Still, Antônia's perceived age fueled Brann's rhetoric and moral outrage (cf. Brann, *Complete Works*, 3:31).

headlined "Baylor in Bad Business," but it opened with one more shot at Steen Morris. The man may have been released from custody, but Brann couldn't help but wonder:

> If he never had carnal intercourse with the child why does she accuse him of being the father of her illegitimate babe? What has she to gain by shielding the real criminal and accusing an innocent man of the terrible crime? She is evidently not seeking to recover pecuniary damages, for Morris has no money. She cannot expect to coerce him into marrying her, for he is already a benedict. Her accusation is evidently not the result of enmity, for she entered no complaint against him until requested by the court to disclose the author of her disgrace. Why then did she accuse the defendant and stick to her story despite the efforts of the Morrises to bluff and bullyrag her into a recantation?[17]

Men of means and reputation "are sometimes wrongly accused of sexual crimes by brazen adventuresses," Brann went on, "but Morris is neither wealthy nor distinguished, and it is inconceivable that a child in short dresses should learn to play the adventuress in a Baptist college—or even in Dr. Burleson's kitchen."[18]

He then turned to the issue of Baylor's complicity in Antônia's treatment:

> Baylor college will have to answer at the bar of public opinion for its brutal and unchristian treatment of the Brazilian girl. She was committed to its care, a child of 13, unversed in this world's wickedness. She was utterly alone, and Baylor was to be father and mother, sister and brother to her until she developed into noble womanhood and was safely returned to her kindred across the far seas, consecrated to the cause of Christ. Instead of being carefully educated she was consigned to the kitchen.[19]

Brann then turned back to Burleson: "the aged president of Baylor denounced her as a thief and branded her in the public prints as a bawd. During her con-

---

17. Brann, *Complete Works*, 3:30. Brann's reference to a recantation by Antônia is prescient; Antônia did, in fact, recant her testimony one year later.

18. Brann, *Complete Works*, 3:31.

19. Brann, *Complete Works*, 3:31–32.

finement she was shown less consideration by Baylor than is due a wolf about to become a mother—and she the duly ordained 'ward of the Baptist church!'" Finally, Brann offered a more general comment that would eventually bring the ire of the entire Baylor empire down on him and cost him dearly:

> There is not enough water in all the oceans to wash the dark stain from the escutcheon of this Baptist college; there are not words enough in the English language to convince the American people that Baylor is a proper custodian for their daughters. The credit of the Morris family may be preserved; Steen may escape the penitentiary; the unfortunate girl and her Baptist bastard may disappear from the face of the earth, but Baylor college will stink in the nostrils of Christendom—it is "damned to everlasting fame."[20]

The news that Judge Goodrich had released Morris without bail—this "Scotch verdict"—also triggered Brann's outrage: "One judicial tribunal, after an exhaustive hearing of the case, decided that the girl was telling the truth and ordered the defendant held; another, after a cursory examination of the matter, and without calling the complainant to combat the witnesses for the defense, ordered that he be discharged. So ends the suit. No one will be punished for the ruin of Antônia Teixeira, the 'ward of the Baptist Church.'"[21] In Brann's eyes, Baylor thought it had discharged its responsibilities to Antônia Teixeira by "establishing, to the satisfaction of the court, not who is, but who is not responsible for her ruin." He lamented: "Poor Antônia! Miserable little waif, adrift among the Baptist wolves. She can now beg money of the publicans and sinners to carry her to her native land, and there lay her ill-begotten babe on her old mother's breast—as her diploma from Baylor!" Hypocrites like "Dr. Burleson will doubtless continue to 'weep and pray' over erring girls" while all the while lambasting them "in the public press."[22] Brann's conclusion unleashed his whole arsenal: "The Baptists will continue to send missionaries to Brazil to teach the . . . heathen what to do with their young daughters, and the godly people to rail at prize-fighting as a public disgrace—while Antônia

---

20. Brann, *Complete Works*, 3:32.

21. Brann, *Complete Works*, 3:33. A "Scotch verdict" was a third verdict of "not proven" allowed by Scottish criminal courts in addition to innocent or guilty.

22. Brann, *Complete Works*, 3:33, 34.

Teixeira clasps her fatherless babe to her childish breast, wets its face with bitter tears and wonders if God knows there's such a place as Texas."[23]

The courts may have released Steen Morris without bail, but public opinion regarding the case, especially in the secular papers, began to turn toward Brann's view and against Baylor and Burleson. The August 1, 1895, issue of the *Lagrange Journal* declaimed: "The justice who held the examining trial, held Morris to bail in the sum of five thousand dollars, and the district judge, on the same testimony, discharges him without bail, virtually saying that Morris had committed no crime for which he was amenable to the law." It uttered a prayer by way of prediction: "It is to be hoped that Brann will in the August number of his *Iconoclast*, thoroughly ventilate this scandalous proceeding, by which a seducer, at least, is turned loose on the community."[24]

Even those papers who rejected Brann's broadsides against the university and/or the Baptist denomination showed some sympathies with his critique of Burleson and the Morrises. The editor of the *Temple Times* wrote:

> The text is the Morris-Texeira case. That a cruel injustice has been done can hardly be denied. That Burleson, Morris and brother are at fault, he has assumed. But that the members of the denomination are culpable, is false or that the college is culpable is false. The man loses the effect of his shot when he hits an innocent person. . . . *Granting to be true all that Brann says of Burleson and Morris*, then what right has he to hurl his invectives against those who are as ignorant of the facts as a babe?[25]

Some Baptist laity wrote Burleson sympathizing with Antônia, such as S. G. Halloway from Firestone County:

> Kind Sir
>
> Seeing in the Fort Worth Gazette a report of the melancholy calamity which has overtaken the lonely and seemingly friendless Portuguese girl—which seems to have been a ward of yours—I desired additional facts in the case and

23. Brann, *Complete Works*, 3:34.

24. *The Lagrange Journal* 16, no. 31 (August 1, 1895), cited from the Texas Digital Paper Program at the University of North Texas, https://texashistory.unt.edu/explore/collections/TDNP/.

25. *The Temple Times*, August 30, 1895 (emphasis added).

desire to place myself in correspondence with the girl and only ask the favor at your hands to secure to me her consent to a correspondence and in compensation for your trouble I promise you my lasting gratitude. Well knowing the many devices and snares to lead astray innocent virtue which lurks in all great cities; it is the duty of the strong to shield the weak and endeavor to reclaim those on the very verge of the breakers on which so many are wrecked.[26]

Such correspondence, if lacking any direct criticism, must have given Burleson real concern.

Rufus Burleson, "The Brazilian Girl and Baylor University"

The public debate with Brann left President Rufus Burleson in a somewhat vulnerable position. His relationship with the Baylor Board of Trustees had long been strained, dating back to his initial resignation as president of the university in Independence in 1861. The matter was a perennial topic of discussion in the *Baptist Standard*, the denominational paper of Texas Baptists. More recently, Burleson had sided with Samuel Augustus Hayden over against B. H. Carroll, J. B. Cranfill, and other Baylor trustees over issues of ecclesiology, power, and influence. Thus Burleson issued a cryptic letter to Trustee Chair J. B. Cranfill, published in the July 25, 1895, issue of the *Baptist Standard*, barely referencing but hardly ignoring the latest imbroglio. He stated that "after a full, free and frank conference with the board I can say that the board of trustees do not now and have never desired or even discussed my removal as president of the University." At the same time he admitted that neither "[B. H.] Carroll nor any member of the board made any pledge whatever to keep me in that position [the presidency] for life, nor would I have accepted such pledge had it been made, though members of the board present did express the hope that I would remain in the presidency so long as I lived." He perhaps gave away the game by concluding: "I take pleasure in adding that I do not in any way connect Dr. Carroll with the attack on me by the secular press in regard to the Brazilian girl."[27]

---

26. S. G. Holloway to Rufus Burleson, Brewer Firestone Co., June 24, 1895, box 2, folder 33, Rufus Burleson Correspondence, Texas Collection, Baylor University.

27. *Baptist Standard*, July 25, 1895. On the Hayden controversy that had engulfed all of Texas

Yet Burleson felt pressure to respond to criticisms of his role in the affair, especially those coming from his fellow Wacoan, William Cowper Brann. As a result, in August 1895, Burleson published a pamphlet that sought to justify his and Baylor's role in the Antônia Teixeira controversy. He was primarily concerned to counter such charges as Brann's that "Baylor University is an unsafe place to educate young ladies." No doubt he was also heartened by the recent decision of Judge Goodrich, who "so wisely decided the infamous charges against Steen Morris for raping the Brazilian girl utterly groundless and without a particle of evidence, and dismissed the case."[28]

Baptists at the time, including Carroll and Burleson, see Joseph E. Early Jr., *A Texas Baptist Power Struggle: The Hayden Controversy* (Denton: University of North Texas Press, 2005).

Burleson's comments take on a different light when considering that in less than two years' time, on June 10, 1897, he would "step down" from the Baylor presidency against his will and reluctantly accept a position as president emeritus with a full salary of $2,000. The vitriolic character of his exchange with Carroll on that occasion can be seen in Burleson's letter published in the August 5, 1897, edition of the *Texas Baptist and Herald*, two months after Burleson's forced retirement. Burleson wrote that Carroll

> had a morbid and long indulged habit of ambition coupled with a physical infirmity which physicians admit does sometimes involve the intellectual perceptions of moral questions, without affecting the strength of the thinking faculties themselves. This has been aggravated by a morbid taste for reading novels of every description, covering the larger portion of his life, covering at times by his own boast a novel a day for months and years in succession. It would be unchristian in me to make these statements in the public prints had it not become necessary by his own publications. (*Texas Baptist and Herald*, August 5, 1897)

Carroll responded two weeks later in the *Baptist Standard* (August 19, 1897):

> He [Burleson] was not re-elected president simply because the impairment of his once vigorous faculties by old age utterly unfitted him for the active duties . . . and responsibilities of the presidency of a great university. That because he was not properly himself we did not hold him responsible for many strange and contradictory things done and said, particularly when played on by the designing who had an ax to grind. In the hands of such men . . . he is as helpless as a little child.

Carroll did not name W. C. Brann as one such ax wielder, but it is not difficult to imagine that the Morris-Teixeira incident which had unfolded in a very public way over the previous two years played a role in the Trustees' decision, Carroll's protestations to the contrary notwithstanding. Apparently, Burleson also partially blamed his transition to emeritus status on the Teixeira-Morris affair (see John Nova Lomax, "The Apostle of the Devil," *Texas Monthly*, June 3, 2016, https://www .texasmonthly.com/the-daily-post/the-apostle-of-the-devil/).

28. Burleson, "The Brazilian Girl." All Burleson quotations in this section are taken from this pamphlet. Elsewhere in it, Burleson challenges Brann's claim that Judge Goodrich was a Baptist. The pamphlet did little to stem the tide against Burleson and Baylor, however. The October 6, 1895,

Burleson began the pamphlet as he did the *Waco Morning News* interview, by expressing regret at having to make negative comments about a student: "Nothing grieves my heart more than to publish or even say anything disparaging a student." But that did not deter him from disparaging Antônia over and over again in these pages. The very title of Burleson's pamphlet dehumanizes her. She is not Antônia or Antônia Teixeira; she is "the Brazilian girl." Even when Burleson did call her by name, he several times misspelled her name, using the masculine form, "Antônio."

Burleson recounted how he had responded to Z. C. Taylor's query regarding the resources Baylor might provide for Antônia: Baylor had no endowment for support beyond that provided for ministerial students or the children of Texas pastors. Nonetheless, Burleson continued, he and Mrs. Burleson had offered personally to "take her in our family and furnish her board, tuition, books and clothing, and teach her housekeeping." Burleson apparently kept detailed records of expenses incurred by Antônia, for he reported that he and Mrs. Burleson had spent at least $320 on her. With this move, Burleson tried to refute Brann's persistent claim that Antônia was "the ward of Baylor University or the Baptists of Texas." She was, rather, a personal burden to the Burlesons alone: "Mrs. Burleson and I are the only persons that ever assumed any responsibility, or paid any money and all the blame, if there be any, rests on us." Yet he asserted, "how utterly blameless we are, 'let facts be submitted to a candid world,' facts that will stand the test of Judgment Day." Burleson proceeded to list those "facts": Antônia was treated like a daughter by his family; she slept in the "best room" with Mrs. Burleson's mother; she was given a seat at the dinner table (though, according to Burleson, she preferred to wait and dine with the Black servants); she dressed as one of their grandchildren and in bad weather rode to the university with Burleson in his buggy. "No daughter was ever treated more kindly. We thought of her as the orphan daughter of a Baptist preacher who had died five thousand miles away."

Yet, he went on, Antônia returned all these kindnesses with "trouble and annoyance." She "loathed study and all kinds of work"; her housekeeping was hardly worth one dollar a month. And eventually she manifested what

---

issue of *The Sunday Gazetteer* (Denison, TX) reported: "A bad feature in this case is that although Antonia was brought from Brazil to be educated for a missionary and had lived in Dr. Burleson's family, no attempt was apparently made by the college officials to discover and bring to punishment the perpetrator of the heinous crime."

Burleson labeled "the three besetting sins of Brazilians": "lust, a want of veracity and honesty."[29] Burleson supplied examples of each of these flaws from Antônia's behavior, underscoring the matter of "shameful talk" caused by her "passion for boys." Confronted with this behavior by Mrs. Burleson, she responded (in Burleson's words): "Why Mamie I am ashamed for you to suspect me I will lay my hand on this Bible and swear no man ever touched me." Since they could not find someone to return Antônia to her family in Brazil, the Burlesons had to give her "closer attention than we ever gave to any ten girls in Baylor University during the last forty-four years." The next sentence perhaps spoke more ominously than Burleson knew: "The only way we could have guarded her more closely would have been to chain her in a cell with bars."

Burleson came then to the nub of the matter, revealing where his allegiances lay: "Yet on her single testimony an honorable young man was thrown into jail, and his young wife, and aged parents and family made inexpressibly miserable." Later in the document, citing Mrs. C. D. Daniel, a former missionary to Brazil, Burleson expanded his slander to label Antônia's family as "the filthiest and most depraved she ever knew."[30] In short, Burleson's pamphlet provides a case study of victim-blaming rooted in racism and xenophobia.

After Antônia's pregnancy was confirmed by the family doctor, Burleson undertook actions that would draw sharp attack by Brann and others: "We immediately wrote Galveston, Dallas and Ft. Worth to find some safe Reformatory where she could be placed." He apparently also wrote the Texas State Reformatory up the road in Gatesville, Texas. His former student, Y. S. Jenkins, had to reply:

> I am just in rect of yr. letter mentioning a certain very sad occurrence. There is no way by which any person can become an occupant of the State Reformatory except by violating the criminal laws of the state. It is the same thing as the state Penitentiary, only differing in the age of its occupants. All persons

29. Burleson here claimed to be quoting the views of Z. C. Taylor. That Taylor was capable of slandering the entirety of the Brazilian population is evidenced in his personal correspondence. See for example Z. C. Taylor to Misses Wilcox and Stenger, in which the Brazilian people are "idolatrous Catholics, the masses ignorant and superstitious" (Z. C. Taylor to Misses Wilcox and Stenger, May 1, 1895, Z. C. Taylor Correspondence, IMB Archives).

30. Burleson also cited Mrs. Daniel as a witness to the claim that Antônia was older than depicted in the papers and by Brann.

in the state found guilty of a Penitentiary offence under the age of 16 years are sent to the state Reformatory. [signed] Jenkins "grateful student"[31]

By all appearances the Burlesons did not take seriously Antônia's complaints that she was assaulted; rather, the intention was to place Antônia and her condition out of the public eye. Yet Burleson thought his explanation to be an adequate defense against the two foremost criticisms levelled against Baylor and himself personally: "These facts will demonstrate how malicious and black are the false-hoods sent broad-cast over Texas: first; that Baylor and the Baptists were ever responsible for this unfortunate girl." Yet it seems inescapable to reach any conclusion other than that Baylor *was* responsible for a young woman transported thousands of miles from her homeland to live in a foreign country and attend a foreign college—indeed, to take up residence in the home of that college's president and his family. To deny any responsibility for the welfare of that person would appear to be the very definition of shirking Christian duty, not to mention Christian hospitality. Burleson's pamphlet does little to allay these concerns, despite his charge that the Waco papers (no doubt especially the *Iconoclast*) were "slandering and vilifying an institution that has done so much for the moral and material development of Waco."

The second criticism Burleson addressed in greater detail, sounding a classic trope of patriarchy:

> second how equally black and damnable are the lies that Mrs. Burlson and I made her a cook, and cast her off in the kitchen to be ruined and then thrust her into the streets to be picked up by Catholics and other "publicans and sinners." I learned from my Welch ancestors and my Father that "Next to God every man should worship his wife, his mother and his daughter, and should ever be ready to defend a woman's honor with his life's blood"; and there was never a time when I would not have slain any man if I found him outraging a woman. I ever guard the character and persons of my students, especially females, with sleepless fatherly vigilance. For years I have advocated enacting a law to make every rapist a eunuch and then confine him to hard work in the Penitentiary for life. And the man who publishes that I have carelessly permitted this crime in my own house, deserves to be cow-hided out of Texas.

31. Y. S. Jenkins to Rufus Burleson, April 18, 1895, box 2, folder 29, Rufus Burleson Correspondence, Texas Collection, Baylor University.

Despite his bravado, however, at no time did Burleson seriously entertain the idea that Antônia Teixeira was the victim of a brutal sexual assault; instead, several times over he dismissed the notion out of hand as "preposterous."

Burleson then turned to a conventional theological defense, exonerating his inaction with the claim that "the Lord himself did not prevent Eve from going astray with the Devil nor will any watch care prevent some student from going astray." Blaming Eve for original (or sexual) sin and then extending that to the entire female population is a familiar move.[32] Steen Morris was innocent of all charges; Antônia Teixeira brought on herself through her "actions or words" whatever shame and hurt accompanied her pregnancy by some other unknown male. Twice Burleson caustically remarked that Antônia was not the "little Missionary Angel" so many thought her to be.

On the last page of the pamphlet, Burleson returned to his prime concern and made it clear that his commitment was not to determining the facts of the case of Antônia Teixeira but to damage control in defense of the reputation of Baylor University: "our persecutors say because one frail Brazilian girl out of the vast army of students, has gone astray, 'Baylor University is an unsafe place to educate young ladies.'" Burleson feared the incident could cause Texas Baptists to withdraw their daughters from enrollment in the school and further weaken his presidency.[33] He countered: "I can and do challenge any school in or out of Texas, Catholic or Protestant, to show purer brighter jewels than the daughters of Baylor University."

He concluded with a plea and a warning: "I sincerely hope . . . that all good students and citizens will rise up and vindicate Baylor University, and that those who have thoughtlessly or maliciously slandered her spotless character will repent and confess openly their sins and receive forgiveness, before they are everlastingly lost."

---

32. For an alternative, and compelling, reading of Gen. 2–3, see Julie Faith Parker, "Blaming Eve Alone," *JBL* 132 (2013): 729–47; for a history of this view in early Christian and Jewish sources, see Gary A. Anderson, *The Genesis of Perfection: Adam and Eve in Jewish and Christian Imagination* (Louisville: Westminster John Knox, 2001).

33. Burleson's fear was not completely unfounded: by some accounts, more than thirty women did withdraw from the university in the immediate aftermath (Lomax, "The Apostle of the Devil").

William Buck Bagby
(1855-1939), missionary to
Brazil *(TC)*

Anne Luther Bagby
(1859-1942), missionary to
Brazil *(TC)*

Above, Zachary C. Taylor (1850-1919), missionary to Brazil *(IMB); right,* Zachary C. Taylor and Kate Crawford Taylor (1862-1894), missionaries to Brazil *(TC)*

Mission meeting, 1892; pictured are the Bagbys, the Entzmingers, the J. J. Taylors, the Ginsburgs, the Sopers, and the Downings *(IMB)*

W. B. Bagby and Brazilian nationals *(IMB)*

Antônio Teixeira de Albuquerque (1840-1887) and his family. The original photo has no identification, but it is understood by some descendants of Antônio T. Albuquerque as being a picture of his family, ca. 1882. From left to right, behind: Antônio and son João; an unknown young woman, perhaps a servant. In front: Antônia, who is called simply "the firstborn"; D. Senhorinha; Antonio Junior; Pedro, in an older woman's lap (perhaps a close relative—mother? sister?—of D. Senhorinha); Madã. (Betty Antunes de Oliveira, *Antonio Teixeira de Albuquerque: O Primeiro Pastor Batista Brasileiro* [Rio de Janeiro: self-published, 1982], image 10)

Left, Georgia Jenkins Burleson
(1833-1924), wife of Rufus
Burleson *(TC); below,* Rufus
Burleson (1823-1901), president
of Baylor University (1851-1861;
1886-1897) *(TC)*

Left, Hallie Burleson Morris
(1865-1952), daughter of Rufus
and Georgia Burleson and wife
of S. L. Morris *(TC)*

Home of President and Mrs. Burleson, 912 Baylor Avenue *(TC)*

William Cowper Brann
(1855-1898), editor
of *The Iconoclast,*
1895 *(TC)*

Provident Building, at the corner of Fourth and Franklin Avenues, completed 1890, where W. C. Brann's *Iconoclast* offices were housed *(TC)*

McLennan County Courthouse, at the corner of Second and Franklin Avenues, designed by architect W. C. Dodson, completed 1877 *(TC)*

Bronze statue of Rufus Burleson, unveiled in 1905, with the inscription, "A Tribute from His Students and Friends." The statue was removed from its location in the Quadrangle on July 13, 2022. Later that same day, the inscribed base of the monument (pictured on the right) was also removed. (TC)

Brann's Response

Brann, known to his contemporaries as the "Apostle of the Devil" (a title he apparently willingly and enthusiastically embraced), was hardly fazed by Burleson's warning regarding his eternal destiny. His reply, published in the October 1895 issue of the *Iconoclast*, began with an "apology":

> The *Iconoclast* must beg the forbearance of its readers for again referring to the pitiful case of Antônia Tiexiera [sic], the duly ordained "ward of the Baptist Church," who, while being educated at Baylor University for missionary work in Brazil, became the mother of an illegitimate babe. She was not the first young girl to get at Baylor more "education" than she could comfortably carry; but, owing to careful concealment "for the sake of Christ," hers is the only mishap that became a *cause celebre*, and therefore legitimately within the pale of journalistic criticism.[34]

Brann then claimed his previous critique focused specifically on Burleson, excusing Baylor because "accidents will occasionally occur even in the best regulated sectarian seminaries."[35] Burleson, on the other hand, sought to protect the college by casting aspersions on the victim of assault: "instead of striving to bring to justice the lecherous scoundrel who dared invade the sacred precincts of Baylor and debauch a child, Dr. Burleson employed all his energy and influence to protect the man accused of the crime—to so prejudice the public mind that an impartial trial of the case would be impossible."[36] Furthermore, Brann mused:

> had Antônia been really so bad as Dr. Burleson painted her, it was his duty as a Christian gentleman to shield her, so far as possible, from public shame, and attempt by every legitimate means to effect her reformation, instead of denouncing her in public and turning her adrift to go headlong to the devil. Mary Magdalen was a professional prostitute, an experienced woman of the

---

34. Brann, *Complete Works*, 3:150.

35. Brann, *Complete Works*, 3:150–51. Brann's characterization of his previous criticisms is not altogether accurate since at more than one point, the university had drawn his ire for its part in the reprehensible treatment of Antônia.

36. Brann, *Complete Works*, 3:151.

world; yet the Son of God freely forgave her—never once thought of cataloguing her crimes in the public prints. Cannot his professed disciples do as much for an ignorant child in short dresses?[37]

With that the war of words between W. C. Brann and Burleson went into hiatus, but not before a reversal in judgment by the McLennan County District Court sent shock waves through the local community and beyond.[38]

37. Brann, *Complete Works*, 3:151.

38. Events subsequent to the Teixeira-Morris case have garnered as much or more attention than the case itself. Much of the attention has centered on the (mis)fortunes of Brann and his adversaries. Brann soon broadened his attack on the university:

> I note with unfeigned pleasure that, according to claims of Baylor University, it opens the present season with a larger contingent of students, male and female, than ever before. This proves that Texas Baptists are determined to support it at any sacrifice—that they believe it better that their daughters should be exposed to its historic dangers and their sons condemned to grow up in ignorance than that this manufactory of ministers and Magdalens should be permitted to perish. It is to be devoutly hoped that the recent expose of Baylor's criminal carelessness will have a beneficial effort that hence forth orphan girls will not be ravished on the premises of its president, and that fewer young lady students will be sent home enciente. . . . Probably Baylor has never been so bad as many imagined, that the joint keepers in the Reservation have been mistaken in regarding it as a rival. (Brann, *Complete Works*, 10:63–64)

The "Reservation" was the "red-light district" in Waco, where prostitution was and would remain legal until 1917.

By insulting Baylor's female students as Magdalens, Brann had finally gone too far. In October 1897, he was abducted from his office by Baylor students and taken to campus where he was beaten and threatened with a gun. John Randolph, "The Apostle of the Devil: A Biography of William Cowper Brann" (PhD diss., Vanderbilt University, 1939), 208–9. Only days later, Brann was beaten by Baylor trustee Judge John Scarborough and his son, George. Brann met his demise on April 1, 1898, in a gun duel on South Fourth Street with the real estate developer Tom Davis, each man fatally wounding the other. An earlier gun fight between the Brann ally Judge George "Big Sandy" Gerald and James Harris, editor of the pro-Baylor *Waco Times-Herald*, also resulted in fatalities. Gerald shot and killed both James Harris and his brother Bill in November 1897; see Lomax, "The Apostle of the Devil"; Carver, *Brann and the Iconoclast*, 140–85; and box 2, folder 6, William Cowper Brann Collection, Texas Collection, Baylor University. Showing that public interest in these two gun-duels tended to eclipse the tragedy of Antônia Teixeira's assault, two Texas historical markers stand in downtown Waco detailing the circumstances of these shoot-outs. Thus, we relegate these events to a footnote to keep the focus on Antônia's plight.

7

The Jury Trial:
The Verdict and Its Aftermath

O n September 28, 1895, an indictment charging Steen Morris with rape was issued by Sheriff J. W. Baker. Deputy Sheriff Lee Davis arrested Morris, who duly appeared before Judge Samuel Scott of the Fifty-Fourth District Court. Unable to make the $3000 bail, Morris spent the night in jail.[1] Since no new evidence had been found after the case was dismissed, it is reasonable to conclude that Brann's public railings about the case had changed public opinion to the point that the prosecution decided to pursue the case.[2] Over the next few months, the state and defense issued their subpoenas for witnesses to appear in court.[3] Most had previously testified (e.g., Antônia Teixeira, Mrs. Ollie Jenkins, Dr. C. T. Young, Dr. O. I. Halbert, Dr. R. C. Burleson, Mrs. R. C. Burleson, etc.), but one was new: Mr. Ora Leesburg, the schoolmate of Antônia with whom S. L. Morris had accused her of having a sexual relationship. Notably, however, Leesburg was summoned as a witness for the *state* and not for the defense. Apparently, prosecutors were confident that he would confirm Antônia's contention that she had no relationship with him. Yet Ora

1. Writ to Serve Copy of Indictment and Capias, September 28, 1895, case 1165, The State of Texas v. Steen Morris, Fifty-Fourth District Court in McLennan County, McLennan County Archives; *Waco Morning News*, September 29, 1895.

2. This is also the conclusion of Randolph, "Apostle of the Devil," 152.

3. Subpoenas for State, September 1895, case 1165, The State of Texas v. Steen Morris, Fifty-Fourth District Court in McLennan County, McLennan County Archives; Subpoenas for Defense, various dates, case 1165, State of Texas v. Steen Morris, Fifty-Fourth District Court in McLennan County, McLennan County Archives.

had moved to Donley County, and the sheriff there was unable to locate him.[4] There is no record that Leesburg was ever found to testify at trial.

In addition to the subpoenas and witness attachments issued by the prosecution, the defense attorneys E. E. Easterling and T. A. Blair presented a written interrogatory to be answered by Mrs. Hattie Johnson for use at the trial on the defendant's behalf. According to the contemporary city directory, Hattie Johnson was an African American woman living in Waco.[5] After questions establishing (1) the witness's identity and (2) her relationships to Antônia and Morris, three more were posed. Their text, and Mrs. Johnson's responses to them, give us a good idea of courtroom exchanges at the time:

> 3. State if you ever had any conversation with Antônia Texera [sic] in regard to any man or men visiting her. If so, state when the conversation occurred and where, and who were present, as near as you can. State fully all of said conversation.
>
> 4. State whether or not Antônia Texera [sic] ever told you that a man unknown to her had come to her in Mrs. R. C. Burleson's backyard in the night time and offered her some thing good to drink, which she drank; and state whether or not at another time she stated to you that a man unknown to her came to her in Mrs. Burleson's backyard and gave her some candy, which she accepted. Answer fully, stating time and place and who were present.
>
> 5. State whether or not Antônia Texera [sic] ever stated to you that H. S. (Steen) Morris was going to marry soon, and that she, Antônia Texera [sic] was going to give him trouble. If so, state all of the conversation as near as you can in which she made this statement; when and where it was and who were present.[6]

4. Witness attachment, December 11, 1895, case 1165, The State of Texas v. Steen Morris, Fifty-Fourth District Court in McLennan County, McLennan County Archives.

5. "Morrison & Fourmy's General Directory of the City of Waco, 1896–1897," 188, Waco City Directories, Texas Collection, Baylor University Digital Collections, https://digitalcollections-baylor.quartexcollections.com/Documents/Detail/morrison-fourmys-general-directory-of-the-city-of-waco-1896-1897/166764. African Americans in the directory were indicated by the "(c)" following their names. There are two residential addresses given for Hattie Johnson: rooms 827 N. 6th street and "rear" 811 Jefferson. Louis and Mary Bailey, Skip Jennings (who worked at Waco Ice and Rfg. Co.), and Richard Lewis (a laborer for Nash, Robinson & Co.; mercantile goods)—all African Americans—are also listed at the latter address. It is unclear why Johnson gave written testimony rather than appearing in court; a request for a written interrogatory would have been made by the attorneys for the defense. Gerald Powell, email to author, September 7, 2021.

6. Interrogatories, December 16, 1895, case 1165, The State of Texas v. Steen Morris, Fifty-

On December 17, 1895, a notary public recorded and submitted Hattie Johnson's responses. She stated that she had known Antônia "Teixera" since September 1894 but did not know H. S. Steen Morris. She answered the other questions as follows:

> 3. I had a conversation with Antônia Texeira [sic] about the 7th of October 1894 about a man coming to the back door several times and offering her some candy and asking her to be his sweetheart and asking her to go walking with him. She said she did not know who he was. No one was present but a grandchild of mine who has since died.
>
> 4. She stated that a man offered her something to drink which she drank but that she did not go out of the house with him. This was stated at the same time as the conversation had in answer to no. 3 above.
>
> 5. She and the little daughter of Mr. S. L. were at my house one day, and while . . . playing some conversation came up as to who her sweetheart is and Antônia Texeira [sic] said that Steen Morris used to be her sweetheart and that she claimed him as her sweetheart, but that he had married and that she was going to make him sorry for it. Mr. Morris' little daughter said that Steen Morris once slapped her (Antônia) for trying to kiss him, and she (Antônia) was going to make him sorry for that too. All this was a part of said conversation. There were two or three different children here at the time but I don't remember their names.[7]

It is difficult to know how to assess this testimony since the May 1896 jury trial left no written record. At the preliminary hearing, Antônia denied the allegations under cross examination: "I know Mrs. Sam Johnson. I did not tell her that a man whom I didn't know had on two occasions come to the house where I was working and tried to get me out of the house." She also testified that she had rebuffed Morris's advances prior to the assaults of November and December 1894. At one point in the preliminary hearing, presumably in response to a question during cross examination, she asserted: "I didn't love

---

Fourth District Court in McLennan County, McLennan County Archives. The McLennan County attorney at the time, J. W. Taylor, signed an agreement allowing the witness's answers to be taken by any "qualified officer" and presumably to be presented as written testimony at the jury trial.

7. Answers, December 17, 1895, case 1165, The State of Texas v. Steen Morris, Fifty-Fourth District Court in McLennan County, McLennan County Archives.

anything about the defendant."[8] There also appear to be no corroborating witnesses of her alleged flirting other than, of course, Steen Morris himself, who had not testified at the preliminary hearing about having to ward off Antônia's advances instead of vice versa.[9]

The jury trial did not begin until May 1896, the delay due in part to the death of Antônia's premature infant in March 1896. Brann commented: "The babe of Antônia Teixeira the duly ordained 'ward of the Baptist Church,' who was 'educated' in Dr. Burleson's kitchen sleeps in a nameless grave."[10] His caustic and callous criticism of Baylor showed little empathy for the bereaved mother:

> Having waited in vain for the Baptist Church to build it a monument, I have decided to take up the good work myself. It was no common babe, and deserves something better than pauper burial. It was begotten in a sacred institution, of a mother duly consecrated to the work of rescuing poor Catholics from the remorseless grip of Papacy. The Babe of the Alamo is celebrated in song and story; but no poet tunes the harp to sing the Babe of Baylor.

He sarcastically continued:

> It seems to me that the great Baptist seminary has been strangely derelict in its duty . . . [having] failed to properly advertise itself as a place where souls are made as well as saved. . . . It received an ignorant little Catholic as raw material, and sent forth two Baptists as the finished product. That important

---

8. Testimonies, September 2, 1895, case 1165, The State of Texas v. Steen Morris, Fifty-Fourth District Court in McLennan County, McLennan County Archives.

9. Morris actually had two chances to set the record straight concerning Antônia's infatuation with him. He was also interviewed in the June 18, 1895, issue of the *Waco Morning News*: "When asked as to his guilt or innocence of the charge he said: 'I'm entirely innocent of the crime charged against me and will prove it whenever the opportunity is given me.' 'Do you deny responsibility for the girl's condition?' asked the reporter. 'Yes sir, I deny any kind or character with the girl, having never had aught to do with her in that way'" (*Waco Morning News*, June 18, 1895). It would have seemed the appropriate moment at this interview for Morris to mention that he had to rebuff Antônia's attempt to kiss him, establishing a failed romantic interlude initiated by Antônia that would have gone a long way in establishing his innocence.

10. *Iconoclast*, March 1896, quoted by Carver, *Brann and the Iconoclast*, 109. In the January issue of the paper (Brann, *Complete Works*, 6:31), Brann honed his knife further: "The case of the State vs. Steen Morris, charged with outraging a half-grown girl under the very nose of the good Dr. Burleson of Baylor, has been continued to the next term of court because one of the defendant's three attorneys had a pain in the umbilicus."

triumph of mind over matter should be preserved in imperishable marble that will forever "shine like a good deed in a naughty world."

Brann then made a "generous" offer:

> the *Iconoclast* herewith opens a subscription to build a monument to the dead babe's memory. I will contribute $50 if permitted to draw the design and write the inscription. I suggest a rectangular pyramid of pure white marble, surmounted by a life-size bust of Dr. Burleson, and bearing this inscription: "Sacred to the memory of the infant daughter of the 14-year-old ward of the Baptist Church, and an unknown member of the Baylor University Stud."

But where to place the monument? It "should, of course, be located at the most conspicuous point in the grounds of that institution whose greatness and glory it is destined to commemorate. All subscriptions should be sent to Dr. Burleson, the monument, when completed, to be dedicated to his dutiful son-in-law, the Rev. S. L. Morris."[11]

With tempers rising on both sides, the jury trial commenced on May 18, 1896.[12] There are no extant records of the testimony given there, so we can assume it was similar to that rendered at the preliminary hearing.[13] On May 19, after both sides had rested, the defense made a motion for the judge to instruct

11. *Iconoclast*, March 1896, quoted from Carver, *Brann and the Iconoclast*, 109–10. Brann would later (*Iconoclast*, June 1896) correct himself to say that Antônia's child was not buried in a pauper's grave but given proper burial albeit not by her "*alma mater*," Baylor, and its allies, but by the same persons who had footed the medical expenses—the "Catholics, Jews, and Atheists . . . while the sainted Baylorians closed their purses and sighed for the wickedness of the world" (Brann, *Complete Works*, 5:87).

12. The minute book pages for case 1165 as well as the judge's docket sheet are missing from the McLennan County Archives.

13. It is noteworthy that the *Waco Morning News*, which had broken the story in the first place, reported very little of the jury trial. There is a short article in the May 19, 1896, issue noting that the "celebrated case went to trial yesterday" and mentioning that Morris sat with his wife and newborn infant while the jury was impaneled (*Waco Morning News*, May 19, 1896). An even shorter article appeared in the same paper the next day, reporting that the "Stein [sic] Morris case was given to the jury about noon yesterday and the jury is still 'rasslin' with it. Late in the afternoon the jury came in and told Judge Scott that no agreement could be had and he did not agree either, telling them to go back and try it again" (*Waco Morning News*, May 20, 1896). The newspaper did not report the final outcome of a hung jury. One cannot help but wonder if pressure from Baylor supporters had dampened the newspaper editors' interest in the case. In support of that supposition is the killing of James Harris, pro-Baylor editor of the Waco paper, by the Brann ally George "Big Sandy" Gerald in

the jury that they could not convict the defendant based on the testimony of Antônia Teixeira because it was "unsupported by other witnesses and not corroborated by circumstances." The presiding judge, D. R. Scott, refused the request.[14] Instead, he issued a charge to the jury, detailing exactly what constituted legal rape and what had to be proven to substantiate guilt in the case.[15] Their role was simply to pass judgment:

> The defendant in a criminal case is presumed innocent until his guilt is established by legal evidence, beyond a reasonable doubt; and in case you have reasonable doubt as to the defendant's guilt you will acquit him, and say by your verdict, "Not Guilty."
>
> You are the exclusive judges of the facts proved, of the credibility of the witnesses and of the weight to be given to the testimony, but you are bound to receive the law from the Court, which is herein given you, and be governed thereby.

So charged, the jury retired to deliberate at noon on May 19.[16] On the following day, the jury informed the court that "though they had carefully considered the case . . . they were unable to agree, and that there was no probability

---

a November 1897 gun duel, when tensions between Brann and Baylor were obviously still running high. See box 2, folder 6, William Cowper Brann Collection, Texas Collection, Baylor University.

14. Defendant's request, May 19, 1896, case 1165, The State of Texas v. Steen Morris, Fifty-Fourth District Court in McLennan County, McLennan County Archives.

15. Gentlemen of the jury:

By indictment filed in this case, the defendant stands charged with the crime of "rape."

To this charge the defendant pleads not guilty.

Rape is the carnal knowledge of a woman without her consent, obtained by force.

The degree of force, used in each case, must have been as might reasonably be supposed by the assailant self-sufficient to overcome resistance, taking into consideration the relative strength of the parties, and other circumstances of the case.

Penetration is essential and must be proved beyond a reasonable doubt, to constitute "rape."

Whoever shall be guilty of "rape" shall be punished by death or the confinement in the penitentiary for life, or for any term of years not less than five, in the discretion of the jury.

Now if you believe from the evidence, beyond a reasonable doubt, that the defendant Steen Morris, did at the time and place charged in and upon Antônia Teixeira . . . by force, and without the consent of the said Antônia Teixeira, have carnal knowledge of the said Antônia Teixeira, then if you so find you find the defendant guilty as charged in the indictment and assess his penalty as heretofore stated, otherwise you will acquit him.

16. *Galveston Daily News*, May 22, 1896.

of them agreeing should they be kept together longer, and requested that they be discharged." Judge Scott agreed and dismissed the jury, putting the case on the docket for its next term.[17] Handwritten on the cover of the case in the archive are simply the words, "May 20. Hung jury."[18] It was widely reported in the press that the vote had been seven to five in favor of finding Steen Morris guilty, a remarkable count given the white male make-up of the jury, but not enough to keep the case out of legal limbo.[19]

Predictably, Brann was outraged:

> Steen Morris, a young man who parts his name on the side, was tried in this city a few days ago on the charge of raping Antônia Teixeira. . . . All the influence of Baylor was brought to bear in favor of the man accused of invading its supposed sacred precincts to feed his unholy lust by the debauchment of a babe. As the Baptists are all-powerful in this county, and can easily make or break any man engaged in a purely local business, his acquittal seemed a foregone conclusion.[20]

Brann went on to disparage Burleson on this point too: "No wonder the president of Baylor gleefully rubbed his hands and predicted that the alleged rape-fiend 'would have easy rolling,' for to oppose the wishes of the Baptist bosses were to court a social, political and business boycott by those who boast that their cult holds a copyright on freedom of conscience." At least the jury had thrown a wrench into these prognostications, Brann continued: "When the case was submitted to the jury it developed that the defendant did not have such 'easy rolling' as the eminent divine had predicted. Seven of the jurors were not willing to turn him loose even to please the dominant political power while the remaining five could not quite make up their minds that it was proper to put the brother of Dr. Burleson's pious son-in-law in the penitentiary."[21]

17. Judgment, vol. 1, p. 194, May 20, 1896, case 1165, The State of Texas v. Steen Morris, Fifty-Fourth District Court in McLennan County, McLennan County Archives.

18. Cover, uncategorized, case 1165, The State of Texas v. Steen Morris, Fifty-Fourth District Court in McLennan County, McLennan County Archives.

19. *The Sunday Gazetteer* (Denison, TX), May 24, 1896; Brann, *Complete Works*, 5:83; cf. Randolph, "Apostle of the Devil," 172.

20. Brann, *Iconoclast*, June 1896, in Brann, *Complete Works*, 5:81.

21. Brann, *Complete Works*, 5:83.

The editor now brought Zachary Taylor, Antônia's original sponsor, into the mix as well. Citing an unpublished article of Taylor's, Brann charged the missionary with knowing "at the time that she was a foul prostitute." Yet now Taylor was

> back in Brazil writing letters imploring her to return to her kith and kin in that faraway country. Why? He declared while here that her mother was a courtesan and all her relatives a very bad lot. Why should the poor girl return to such immoral surroundings—after enjoying for three years the elevating influence of Baylor University? Does he consider that her "education" is complete—that illegitimate childbirth constitutes Baylor's graduating exercises—and that she should enter at once upon the work of converting the Brazilian Catholics? Or does he want her to resume her duties as companion to his wife?

Brann protested to be flummoxed by

> this good man Taylor. When he brought Antônia here, he gave her a certificate of good character. When her downfall casts a shadow over the great Baptist University, he declared that she had been bad from babyhood, and that, knowing this, he first made her an inmate of his family, then consigned her to the companionship of scores of pure young girls, well knowing—if he knows anything—that one wanton can work more mischief among innocent maids than can a dozen men.

Brann sarcastically concluded: "I much fear that Rev. Zechariah [sic] would be a first-class fraud if God hadn't intended him for a fool."[22]

While the rhetoric remained as hot as the Waco summer, plans went ahead to retry the case in the November 1896 term. Subpoenas were issued as late as October and potential jury lists were being draw up in early December 1896.[23]

---

22. Brann, *Complete Works*, 5:83–84.

23. Subpoenas for State, October 22, 1896, case 1165, The State of Texas v. Steen Morris, Fifty-Fourth District Court in McLennan County, McLennan County Archives; Subpoenas for Defendant, October 20, 1896, case 1165, The State of Texas v. Steen Morris, Fifty-Fourth District Court in McLennan County, McLennan County Archives. For jury lists, see box 2, Teixeira-Morris controversy, 1893–1896, William Cowper Brann Collection, Texas Collection, Baylor University.

But then the case was suddenly dismissed.[24] What happened? In August 1896, Antônia signed a sworn affidavit revoking her previous charges. "On her oath," the affidavit read, she stated that the accusations she had made against Steen Morris were "untrue and false." She swore that "there was no force used by the defendant Steen Morris in any or either of said transactions and that she was not in any way coerced or forced by said defendant to gratify his said desire and that in all of said transactions heretofore charged against the defendant she was a willing party to." Furthermore, the affidavit read, "this statement is made of her own free will, without any consideration coming to her from the De-fendant or anyone, and without any threat or coercion on the part of anyone." Rather, "she was told by another person to testify on the witness stand what she has heretofore testified to relative force having been used by the Defendant Steen Morris in accomplishing sexual intercourse with her," even though she then knew that testimony "to be false and untrue." The document was signed "Antônia Teixeira" and attested to by the notary public on August 11, 1896.[25]

How are we to judge this statement, especially in light of the flurry of sub-poenas issued in October 1896? Recent studies have shown that nearly 25 per-cent of victims who disclose instances of sexual assault or abuse later recant.[26] Retraction is a common feature among victims of sexual assault who attempt to deal with the secondary trauma of "disbelief, blame and rejection" on the part of the public or even their own families.[27] In this case, Antônia had not only suffered the loss of her child but had endured verbal insults and injuries

24. Cover, uncategorized, case 1165, The State of Texas v. Steen Morris, Fifty-Fourth District Court in McLennan County, McLennan County Archives.

25. Antônia Teixeira, sworn affidavit, box 2, folder 7, William Cowper Brann Collection, Texas Collection, Baylor University.

26. See T. Sorenson and B. Snow, "How Children Tell: The Process of Disclosure in Child Sexual Abuse," *Child Welfare: Journal of Policy, Practice, and Program* 70 (1991): 3–15. In this highly cited study, Sorensen and Snow's analysis was based on 630 cases of reported sexual abuse. See also L. C. Malloy, T. D. Lyon, and J. A. Quas, "Filial Dependency and Recantation of Child Sexual Abuse Allegations," *Journal of the Academy of Child and Adolescent Psychiatry* 46 (2007): 162–70.

27. The landmark study in this regard is R. C. Summit, "The Child Sexual Abuse Accommoda-tion Syndrome," *Child Abuse and Neglect* 7, no. 2 (1983): 177–93. The use of CSAAS as a diagnostic tool in cases of sexual abuse is controversial. Here, we simply reference it to provide a framework for understanding the dubious nature of Antônia's recantation: she had, at this point, every reason to recant and no real incentive to proceed with a retrial given the unlikelihood of a conviction despite the circumstantial evidence.

at both the preliminary hearing and the jury trial, not to mention a public shaming at the hands of Rufus Burleson and others.

Soon after signing her affidavit, Antônia Teixeira left Waco for Memphis, Tennessee.[28] Brann, predictably but also not without cause, raised questions of impropriety: "When Capt. Blair (Morris's attorney) asks the court to dismiss the case . . . let him be required to state why the drawer of the remarkable document purchased Antônia's ticket, and who furnished the funds."[29] It was (and is) highly irregular for defense attorneys to contact the state's key witness and to meet with her without the state's attorneys being present, redoubling suspicions about the motive for and validity of Antônia's recantation.[30] If Brann is to be believed, she was enticed or bribed to leave all this behind for a new start in a new place. Her increased vulnerability as an immigrant woman further compounded the issue.[31] The price for Antônia's new start? Her recantation.

But why Memphis? It was a six-hundred-mile train ride away, and Antônia had no relatives or acquaintances there. Yet three days after signing the affidavit, Antônia was mentioned in a brief notice in the August 14 edition of the *Commercial Appeal*, a local Memphis paper: "Antônia Teixeira, an 18-year-old girl, who came to this country four years ago from Portugal, is at the police station, a stranger in the city. She came to Memphis yesterday from Waco, Tex., expecting to meet James Stratton who, she says, promised to meet her at the passenger station. She is very much in love with Stratton. He is said to be a baker."[32]

Who was James Stratton, whom Antônia allegedly hoped to marry? Another *Commercial Appeal* article, printed a week later and entitled "Unhappy Antônia," filled in the picture: "Antônia Teixeira is again deserted in a strange city and without money or friends. James Stratton, whom she came here to

28. Brann, *Iconoclast*, September 1896, citing the *Waco Telephone* newspaper (Brann, *Complete Works*, 6:126). Lomax, "The Apostle of the Devil," claims Antônia left the very same day that she signed the affidavit.

29. Brann, *Complete Works*, 6:8.

30. Gerald Powell, interview with the author, August 19, 2021.

31. Jessica Mindlin et al., "Dynamics of Sexual Assault and the Implications for Immigrant Women," *National Immigrant Women's Advocacy Project* (NIWAP), https://niwaplibrary.wcl .american.edu/wp-content/uploads/2015/CULT-Man-Ch1-DyanimcsSexualAssaultImplications -07.10.13.pdf.

32. *Commercial Appeal* (Memphis, TN), August 14, 1896. Our appreciation to Wayne Dowdy, archivist at the Memphis and Shelby County Room, Central Library, Memphis, TN, for locating and sending copies of the *Commercial Appeal* articles. The first article mistakenly identifies Antônia as being from Portugal; this error is corrected in the subsequent articles.

marry, has fled to parts unknown. It is the old story with few variations, except in this case it is worse than usual."

The reporter carefully mixed sentiment with hard data: "The girl was desperately in love with Stratton in Waco, Tex. . . . He then deserted her and came to Memphis. From here he wrote to her to come to Memphis and he would marry her. This letter she showed to Chief Moseley and an officer was sent to hunt up Stratton. The girl appeared perfectly happy to once more look upon her lover's face and told the officer everything was all right."[33] That was Thursday, August 13. By the following Sunday, the sixteenth, the *Commercial Appeal* reporter looked up Antônia again since no marriage license had been filed for the couple. "She again said everything was all right, and gave the reporter to understand that a marriage had been performed." But then, the next Thursday,

Antônia was at the police station asking "for protection and help to enable her to go back to her home or at least to where she has acquaintances." The reporter found her sadly changed: The bright, happy light had left her face and one of deepest despondency had settled there instead. She told her story amid deepest sobs and when counseled not to cry she answered, "I can't help it. My heart is broken. To think that he should have left me this way after sending for me."

The reporter rejoined: "If you had told me Sunday that you were not married there would have been a wedding out here before night." Antônia replied: "He told me to say that and then we would be married Monday."

It turned out that Stratton had given one excuse after another for delaying the wedding until Wednesday, the nineteenth, "when he left her and said he was coming down to town for a while. He went to the bakery where he was employed and told his employer he was sick with boils and could not work. The next seen of him was on the train bound for Chattanooga, so one of the boarders said who knew him."

The reporter urged Antônia "to seek shelter in one of the charitable institutions for women in Memphis," and indeed she was taken in at the House of the Good Shepherd. Yet "her one thought is to go home," so she was waiting "until the Waco people could be heard from."[34]

---

33. "Unhappy Antônia," *Commercial Appeal* (Memphis, TN), August 21, 1896.
34. *Commercial Appeal* (Memphis, TN), August 21, 1896.

There are several unexpected turns in this story and, given the scant available evidence, it may not be possible fully to unravel them all. First, who was James Stratton? In the 1894–95 Waco city directory, he is listed as an employee at the Waco Bakery at 721 Austin. His presumed relatives Ross Stratton (manager) and William Stratton (driver) are also listed, with Michael Mihalski designated as the proprietor.[35] Stratton is listed again as a baker at the Waco Bakery in 1896–97, with Ross H. Stratton now listed as the proprietor.[36] James is still a baker in the city directories for 1898–99, 1900–01, and 1904–05 along with Leonard Stratton, driver, and William Stratton, baker; Lucy Clay is now listed as proprietor. But in 1906–7, James has become the proprietor, with William Ripley and J. Ross Bailey working for him alongside William and Leonard Stratton. By 1910, however, James Stratton has dropped from view, with one John Koller having taken over the Waco Bakery. In short, James Stratton left for Memphis for a brief period in 1896; while he may have traveled to Chattanooga (and other locations?) that August, he was soon back at the Waco Bakery and apparently stayed there for another ten years.[37]

When did the relationship between Stratton and Antônia begin and what was its nature? There are several possibilities to be explored:

1. Stratton was involved with Antônia by late 1894, and Antônia's child was the result of their consensual relationship and not from an assault by Steen Morris. While possible, there is little evidence pointing in this direction. Morris's defenders suggested a variety of alternatives to Morris as biological father—

---

35. "Morrison & Fourmy's General Directory of the City of Waco 1894–95," 261. The Waco Bakery is one of nine bakeries listed in the Waco directory ("Morrison & Fourmy's," 301).

36. "Morrison & Fourmy's General Directory of the City of Waco, 1896–1897," 287. William Stratton is again listed as a driver of the bakery wagon, and the bakery has expanded to include groceries and produce.

37. See the following documents in Waco City Directories, Texas Collection, Baylor University Digital Collection, https://digitalcollections-baylor.quartexcollections.com/explore-the -collections/list/collections/12: "Morrison & Fourmy's General Directory of the City of Waco, 1898–99," 201; "Morrison & Fourmy's General Directory of the City of Waco, 1900–01," 167; "Morrison & Fourmy's General Directory of the City of Waco, 1904–05," 189–90; "Morrison & Fourmy's General Directory of the City of Waco, 1906–07," 232; "Morrison & Fourmy's General Directory of the City of Waco, 1910," 2, 268.

The directory for 1895–96 is not extant (and possibly was never published for that year; Amie Oliver, email to author, September 10, 2021).

from a Black servant, to an unnamed Baylor student, to Ora Leesburg. James Stratton is never mentioned in any document. Furthermore, if Stratton were the father, why did he and Antônia not marry and move elsewhere when she became pregnant? What did Antônia have to gain from falsely accusing Morris? Still, while unlikely, this possibility cannot be conclusively dismissed.

2. Stratton and Antônia developed a relationship after the assault. The likelihood of this scenario increases when one considers that Mrs. Ollie Jenkins, with whom Antônia lived from April 1895 until August 1896, resided at 717½ Austin Avenue, in very close proximity to 721 Austin Avenue, where Stratton both worked at the Waco Bakery and lived with other members of the Stratton family.[38]

Assuming the latter scenario to be more plausible, what was the nature of this relationship?

1. If one takes the *Commercial Appeal* account at face value, Antônia had a deep romantic attachment to Stratton, strong enough to cause her to leave Waco and join him in Memphis at his invitation for matrimony. What about the relationship from Stratton's point of view?

2. Perhaps Stratton's intentions to move to Memphis and then send for Antônia to join him and marry were sincere, but before she arrived he developed cold feet. Presumably his reluctance had grown between the time of sending the letter to Antônia and her arrival there as he made no effort to meet her at the train station to tell her of his change of heart. Instead, the police had to "hunt for" Stratton in order to deliver Antônia to him. Stratton then spent the next several days plotting his escape, including instructing her to lie to a reporter about having already married on a Saturday with the promise of a wedding on the next day. Within three days, Stratton had abandoned Antônia entirely, quitting his job at a Memphis bakery and making his way first to Chattanooga (if the report of his fellow boarders is accurate) before returning to Waco and resuming his position at the Waco Bakery.

There is, of course, a more nefarious scenario to consider:

38. "Morrison and Fourmy's General Directory of the City of Waco, 1896–97," 186, 261.

3. It is possible that Steen Morris's defenders (the most likely candidate being his brother, the Rev. Silas L. Morris, but with possible financial assistance from others), upon learning of Antônia's romantic interests in James Stratton, arranged for him to relocate temporarily to Memphis in the summer of 1896 and then invite Antônia to join him on promise of marriage (in the form of a letter, which Antônia produced to the police upon her arrival in Memphis).[39] Knowing she had a written marriage proposal in hand, Morris's attorneys then met with Antônia, promising her train fare to Memphis to join Stratton in return for a signed affidavit recanting her previous accusations against Morris. For his part, Stratton had no intention of a rendezvous with Antônia in Memphis, though he was forced to improvise on his plans when the police showed up at his door with Antônia in tow. He then proceeded to lie to her, the police, and his employer, while he made plans to abandon Antônia and make his return (however circuitously) to Waco and his old job.[40] In this worst-case scenario, Antônia was sexually assaulted in Waco and emotionally and physically abandoned in Memphis with malice aforethought.

Whichever scenario (or some other) one finds most compelling, the results are the same. Antônia was left abandoned and penniless in Memphis and found temporary refuge in the House of the Good Shepherd, a home for "troubled girls" run by the Catholic Sisters of the Good Shepherd.[41] The headlines of the article in the *Commercial Appeal* claimed Antônia "wants to return to Waco," which apparently she did. A marriage license issued in McLennan County (where Waco is located) indicates a Mr. J. R. Cook married Miss Antônia "Teiziera" (sic) on October 15, 1896, thus confirming a conjecture that Antônia had eventually married a US citizen.[42] No further record has yet been uncovered.

---

39. This scenario would rule out Stratton as a potential candidate for the biological father of Antônia's child since, if the defense attorneys thought this was a possibility, they likely would have introduced that theory at the jury trial in May or the one rescheduled for fall 1896.

40. Were one inclined to even more conspiratorial thinking, it would be plausible to imagine some pecuniary incentive for Stratton as well.

41. Our Lady of Charity of the Good Shepherd was founded by Sister Mary Euphrasia in France in 1835. A group of five sisters migrated to Louisville, Kentucky, in 1842 and established multiple homes across the United States. See https://sistersofthegoodshepherd.com/.

42. Marriage Records, vol. 00J, Page 467A, The State of Texas, McLennan County. The record states the "rites of matrimony" occurred between J. R. Cook and Antônia "Teiziera" (sic) on Oc-

At this point, one can only say that Antônia Teixeira disappeared not only from Waco and Memphis but for all practical purposes "from the face of the earth" as well, just as Brann had predicted.[43]

tober 15, 1896, and returned to the county clerk on November 11, 1896. Oliveira further suggested that Antônia attempted to contact her family in Brazil in 1915 (*Antonio Teixeira de Albuquerque*, 23).

43. Brann, *Complete Works*, 3:32. Little is known of the fate of Steen Morris either. On January 13, 1895, he married Amanda Antoinette "Nettie" Tony. Moses D. A. Steen, *The Steen Family in Europe and America* (Cincinnati: Monfort & Co., 1900), 227. Apparently, the infant child reported at the preliminary hearing (eight months old) died on June 30, 1896. *Waco Weekly Tribune*, August 2, 1896, cited in John M. Usry, ed., *Early Waco Obituaries and Various Related Items 1874–1908* (Waco, TX: Central Texas Genealogical Society, 1980). Morris (1867–1911) and Nettie Tony migrated to Louisiana, where they had two children. He is buried in Nolley Memorial Methodist Cemetery in Jena, La Salle Parrish, Louisiana.

8

Constructing and Protecting Institutional Memory:
Beyond Antônio and Antônia

I f Antônia was forgotten, other characters in this story were not only remembered but celebrated. Rufus C. Burleson went on to be arguably the most honored president in Baylor University history, a legacy also linked to the memorialization of Southern Whiteness, including the celebration of Confederate and Lost Cause ideals, which Burleson shared with most of his Baylor contemporaries. To all of these and other ideals as well—commitment to Christian education, love for Baptists, missionary zeal, etc.—the story of Antônia stood as an embarrassing contradiction. Zachary Taylor, who brought Antônia to Waco and became a Baptist icon in Brazil, likewise stood in contradiction to these ideals. The sexual scandals Taylor knew about did not appear in his public presentations; missionary promotion and legacy are shy of public confession.

The construction of transnational religious memories, however, goes well beyond individuals, in this case individuals who benefited from the forgetting of Antônia. Many other unfortunate episodes lie hidden in the records of the institutions transnational religious workers built. This chapter explores the legacies of Rufus C. Burleson and Zachary Taylor as case studies in selective remembering and active forgetting.

The Legacy of Rufus C. Burleson

Historically, one of the most prominent sites at Baylor University has been Burleson Quadrangle. At the main entrance to the square stood the statue of its namesake, looking over the passing parade of students who would do impressive things all over the globe in an array of fields. Burleson's bronze figure, created by the renowned Italian sculptor Pompeo Coppini, was unveiled in 1905.[1] The page dedicated to his legacy on the university's website lists his accomplishments although of late has added the recognition that Burleson "arguably stands as the most controversial of all of Baylor's early leaders due to his attitudes and behaviors with regard to slavery and the Confederate Army's role in the American Civil War."[2] The current version of the article acknowledged Burleson's anti-Black racism and commitment to Lost Cause ideals, stating that "age and 'modern ways of doing things' caught up with him so that, at the request of the trustees, he reluctantly stepped down from the presidency of the University" in 1897.[3] "In spite of the loss of personal prestige, administrative authority and teaching privileges," however, "Burleson kept his promise and worked diligently for Baylor until his death four years later."[4] As of the time of this writing, the website makes no mention of Antônia.

1. The full text of the Texas Historical Commission sign in the Quadrangle reads as follows:

Burleson Quadrangle: Dr. Rufus C. Burleson was the first president of Baylor's Waco campus and Burleson Quadrangle was named in his honor. With the completion of Baylor's four original buildings—Old Main (1886), Georgia Burleson Hall (1888), The F. L. Carroll Chapel and Library (1903), and the George Carroll Science Building (1903), the Quadrangle took on its current appearance, and has since that time served as a social area and a link to Baylor's history and tradition.

Burleson Quadrangle has often been the site of the evolving social norms and customs at Baylor. During the 1920s the "Ring Out" ceremony, held every Spring in Burleson Quadrangle, became a Baylor tradition and is still performed today. The ceremony involves the passing of an ivy chain from senior students to junior students and symbolizes the passing of custodianship of the historic bells that are located in the Quadrangle to Baylor's next graduating class. The ceremony was originally performed by female students but has since grown to also include male students. Since 1945, students have participated in the passing of the Key Ceremony, also held in the Quadrangle at graduation time. The Key opens a Baylor time capsule that was placed in the Quadrangle during the University's 1945 centennial.

Burleson Quadrangle is the location of a bronze sculpture of Dr. Burleson, unveiled in 1905 and created by renowned Italian-born Texas sculptor Pompeo Coppini (1870–1957). The Centennial Monument, also located within the Quadrangle, was constructed in 1945 using stones from Tyron Hall (formerly located at the Independence Campus) and several buildings on the Waco Campus.

2. "Rufus C. Burleson, Baylor President (1886–1897)," Baylor University, About Baylor, accessed on December 29, 2021, https://www.baylor.edu/about/index.php?id=89259.

3. "Rufus C. Burleson, Baylor President (1886–1897)."

4. "Rufus C. Burleson, Baylor President (1886–1897)."

Yet it was not the board of trustees' realization of Burleson's unpalatable racism that moved them to ask Burleson to resign, as the language on the Baylor website may imply. On the contrary, all indications are that his Lost Cause convictions and racist commitments were enthusiastically supported by the trustees. In fact, Burleson's statue was erected almost a decade after he stepped down from the presidency; it stood as an affirmation, not a denial, of Burleson's broadly known Lost Cause sensibilities. As the historian Karen L. Cox has pointed out, statues of pro-Confederate men such as Burleson "were placed by white southerners whose intentions were not to preserve history but to glorify a heritage that did not resemble historical facts."[5] Although Burleson's legacy carries a heavy dose of appreciation for what he had done specifically for Baylor, his memory cannot be dissociated from the pro-Confederate memorializations so common in the South during the time his statue was unveiled. His sculpture was not a "Confederate statue" in the classical sense but nonetheless fits the pattern that Cox identifies: "By erecting these statues, white southerners have, over time, upheld a past in which the ideals of Confederate nationalism rest on metaphorical pedestals of heroism and sacrifice, while at the same time they negate the legacy of slavery and suggest that all white southerners were committed to the Confederate cause, which they were not."[6] In light of Antônia's story, the sculpture also serves as a reminder that such statues might also memorialize issues of sexual misconduct or gender oppression.

Baylor University's Commission on Historic Representation investigated Rufus Burleson's legacy and concluded that he was a rather common nineteenth-century Southern Baptist White when it came to race relations. Much was made of the report, which appeared to be surprising to otherwise highly educated individuals despite the availability of Burleson's thoroughly pro-Confederate writings. After the report was released, admirable efforts to condemn such racism were made. Burleson descendants and Baylor University employees Blake and Burt Burleson, for example, publicly criticized their "Dear Uncle Rufus" on the grounds of his racism.[7] Antônia's story, however, is only rarely found in such public critiques of his career.

5. Karen L. Cox, *No Common Ground: Confederate Monuments and the Ongoing Fight for Racial Justice* (Chapel Hill: University of North Carolina Press, 2021), 13.

6. Cox, *No Common Ground*, 13.

7. Blake Burleson and Burt Burleson, "Our Letter to Uncle Rufus, Confronting Baylor's Racist Past," *Waco-Tribune-Herald*, April 24, 2021, https://wacotrib.com/opinion/columnists/blake-and

It is far more likely that Burleson would have been removed from office for voicing anti-racist sentiments rather than the opposite. Instead, it was the scandal surrounding the rape of Antônia Teixeira and its possible implications for female enrollment that helped prompt his begrudging transition to "president emeritus."[8] Already at the annual Baptist General Convention meeting in Belton in October 1895, three months after the jury trial, the Baylor trustees acknowledged a decrease in female enrollment from the previous year and attributed the loss directly to the incident involving Antônia Teixeira:

> The Whole state has been diligently sowed down with papers and pamphlets making a most violent and scurrilous attack on Baylor University as a proper school for girls, and particularly on its president as unworthy to have charge of female education. . . . Nothing known in the history of education equals the virus and scurrility of this attack. And as the ostensible occasion of this attack was the case of the Brazilian girl, Antonio Texeira [sic], we deem it not inappropriate, as a Board of Trustees, to make some mention of this matter in our annual report, calmly and dispassionately submitting such exact facts as bear in any just sense on Baylor University.[9]

The "facts" laid out by the Baylor trustees amounted to little more than a vigorous defense of Baylor and denial of any responsibility in the assault on Antônia. They began by withholding any comment concerning the accusations against Steen Morris "pro or con, neither expressly nor by implication, leaving that matter to the adjudication of the courts, where it is now pending."[10] Such judgment was none of their concern because, they claimed, Antônia was not a "ward" of the university, as Brann had asserted. In fact, the trustees had unanimously rejected the proposal by Zachary Taylor to admit her with tuition paid "as a prospective missionary." Tuition remission was offered only to "licensed or ordained ministers and to the children of Texas Baptist pastors."[11] The trustees

---

-burt-burleson-our-letter-to-uncle-rufus-confronting-baylors-racist-past/article_0d91ee96-a3b4
-11eb-a1e3-3b5b9b3a5c8f.html.

8. See Lomax, "Apostle of the Devil."

9. "Proceedings of the Forty-Seventh Annual Session of the Baptist General Convention of Texas," 50.

10. "Proceedings of the Forty-Seventh Annual Session," 51.

11. "Proceedings of the Forty-Seventh Annual Session," 52.

ignored the fact that Antônia was indeed the daughter of a deceased Brazilian Baptist pastor, one who had been vital to the very founding of the Baptist mission in Brazil. Rather, she had come from "poverty stricken and immoral family surroundings."[12] On this account, Zachary Taylor's efforts to bring Antônia to Baylor would appear as a random act of mercy, plucking a penniless urchin from the streets of Brazil. Little could be further from the truth.

Furthermore, the trustees asserted that Antônia was never a resident at Georgia Burleson Hall, thus "dispos[ing] of a false impression . . . that Baylor University did not properly care for the girls entrusted to its charge." Texas Baptist parents could rest assured their daughters were safe so long as they were "in the Hall under school authority." Finally, the trustees maintained that Antônia was not actually enrolled as a student at Baylor when the alleged assault occurred, nor had the incident occurred on grounds under school jurisdiction.[13] By following the letter of the law, the trustees thus relieved themselves of any moral responsibility for Antônia's injury, opting rather to judge that, by becoming pregnant, "shame had come to the girl." Elsewhere they describe her as "fallen" and one who had gone "astray," bearing "antecedent tendencies to vice, arising from early evil environment and custom."[14] In short, having explicitly refused to make judgment on Steen Morris's guilt or innocence, they had transferred all blame to Antônia, her family, and her culture.

But had the trustees not inadvertently also shifted blame from the university to President Burleson, in whose house Antônia Teixeira had resided at the time of the incident? Anticipating this inference, the trustees acknowledged that if "there was credible evidence that shame [had come] to this girl, with or without her consent, from culpable neglect of that vigilance and supervision on the part of Dr. Burleson or his family, which duty requires," the board would have promptly recommended his removal from the presidency.[15] But no, they had found "no evidence whatever, that either he or his good wife were wanting in prudence, counsel, good treatment, or oversight."[16]

Given all that transpired during and after Morris's assault on Antônia, that claim is astounding. Burleson had denied even the possibility that Morris could

---

12. "Proceedings of the Forty-Seventh Annual Session," 50.
13. "Proceedings of the Forty-Seventh Annual Session," 53.
14. "Proceedings of the Forty-Seventh Annual Session," 54.
15. "Proceedings of the Forty-Seventh Annual Session," 53.
16. "Proceedings of the Forty-Seventh Annual Session," 53.

be guilty; as soon as he discovered Antônia was pregnant, he made inquiries of where she could be hidden from view, including the reformatory in Gatesville. He and the Morris brothers had confronted the girl at his residence; he had blamed her for the assault in a pamphlet and smeared her family; and he had done nothing to identify Antônia's assailant, despite being convinced it could not have been Steen Morris. Still, the trustees could conclude: "Whatever may be his faults in other matters, no man within our knowledge has a clearer record in the oversight of the manners and morals of girls."[17] The trustees concluded with a lament that it was not Antônia Teixeria who had been violated; rather, "both Dr. Burleson and the institution have been wronged, and one of the best women in the world most cruelly grieved." This assertion they made "as a matter of history" along with a request for the convention messengers' "approval of it" so that it "may go to record."[18]

The public silence of Baylor president's pastor, B. H. Carroll, on the matter was as telling as the trustees' report, a matter that did not escape the notice of his contemporaries. One San Antonio Baptist wrote Carroll:

> It is talked about here, and matter of great surprise to brethren why you have remained perfectly silent, as a graduate of Baylor University and one of its Trustees, and pastor of the church of its President and his wife and of the Trustees and of the denomination—when they have been scandalized and held up to public ridicule by that moral abortion and physical coward and intellectual "lusers natural"—W. C. Brown [sic for Brann], and his friends. We cannot understand it. Can you relieve our amazement?[19]

In the immediate historical context, it is difficult to read B. H. Carroll's description of Burleson as a "helpless child" in the hands of men "with an axe to grind" as not including Burleson's exchanges about Antônia with W. C. Brann.[20] But even here Carroll's critique of Burleson was that he was ineffective in protecting the Baylor brand, not that he failed to protect a vulnerable immigrant under his care.

17. "Proceedings of the Forty-Seventh Annual Session," 54.
18. "Proceedings of the Forty-Seventh Annual Session," 54.
19. D. S. Snodgrass to B. H. Carroll, December 3, 1895, box 1, folder 3, Correspondence: General, 1894–1896, B. H. Carroll Papers #0089, Texas Collection, Baylor University.
20. *Texas Baptist Herald*, August 5, 1897.

Unsurprisingly, Antônia appears in none of the memorializations of Rufus Burleson, whether it be a 1901 compilation of his works-cum-biography put together by his wife Georgia, or biographies and biographical sketches written by scholars and denominational leaders (including one by the prominent Baptist leader J. M. Dawson), or unqualified praises from missionaries, denominational figures, and scholars who have insisted that Burleson be remembered and celebrated.[21] On the occasion of Burleson's death, Baylor's faculty committed to carrying his torch into the future. In a tribute published in the memorial volume organized by Georgia Burleson, the faculty, who most certainly knew of Antônia's story, pledged:

> In view of his great work for Baylor University, his wonderful success as an educator, and his glorious labors as a Christian minister, be it resolved by the faculty of Baylor University:
>
> 1. That we thank God that so good and so great a man has been permitted to live among us so long, and that we have the privilege of enjoying the precious heritage of his labors.
> 2. That we recognize fully the debt of gratitude we owe to his memory and great life-work in planting the foundations of this school on the solid basis of prayer and Christian watchfulness.
> 3. That we pledge our efforts to perpetuating the great principles of Christian education to which he devoted his whole life.[22]

Four years later, a Baylor committee commissioned the statue that stood in the quadrangle until 2022, watching over the university's most celebrated tra-

---

21. Georgia Burleson, ed., *The Life and Writings of Rufus C. Burleson, Containing a Biography of Dr. Burleson by Hon. Harry Haynes* (Texas: Compiled and Published by Georgia J. Burleson, 1901); Jack Winton Gunn, "The Life of Rufus C. Burleson" (PhD diss., University of Texas, 1951); Joseph Martin Dawson, *Rufus C. Burleson: Pro Ecclesia, Pro Texana* (Dallas: Baptist Standard Pub. Co., 1956); and Neil Wood, *Burleson at Houston: A Personality Sketch of Rufus C. Burleson as Revealed in His Personal Writings During the Years of His Houston Ministry, 1848–1851* (Waco, TX: Baylor University, 1957).

22. Resolutions of Baylor Faculty, in Burleson, *Life and Writings*, 507–8. The tribute went on to express "profound condolences" to the widow and family with the assurances that Burleson's "memory will ever be dear to our hearts."

ditions.[23] The case of Antônia was intentionally forgotten at that moment and has largely remained so for well over a century.

A twelve-page essay written by Burleson's biographer, Harry Haynes, and published by the journal of the Texas State Historical Association in 1901, praised Burleson's life enthusiastically. Haynes concluded by quoting from a piece printed in the *Galveston News* on May 15, 1901, the morning Burleson's death was announced: "There are in all portions of Texas men and women who will remember with a tear the earnest and zealous old man whom they learned to love during their college days. Other will recall the venerable man of the pulpit to whose sermons they have listened, the genial old preacher who delighted to recall the adventures and triumphs of early days in Texas."[24] Indeed, the very landscape joined its citizens in singing his glory: "Evidences of the zeal and energy of the deceased are to be found in many places, and thousands of living witnesses stand ready to honor the dead. It is set down that Baylor University is 'a monument to his genius and industry.'"[25]

So Rufus C. Burleson has been remembered, his stance on race and the rape in his household forgotten. Many people had a stake in that endeavor.

The Legacies of SBC Missionaries in Brazil

Missionary legacies in Brazil also benefited from forgetting Antônia. Z. C. Taylor, who brought her to Waco, went on to become one of the most celebrated agents of the Foreign Mission Board and is today considered a pioneer of Baptist history in Brazil second in importance only to William Buck Bagby. He is particularly celebrated for his legacy in theological education, as the father of denominational publications, and for promoting evangelization as the first secretary of the National Mission Board of the Brazilian Baptist Convention.[26] His autobiography mentions those aspects of Antônio—Antônia's father—that Taylor chose to remember but nothing about the sexual scan-

---

23. See Mikeal C. Parsons, "Rufus Burleson and the Brazilian Girl," *Baptist History and Heritage* 56, no. 1 (March 2021): 26–38.

24. *Galveston Daily News*, May 15, 1901.

25. Harry Haynes, "Dr. Rufus C. Burleson," *The Quarterly of the Texas State Historical Association* 5, no. 1 (1901): 60.

26. See Oliveira, "Perfil Histórico"; Crabtree, *História*, vol. 1; and Pereira, *História dos Batistas no Brasil*, 15–48.

dal in which Antônio was involved nor anything about Antônia. But Rufus Burleson looms large. Taylor praised him profusely and took great pride in having translated one of Burleson's books into Portuguese to help educate potential Brazilian pastors.[27] Ironically, in light of Antônia's case, the volume treated *Family Government.*

Taylor was hardly the only Southern Baptist missionary to benefit from the covering up of sexual scandals in Brazil. Improprieties between missionaries and locals, including potential sexual misconduct, often appear in missionary correspondence, though of course not in FMB publicity. For example, when the missionary D. L. Hamilton tried to explain to his mother why other missionaries did not like him, he told her of an episode that occurred during his time on the faculty at the Baptist seminary in Recife:

> One of our missionaries recently got into trouble about women, and the natives involved called on me to stand by them in the investigation. It was a very delicate undertaking. All the other missionaries were against me. So, it turned out that I was on one side with all the natives, and all the missionaries, practically all, were on the other side with the offender. Every effort was made to cover up the matter, but I was armed with documents of which they knew nothing. So, I forced them to uncover the thing.[28]

The missionary in question departed—although he was later reassigned to the same field—and the missionaries in general were most disappointed in Hamilton for not letting the matter slide. This was one of the many incidents that led Hamilton to side with local Baptists against most Southern Baptist missionaries during a controversy that split the Brazilian Baptist Convention for over a decade.[29] The misconduct Hamilton helped locals uncover, of course, never made it into missionary news or publications. Much more often the perpetrators were reassigned and, later, celebrated. Hamilton's digression

---

27. Taylor, "Rise and Progress," 238 (in the Grober manuscript).

28. D. L. Hamilton to Lydia Hamilton, July 3, 1921, IMB Archives.

29. For more, see Chaves, *Global Mission*, chapter 3; and João B. Chaves and C. Douglas Weaver, "Baptists and Their Polarizing Ways: Transnational Polarization Between Southern Baptist Missionaries and Brazilian Baptists," *Review and Expositor* 116, no. 2 (2019): 160–74.

from fellow Southern Baptist missionaries in this incident and others was repaid by an FMB request that he retire early.[30]

A more notorious case involved Alyne Muirhead, the wife of missionary H. H. Muirhead. A few years before the Muirheads left Brazil permanently to serve in another field, rumors began to emerge that Mrs. Muirhead had an affair with Eduardo Liga, a Brazilian seminary student and the Muirhead family chauffeur. The Board of Trustees of the Rio Baptist College and Seminary (RBCS) convened to deliberate on the matter, and members of the South Brazil Mission communicated with the FMB about Alyne Muirhead's conduct. H. H. Muirhead was president of RBCS at the time and had been a leader of Baptist education efforts in Brazil for decades.

After the Muirheads left for Argentina because of this agitation, H. H. Muirhead received a letter—written in Portuguese—from the RBCS's Board of Trustees. The board was composed overwhelmingly of Southern Baptist missionaries who only rarely exposed fellow Americans to the kind of scrutiny they now leveled upon the Muirheads. The letter invited the Muirheads to an extraordinary session to be held a month hence, on January 14, 1934, to decide the issue.[31] Muirhead's response to the board—written in English from Argentina—made it clear that he was not willing to entertain further deliberations and investigations.[32] He also denied the accusations to his superiors at the FMB, as expected: "The rumors against Mrs. Muirhead's character were absolutely groundless, and were given no credence by the Brazilians, except a small group with axes to grind. The missionaries did not start the rumors, but a few of them did not hesitate to take advantage of the underhanded work of two seminary students who were facing expulsion. Others, outside the student body, for personal reasons, added fuel to the fire."[33]

Alyne Muirhead was facing exclusion not only from the seminary but also from her church—the First Baptist Church in Rio de Janeiro, started by W. B. Bagby when he left Antônio Teixeira and Z. C. Taylor in Bahia in 1884. An anonymous letter sent to the FMB official C. E. Maddry warned that if the

---

30. See Chaves, *Global Mission.*

31. Junta Administrativa do Seminario do Sul to H. H. Muirhead, December 14, 1935, IMB Archives.

32. H. H. Muirhead to Terry, Watson, Cowsert, Stover, Pinto, Porter, Teixeira, Christie, and Cockell, December 18, 1933, IMB Archives.

33. From H. H. Muirhead to C. E. Maddry, August 28, 1934, IMB Archives.

Muirheads returned to the seminary and their church, the outcome would expose the FMB in undesirable and embarrassing ways. After apologizing for presuming to give unrequested advice, the anonymous missionary, writing 320 miles away from Rio de Janeiro, stated: "I am not judging the question of the school for I am far enough away not to have the justice to judge. However, I am near enough to know that there is a big misunderstanding between the Seminary boys and the family of Bro. Muirhead and that Sister Muirhead is up before the deacons of the First Church for exclusion." Given that, a warning seemed due: "There seems to be no doubt but that if she returns to Rio, she must face a Church trial and, as soon as the school opens, a revolt on the part of the Ministerial students." A decision against her in the church trial "will put our Board in a very hard place." So that everything might be clear and above-board, the writer stated that "I am sending a copy of this letter to Bro. Muirhead and enclosing you a copy of my letter to him."[34]

The very next day, the FMB received the following letter from Palpalá, Argentina:

Dear Brethren:

Convinced that my health will not permit me to continue as head of the Rio Baptist College and Seminary, I hereby hand you my resignation as president of that institution, same to take effect immediately.

Fraternally yours,
H. H. Muirhead[35]

Health concerns covered a multitude of sins on the mission field. While invoking that cause, Muirhead made clear that "missionary politics" had led his colleagues to take advantage of the rumors about his wife's conduct. Other missionaries feared that he would expose their misappropriation of funds and mismanagement of FMB resources, or so he claimed, so they sought to undermine him by malicious rumor.[36]

---

34. Anonymous letter to C. E. Maddry and H. H. Muirhead, December 19, 1933, IMB Archives.
35. H. H. Muirhead to Foreign Mission Board, December 20, 1933, IMB Archives.
36. From H. H. Muirhead to C. E. Maddry, August 28, 1934, IMB Archives.

In an official report commissioned by the FMB, however, the missionary A. R. Crabtree did not seem so sure that the accusations could be dismissed as nasty denominational politics. Although Crabtree acknowledged that H. H. Muirhead's health needed attention, he stated: "All, with the exception of the Muirheads, seem to feel that his resignation was made necessary by the social conduct of Mrs. Muirhead."[37] Even the most charitable interpreters of the evidence against her (almost all of them friendly SBC missionaries) were convinced she was at least guilty of "indiscretion, imprudence, and a certain lack of dignity and consideration"; so said the report.[38]

Brazilian observers were generally not so charitable. Crabtree praised H. H. Muirhead's stance defending his wife's honor by all means possible, a step that Crabtree thought Brazilians misunderstood because, in his view, Brazil was not "a man's country" like the United States. Crabtree did not take a definitive stance on the incident, however. Such qualified impartiality is telling, for he was not often shy about defending questionable behavior by missionary colleagues.[39]

Several months after his resignation, H. H. Muirhead was back in Rio doing missionary work, but not for long. He complained to his FMB superiors that he and his wife continued to be persecuted by other missionaries. Despite the fact that the FMB was heavily strained by the Great Depression, the Muirheads left for a trip to Europe because "Alyne is on the verge of a complete breakdown and I am not too far behind."[40] With that, the Muirheads permanently broke their connection to the Brazil mission. After spending time in Italy, Portugal, and Romania, H. H. Muirhead would serve as president of the Mexican Baptist Theological Seminary in Texas, eventually retiring from active missionary work in 1947.[41]

The alleged affair between Alyne Muirhead and Eduardo Liga was not investigated further, nor were the charges of misappropriation of funds that Muirhead made against his fellow missionaries. Business went on as usual;

---

37. A. R. Crabtree, "Report on Dr. Muirhead's Resignation as President of Rio Baptist College and Seminary of Rio" (probably written in early 1934), IMB Archives.

38. Crabtree, "Report on Dr. Muirhead's Resignation."

39. See the event involving Frank Purser in Chaves, *Global Mission*, 89–91.

40. From H. H. Muirhead to W. C. Taylor, September 15, 1936, IMB Archives.

41. "In Memoriam," *The Commission* 21, no. 1 (January 1958): 21. H. Muirhead received an honorary doctorate from Baylor University in the 1920s.

differences were negotiated behind closed doors. Even the most careful readers of denominational publications and reports would most likely not have suspected such scandals.

In like manner a host of other concerns beyond sexual scandals were concealed from the broader public: intentional violations of immigration legislation, missionaries using their passports to import cars and other equipment for sale in the black market, missionaries' aggressive support of dictatorships and explicit demonstration of racial and cultural snobbery are all clearly found in missionary correspondence.[42] Sometimes, the more scandalous elements of such behavior did not reach the offices of the FMB in Richmond, Virginia. Many other times, the FMB overlooked or actively forgot facts that would keep them from telling the most productive story they could tell. Missionary legacies often depended—and still depend—on selective remembering and active forgetting.

---

42. For instances of investigations on missionary contraband, see the personal papers of A. R. Crabtree from 1949 to 1952, IMB Archives. For Baptist support of the dictatorship in Brazil, see Cowan, *Moral Majorities Across the Americas*; Sérgio Dusilek, Clemir Fernandes, and Alexandre Carvalho, "A Igreja e a Farda: Batistas e a Ditadura Militar," *Estudos Teológicos* 57, no. 1 (January/June 2017): 192–212; and Daniel Augusto Cavalcanti, *Protestantismo e Ditadura Militar no Brasil* (São Paulo: Editora Reflexão, 2015). Issues regarding immigration legislation and racial and cultural superiority are covered in João B. Chaves, *Migrational Religion* (Waco, TX: Baylor University Press, 2021); and Chaves, *Global Mission*.

Conclusion

Forgetting Antônia and Narratives
of Institutional Goodness

The systematic erasure of Antônia Teixeira from SBC institutional memories in the United States and in Brazil left her, like Melchizedek, without
beginning or end. We are not certain of her birth date or even the identity of
her birth mother. Her trail after leaving Waco for Memphis runs cold. Did she
marry and have children? Did she ever return to Brazil to visit her family?[1]
The erasure of Antônia from the historical record was successful and from
collective Baptist memory nearly complete. Likewise, aspects of her father's
life were also intentionally "forgotten."

Besides helping to protect the legacies of individuals like Rufus C. Burleson,
Z. C. Taylor, and assorted Southern Baptist missionaries, the eclipse of Antônio's sexual scandal and Antônia Teixeira's rape point to the vigilance with
which institutional stakeholders can mold and maintain narratives of institutional virtue. Burleson, Taylor, Baylor University, and the FMB are hardly iso-
lated instances in this regard but do exemplify a controlling set of assumptions
and behaviors. Institutional mythmaking lay behind the forgetting of Antônio's abduction of Senhorinha because the complexity of his full story would
reflect negatively on the entire SBC missionary enterprise, marring a legacy
constructed to bolster a Southern Baptist narrative of institutional goodness.
Similarly, Antônia had to be forgotten lest the narrative of Baylor University's
virtue—and its function as "a monument to (the) genius and industry" of Ru-

---

1. Oliveira hinted that Antônia may have later attempted (unsuccessfully?) to contact her
Brazilian family (*Antônio Teixeira de Albuquerque*, 23).

fus C. Burleson—be imperiled.[2] Burleson's legacy figured centrally in the definitive story about the Christian university in whose mission his defenders were deeply invested. In praising Burleson, Baylor's supporters were celebrating their university; they were also praising themselves. No immigrant girl could ever stand in the way of such mythmaking, and if contemporary cultural pressures have compelled Baylor to revisit Burleson's place in its story, it is partly because new standards of institutional goodness have been established.

That institutional mythmaking might crush vulnerable people goes much beyond the story of Antônia's rape at Baylor University.[3] Campuses across the nation have experienced their own episodes in which narratives of institutional virtue clashed with actual institutional behavior on the matter of sexual assault. Today, it is estimated that over 80 percent of sexual assault cases are not reported by college students to authorities.[4] Among women of color, that percentage is even higher.[5] Despite the requirement that schools report sexual assault statistics from their campuses, many schools intentionally obscure the extent and gravity of the problem.[6] Even though having a strong and effective Title IX office has become part of universities' standard narratives today, the overwhelming majority of campus sexual assaults go unreported or unpunished.

2. Haynes, "Dr. Rufus C. Burleson," 60.

3. This point was recognized long ago by Reinhold Niebuhr in *Moral Man and Immoral Society: A Study in Ethics and Politics* (New York: Charles Scribner's Sons, 1932), 117:

> The moral attitudes of dominant and privileged groups are characterised by universal self deception and hypocrisy. The unconscious and conscious identification of their special interests with general interests and universal values, which we have noted in analysing national attitudes, is equally obvious in the attitude of classes. The reason why privileged classes are more hypocritical than underprivileged ones is that special privilege can be defended in terms of the rational ideal of equal justice only, by proving that it contributes something to the good of the whole. Since inequalities of privilege are greater than could possibly be defended rationally, the intelligence of privileged groups is usually applied to the task of inventing specious proofs for the theory that universal values spring from, and that general interests are served by, the special privileges which they hold.

Here Niebuhr focuses on class, but it applies, of course, intersectionally as well.

4. David DeMatteo et al., "Sexual Assault on College Campuses: A 50-State Survey of Criminal Sexual Assault Statutes and Their Relevance to Campus Sexual Assault," *Psychology, Public Policy, and Law* 21, no. 3 (August 2015): 227–38.

5. Jessica C. Harris, "Women of Color Undergraduate Students' Experiences with Campus Sexual Assault: An Intersectional Analysis," *Review of Higher Education* 44, no. 1 (Fall 2020): 1–30.

6. Corey Rayburn Young, "Concealing Campus Sexual Assault: An Empirical Examination," *Psychology, Public Policy, and Law* 21, no. 1 (2015): 1–9.

Baylor's own recent rape scandal, of course, cannot help but bring up Antônia's story.[7] In the spring of 2012, the mother of a Baylor female student informed an associate athletic director that multiple Baylor football players had sexually assaulted her daughter at a party, but the student had not reported the assault to the police. The athletics official met with the head football coach, Art Briles, but no action was taken. In 2015, after a Baylor football player was convicted of sexual assault, a law firm was hired by the university to review university policy and practice in handling reports of physical and sexual violence. That report, released in 2016, found systemic failure in Baylor's handling of sexual assault allegations. The football coach was fired, the university president, Ken Starr, was demoted (and later forced to resign), and the athletic director, Ian McCaw, was put on probation. A number of lawsuits claiming sexual assaults by a number of football players were subsequently filed. That scandal, which made headlines across the nation, was linked back to Antônia's rape by John Lomax in the *Texas Monthly*:

> The serious personnel shakeup in the aftermath of the recent rape scandal that's unfolded at Baylor University is shocking, but it isn't a first for the Waco school. As far back as 1897, the forced early retirement of Dr. Rufus Columbus Burleson amid a controversy that attracted national headlines would never have come to fruition if it weren't for the stubbornness of a vitriolic Waco journalist, whose diatribes would result in the violent deaths of four of Waco's leading citizens. Aside from that body count, today's Baylor rape shame shares much with its 1890s forerunner.[8]

Narratives of institutional virtue sit at the center of Antônio's and Antônia's story. Antônio's scandal was forgotten and Antônia's assault was erased because the mythologies of Southern identity combined with desires for Christian purity have been so important to Baylor University, Baptist missionaries, and the SBC in general. Contemporary scholars find that "southerners, more than other Americans, have grounded their identities in distinct images of the past, and the literature charts the ways in which southern communities have used,

---

7. The Associated Press, "Key Dates and Developments in the Baylor Assault Scandal," *AP News*, August 11, 2021, https://apnews.com/article/sports-college-football-violence-lawsuits-sexual-assault-9fe035761dc3d1f3d42c714a87c78a10.

8. Lomax, "Apostle of the Devil."

reimagined, and fought over their history."[9] The mythologies and desires that have gone into Southern institutions and Southern-based transnational projects are deep-seated realities that remain at the heart of historically Southern institutions.

Nevertheless, these traditional commitments have recently been contested by projects trying to replace old memories with new ones. For good reason, this push has centered on issues of race. In his study of the importance of myth and memory in the South, the historian Charles Reagan Wilson reminds us that "January once was best known in the South as the month of Robert E. Lee's birthday, but far more community energy now goes into honoring the birthday that month of Martin Luther King Jr. The contemporary South's passionately fought battles over Lost Cause symbolism suggest the continuing hold it has on some of the region's people and the commitment of others to change that symbolism as inappropriate to a desegregated southern public culture."[10]

The ongoing struggle for better collective identities is complicated by recent developments in the South. Hispanics there march against Confederate symbols while holding up images of Our Lady of Guadalupe. Native Americans push Southern historians to go beyond Black-and-White binaries, while increased attention is given to the fluidity of narratives and identities informed by migration patterns in the Southern borderlands.[11] Antônia's story invites us to move beyond race as the central category from which to challenge traditional Southern memories in general and denominational histories in particular.

The story of Antônia challenges scholars and practitioners to add intersectional concerns in reconsidering individual and institutional legacies. What would happen to our heroes if their value were judged not only according to

9. Andrew Denson, *Monuments to Absence: Cherokee Removal and the Contest over Southern Memory* (Chapel Hill: University of North Carolina Press, 2017), 4. See also David Blight, *Race and Reunion: The Civil War in American Memory* (Cambridge, MA: Belknap Press, 2002); and W. Fitzhugh Brundage, *The Southern Past: A Clash of Race and Memory* (Cambridge, MA: Belknap Press, 2005).

10. Charles Reagan Wilson, "Myth, Manners, and Memory," in *The New Encyclopedia of Southern Culture*, ed. Charles Reagan Wilson, vol. 4, *Myth, Manners, and Memory* (Chapel Hill: University of North Carolina Press, 2006), 6.

11. See Wilson, "Myth, Manners, and Memory"; Denson, *Monuments to Absence*; and Todd W. Wahlstrom, *The Southern Exodus to Mexico: Migration across the Borderlands after the American Civil War* (Lincoln: University of Nebraska Press, 2015).

their racial commitments but also by their views of foreigners? What if the individuals celebrated with monuments were judged by whether they protected or oppressed the most vulnerable? How would we narrate our collective pasts if institutional triumphalism did not stand as the strongest element in the stories we tell about who we were, are, and will be?

In remembering Antônia, we do not do ourselves an immediate favor but may build toward a truer one farther off. The story of the "Brazilian girl" who was raped in Texas reminds us that, when narratives of institutional virtue prevail, those who hold power will most likely continue to have it their way. Nevertheless, the challenge of redemption remains: "Beyond the grave, Antônia Teixeira still cries out for justice. Who will answer?"[12]

---

12. Parsons, "Rufus Burleson and the Brazilian Girl," 35.

Epilogue

The years 2020 and 2021 were extraordinarily challenging times, and the contemporary situation shows no signs of relenting. In addition to the COVID-19 pandemic that has surged across the globe in several waves with devastating results, acts of violence toward persons of color (notably, the brutal murder of George Floyd in May 2020) stirred massive protests in the United States and heightened awareness of the structural racism that is as insidious as it is harmful, even lethal, to people of color. Baylor University's Board of Regents created a Commission on Historic Campus Representations charged with reviewing "the complete historical record and context of the University and its founders and early leaders, including historical connections to slavery and racial injustice."[1] With that, Baylor belatedly joined other universities, such as Brown, Furman, Georgetown, Harvard, and Wake Forest, in examining the entanglement of the university's founders with chattel slavery. This project began as a response to President Linda A. Livingstone's commitment to "the hard work ahead of confronting systemic racism, injustice, and inequality at [Baylor] University."[2] The authors first became aware of this issue when Mikeal became

1. "Baylor University Announces Members, Charges for Commission on Historic Campus Representations," Baylor University: Media and Public Relations, July 6, 2020, https://www.baylor.edu/mediacommunications/news.php?action=story&story=219486.

2. "Baylor University Board of Regents Acknowledges University's History, Ties to Slavery and Confederacy; Unanimously Passes Resolution on Racial Healing and Justice," Baylor University: Media and Public Relations, June 26, 2020, https://www.baylor.edu/mediacommunications/news.php?action=story&story=219405.

interested in the role of Rufus Burleson in perpetuating racial injustice and stumbled upon the story of the sexual assault of Antônia Teixeira. When he realized its connections to Baptist mission work in Brazil, he invited Dr. João Chaves of Austin Presbyterian Theological Seminary and the Hispanic Theological Initiative at Princeton Seminary, a historian of missions and migration studies, to join him in a project to situate Antônia's story within its larger transnational context.

Antônia's story reminds us of the ways in which sexual assault and harassment have recently emerged from the shadows and into the national consciousness through the watershed #MeToo movement. A phrase coined in 2006 by Tarana Burke, a sexual assault survivor, it was embraced in 2017 by Ashley Judd and Alyssa Milano, inter alia, and has since swept through social media, continuing to empower people to name and confront those guilty of harassing and assaulting them.[3] Closer to home are high-profile incidents of sexual violence perpetrated by athletes at Baylor in the 2010s. No fewer than ten female students filed complaints against the university's failure to implement effectively its Title IX–compliance responsibilities.[4] The Regents' *Findings of Fact* report also determined that some administrators and university employees at the time "engaged in conduct that could be perceived as victim-blaming, focusing on the complainant's choices and actions, rather than robustly investigating the allegations."[5] Most recently, the Department of Education fined Baylor $461,656 for Clery violations. President Livingstone indicated that Baylor did "not plan to contest this fine, as we contend it is fair given the circumstances and in comparison to Clery-related penalties levied against other schools."[6]

These events—global, national, and local—arrayed across the transnational context at hand in this story, helped motivate the writing of this book.[7]

---

3. See, e.g., the December 18, 2017, issue of *Time* magazine, in which some of these women were named "persons of the year."

4. Proper implementation, said the university's official report, would have "identified the nature of the risks attendant to sexual and gender-based harassment and violence and interpersonal violence, the likelihood of occurrence, and the adequacy of existing controls to ensure an informed and effective institutional response." Baylor University Board of Regents, *Findings of Fact* (Waco, TX: Baylor University, 2016), 4, https://www.baylor.edu/thefacts/doc.php/266596.pdf.

5. University Board of Regents, *Findings of Fact*, 8.

6. Email from the Office of the President to author, October 9, 2020.

7. After completing this manuscript, we learned of the devastating Guidepost Solutions report concerning widespread sexual abuse and assault by SBC clergy over several decades and the subsequent cover-up by the SBC Executive Committee. The full, over three-hundred-page report is available here: https://www.sataskforce.net/updates/guidepost-solutions-report-of-the

The episode of "The Brazilian Girl and Baylor University," as Rufus Burleson regrettably labeled it, represents a low point in Baylor's history and Burleson's presidency and remains remarkably relevant for understanding the historical roots of the current scene. This project joins other efforts on Baylor's campus to report and address the institution's complicity in racist, sexist, and xenophobic practices and policies over its history. But the significance of the project is neither limited nor provincial. The specifics of Antônia Teixeira's story provide an opportunity to develop themes of more general interest: the roles of race, ethnicity, and gender following Reconstruction in a frontier town like Waco; the complexities and cultural entanglements of Protestant missionary efforts, specifically among the Baptists in Brazil in the second half of the nineteenth century; and the conflicted character of a faith-related institution of higher education that is deeply implicated in White privilege, an institution whose transnational, racialized influence is often celebrated as an uncomplicated aspect of its legacy.

We shared the preliminary results of our research on Antônia with the co-chairs of the Commission on Historic Representation.[8] We hope our findings contributed to the commission's recommendation that the Burleson Quadrangle be renamed and Burleson's statue be moved to "a less prominent location."[9] In addition to Burleson's connections to the "Lost Cause" movement, the report also cited "issues regarding the treatment of Antônia Teixeira, a young woman entrusted to the care of the Burleson family during Rufus Burleson's presidency whose rape and controversy surrounding the related criminal case contributed to Burleson's retirement as Baylor President in 1897."[10] In May 2022, the Baylor regents announced that the Burleson Quadrangle would be renamed simply the "Quadrangle," and the Burleson statue would be moved out of the Quadrangle to a less visible pedestal and given signage that gives a

---

-independent-investigation. We cannot begin to fathom the anguish and outrage experienced by the survivors of these assaults and their families, but we do lament with them in their suffering and stand with them in their quest for justice against the perpetrators of these crimes.

8. Those findings were published as "Rufus Burleson and the Brazilian Girl" in *Baptist History and Heritage* 56, no. 1 (2021): 26–38. We are grateful to the editors for permission to use material from that article.

9. Baylor University Commission on Historic Representation, *Final Report*, December 2020, 47, https://www.baylor.edu/diversity/commission/doc.php/372287.pdf.

10. Baylor University Commission on Historic Representation, *Final Report*, 46.

fuller historical picture of Burleson's conflicted presidency.[11] On July 13, 2022, Burleson's statue was removed from the Quadrangle; Baylor Regents are commended for taking this significant first step in addressing past injustices.

We received funding for this project through Baylor's University Research Committee, which awarded us the Dr. Benjamin Brown IV Fund for Interdisciplinary and Collaborative Scholarship. These funds allowed us to employ Marcelo Oliveira, a Baylor (Truett Seminary) student from Brazil, to partner in the research and supported João's research trips to Brazil. We are grateful to the administrators of the Brown Fund not only for their support but for what it symbolizes. To engage in this kind of institutional self-reflection and analysis with Baylor financial support speaks to the seriousness with which at least some parties at the university take President Livingstone's mandate to examine historical examples of Baylor's racism, sexism, and xenophobia.

Mikeal is grateful for the support of colleagues in the Department of Religion and beyond who have joined together in acts, large and small, to counter systemic racism, sexism, and xenophobia at Baylor and elsewhere. We express appreciation to the medical physicians Dr. Ann Sims and Dr. Craig Keathley for their expert analysis of the medical testimony at Steen Morris's trial and to Gerald Powell, Baylor law professor emeritus, who interpreted for us some of the intricacies of nineteenth-century Texas-courtroom procedure. Appreciation is also due to Wayne Dowdy, archivist at the Memphis Public Library, who located newspaper articles about Antônia's sojourn to Memphis, Tennessee, and Kerry McGuire, researcher at McLennan County Archives, who provided copies of extant court materials related to the trial of Steen Morris. Gratitude is also expressed to John Arnold and his colleagues at NICOM, Inc., especially for discovering the marriage license between J. R. Cook and Antônia Teixeira and for confirming that from that point, without additional resources, Antônia's trail was inaccessible. Dr. Jim Bratt, in his role as Eerdmans development editor, improved the logic, language, and structure of the manuscript; remaining flaws, of course, are our responsibility. A special thanks to the Baylor historians Doug Weaver, Betsy Flowers, Mandy McMichael, and Carlos Cardoza-Orlandi for commenting on various chapter drafts. As always, Mikeal wants to thank his spouse, Heidi Hornik, who, despite her own research projects and heavy administrative duties as chair of Baylor's Department of Art and Art History, listened patiently to and offered constructive insights on

---

11. *Waco Tribune-Herald*, May 21, 2022.

these efforts to untangle the web of Antônia Teixeira's story. Special thanks to Christian Sanchez, who read the page proofs and spotted many errors.

João also extends his gratitude to the Baylor Department of Religion, including professor Mikeal Parsons, who invited him to join this exciting project. In addition, he is thankful for the archivists, pastors, and priests across national and state borders who helped collect the indispensable primary-source material for this manuscript. A multitude of people forwarded materials and/ or opened doors of archives when they were still officially closed due to the COVID-19 pandemic; among them are Jim Berwick at the International Mission Board in Richmond, Virginia; Renata Bertolino and Almira from the Public Archives of the State of Alagoas in Maceió, Alagoas; Luiza Sahara from the Archives of the Curia of Maceió, Alagoas; Diego Rodriguez from the Dom Lamartine Archives in the Archdiocese of Olinda, Pernambuco; Vanessa Varone from the Methodist Cathedral of Rio de Janeiro; Maria Betânia Melo Araújo and Ramos André from the North Brazil Baptist Theological Seminary in Recife, Pernambuco; Tercio Ribeiro and Jovesi de Almeida Costa from the First Evangelical Baptist Church in Maceió, Alagoas; Cláudio Albuquerque from the First Presbyterian Church in Recife, Pernambuco; Marlene Pereira from the Libraries of the Catholic University in Petrópolis, Rio de Janeiro; and Ana Beatriz from the Archives of the Pontifical Catholic University of Pernambuco, in Recife, Pernambuco. He also thanks his research assistants, Britt Hicks and Aiden Diaz, for their diligent work in putting the index together. João is especially thankful to his wife, Clare Duffy, who helped open space for the many hours of travel and writing invested in this project, including six weeks in Brazil. Finally, Joanne Rodíguez, executive director at the Hispanic Theological Initiative at Princeton Theological Seminary, and colleagues from Austin Presbyterian Theological Seminary continued to offer indispensable support for research and writing, for which João is very grateful.

We hope this historical work can bolster ongoing efforts to redress institutional injustices, past and present, and to correct historical narratives that remain incomplete. Antônio Teixeira's role in the history of US missionary presence in Brazil is recognized but not in its full importance. His real significance for Brazilian Protestantism has been overshadowed by narratives that overstate Southern Baptist–missionary autonomy in the country and that forget how his own sexual scandal opened avenues for publicity on which Protestants of different stripes capitalized in Brazil. We scratched enough of the surface of that story here to know that there is more to be done in rethinking the role of ex-priests turned Protestants, of Antônio in particular, in helping ensure the success of Protestant missionary work in Latin America.

Antônia's story has value well beyond its connection to her father and his significance in Brazil. Besides revealing horrible details of her rape, trials, and subsequent oppression by powerful men in Texas, her story opens a window into the processes by which individuals and institutions across borders erase inconvenient memories for the sake of building narratives of institutional goodness. *Remembering Antônia Teixeira* shows how closely transnational Baptist relationships are connected to the construction of religious legacies, both at home and on the mission field. Her rape is also a troubling reality to remember for demonstrating how institutions have used—and still use—selective remembering to build and maintain legacies. May we continue to consider how institutions—Christian and otherwise—might look at themselves to see a myth maintained by the erasure of the powerless they oppressed. In so doing, we honor the full and complex memory of Antônia Teixeira and her family.

Appendix 1

Three Reasons Why I Left the Church of Rome

By Priest Antônio Teixeira de Albuquerque
Translated by Marcelo Oliveira from
the tract *Tres Razões Porque Deixei a Igreja de Roma*

Mass or Transubstantiation
Mandatory Celibacy
Auricular Confession

T he three reasons that serve as an epigraph to this booklet were those that first made me question the veracity of the Church of Rome, even though I thought of myself as far from the Bible and short of full knowledge of it.

Unsettled by reason and conscience, I had a happy moment: I became aware of the duty to study the Word of God seriously and carefully, now comparing the different versions to make sure there was a false Bible, and now meditating on each commandment of God, teachings and precepts of Jesus Christ. I was surprised: for all the versions came from the same original (Greek) and were the same. There was not a false Bible. These things were entirely new to me.

The veil of the Pope's mysteries was being torn down bit by bit as I'd read the Bible, seeing the will of God revealed to men, and in such a way that I was able to find out many other reasons why I should no longer linger in such a church. Bad doctrines are condemned by themselves: errors, su-

Antônio Teixeira de Albuquerque was born in 1840 in Maceió, Alagoas, Brazil, and died April 7, 1887, in Rio Largo, Alagoas. This booklet was probably written in 1884.

perstitions, idolatries, are contradicted in the eyes of the Bible and reason. I saw the condemnation of the church of Rome.

Then came to my ears an imperious, but comforting, warning as in the days of Noah and Lot, a warning of divine salvation, perfect, and eternal: "Come out of her, my people; that ye may not be partakers of her sins, and that ye may not fall in her plagues" (Rev. 18:4).

Educated in the solitude of an old Jesuit convent, under the direction of six company priests, I learned Roman Theology, having to blindly obey all dogmas. I had no time to engulf myself in greed, nor to entangle myself in the political turmoil in which many of the clergy took part, abandoning their vicars to meddle in secular business and elections. Neither secular or religious politics, nor any pretense of ecclesiastical jobs, ranks, or benefits, was the cause of my departure from Romanism. Rather, it was solely its doctrine, mainly the following three points: "Mass or transubstantiation, Mandatory Celibacy, and Auricular Confession."

Dear reader, I must also declare to you, that I was not led to abjure the church of Rome for the promise of money or employment in the evangelical churches; instead, since that time I have suffered privation, and more. Romanism, on the other hand, has always offered me advantages, perks (in the beginning, to return to it), money, home and jobs (even today). Everyone is wrong because I was not dragged or convinced by men but by the Bible, which I also heard said in the Church of Rome to be the Word of God.

It is also important to tell you that I was not banned, expelled, or unauthorized as a priest by any bishop until today (which they could have done, without me bothering about it). I myself sent a letter to the bishop informing him of my definitive withdrawal from his church, asking him to cross me out of the Roman priestly lineage, as it is not known in the Bible that Jesus Christ instituted such an office.

Even more, dear reader; I left Romanism, not because of a woman, as some, finding no other reason, claim. For everyone knows that, at best, a priest may be suspended (rarely) for some time, and then may return to his office, although the crime of honor remains!! Who can dispute such truth? It is a sad and harmful truth; nonetheless, it is truth.

Therefore, I withdrew from Romanism, freely and spontaneously, just as I embraced the Gospel freely, spontaneously and cordially. Now I proceed to explain the three reasons.

I. Mass or Transubstantiation

This extraordinary dogma, upon which the Church of Rome is founded, an effect of the presuppositional [presupposed?] power of the priest, was never entirely believed by me, although I have never read this point in the Bible. I adored all the hosts and chalices consecrated by the priests, perhaps with some degree of belief, but after I myself came to possess the popular rite of transubstantiating them, I could no longer have a single glimmer of belief.

They taught me that those elements (bread and wine), after being consecrated lost their substances, leaving only accidents. Let's see: The truth of the matter was that I would eat the communal wafer, and it tasted like wheat flour. And I would drink the wine, and it tasted the same flavor of grape wine. And even more so, it had the same effect as when drinking it elsewhere. I learned everything out of obligation and not conviction; in the book of tradition, this unfortunate boat wandered without a sail, without a compass, in the batting waves stirred up by the gales, which are the human passions in its pride. Here are the books I studied: practical and theoretical morals, sacramental morality, theoretical and dogmatic theology, ecclesiastical and sacred history (a summary), hermeneutics and exegesis, which deal with those biblical points that are convenient, apparently to better prove the dogmas of the Church of Rome. I didn't study the Bible, because there was not a special course for this. When I ate the communal wafer, already consecrated, I knew and saw that the substance had not changed, because it sustained me in the same way and had the same taste as before. The wine, in addition to retaining the same taste, disturbed my head for a few minutes. (Does blood have this effect?) Then I reflected: How is this? What's with Substance Change? What is the substance of flour? Isn't taste one part of the substance and nutritional strength another? What is the substance of wine? Aren't flavor and alcoholic strength integral to its substance? If the substance was gone, this wine should not disturb me! How many times had I read of the poisoning of priests, placed in the communal wafer and the cup?! But, they would say: As soon as the poison enters, matter becomes corrupt, and therefore invalid. What a misleading excuse! In that case the priest's power would have ended; the poison therefore, is more powerful! Sorry religion, where power resides in men and not in

God! Still, they'd say there are holy priests. Well then, swallow a poison wafer or wine, and see if they would die or not?!

I learned more: the priest's power is such that after he pronounces the words—"This is my body"—Christ comes down from heaven as he is there, in body, soul and divinity, and comes right up to the pater. Then he is offered in favor or to cleanse the venial sins that the blessed souls took to the flames of the fire of purgatory!!! Oh! dear reader, what a convenient remedy for worldly passions and mundane pleasures! Such doctrine gives rise to the fact that man continues in his sins, and intends to destroy the doctrine of Jesus Christ, the only way of salvation: "Repent and believe in the Gospel" (Mark 1:15).

I thought that after I became a priest, I could know which individuals or souls were in purgatory (such a word is never found in the Bible): but which! Neither I nor any of my colleagues ever knew of such a hint, for there has not yet been a priest who said that he no longer needed to say a mass for the souls of so and so, unless there is no more money for it. But if there is, then, dear reader, it is even worse, because purgatory for that soul just turned into hell, and such soul will never leave it. Is it not so? It's a mystery, they would tell me. Since the Bible is God's revelation to men, it seems rather clear to me that there should not be so much mystery. But I will open the Bible, I said, for these mysteries confuse me, and my soul finds no rest in them. In fact, dear reader, when I read the Bible carefully, then I saw with surprise the error of the religion I was brought up in and was following, and in which, unfortunately, I had been ordained!

I did not find the word "mass" anywhere in the Bible, but I clearly saw an "ordinance" instituted by Jesus Christ—a "special supper" of bread and wine offered by him to his disciples—and a command for them to celebrate it in his memory.

See now what our Lord said: "This is my body that is given for you. Do this in remembrance of me" (Luke 22:19). Here we see the clarity with which the divine Master spoke to his apostles. Can we celebrate someone who is present? No, commemoration is an act that is done when someone is absent or dead. It was just what was going to happen:

Jesus was to be delivered that same night, accused, sentenced and killed. That is why he instituted Holy Communion, not only to represent the kind of death he was going to suffer—his injured body and his spilled blood—but to be a memorial, a commemoration of his passion and death.

"Do this in memory of me." It is a mistake and, more than that, it is a sin to adore the communal wafer and the cup after they are consecrated, as the priests teach, because Jesus Christ is not there in body and soul. This doctrine is repugnant to reason and goes against the Holy Scriptures. Converse with me: "Christ is seated at the right hand of God" (Col. 3:1). "I came out of the Father, and came into the world, and I go to the Father" (John 16:28). "And if there was a time when we knew Christ according to the flesh, by now we don't know him in this way" (2 Cor. 5:16). "For you always have the poor with you, but you will not always have me" (Matt. 26:11). This clearly shows that Christ ascended into heaven, where he is "corporeally and in reality." This being the case, he will only come on the last day, and not every day on all altars at the same time, in all wafers and cups and fragments, and at the mercy of any individual who calls himself a priest, or was entitled so. For then Christ would not rule himself—he must obey such, millions who are time and again depraved! This is more than a mistake, it's blasphemy!

It reminds me of an objection from a Dogmatic lens: If a rat breaks into the tabernacle and steals the wafer, what should you do? The ritual is that when the wafer falls on the floor, that it should be swallowed, but today, due to the reform, the place is scraped clean or burned; but, the rat fled, and even an act of disgrace it is unknown; how should we proceed? . . . All the students were stunned, as it was difficult to solve such an objection, if it were not the phlegm of our causative lenses: "God will destroy the mouse." Answer me, gentlemen who were my friends, was it so or not?

Did you know John of the martyrs well? Isn't this ridiculous?

Isn't that blasphemy too? It would be better to answer as Father Antônio Vieira writes very well: "And even God in temples and tabernacles is not safe." (Classic selection in Portuguese, describing the war.)

All Roman Catholics must go to purgatory without fail, because although they receive all oils, holy waters, crosses, blessings and wafers, they must necessarily send orders, masses and suffrages to be said postmortem (after death). But didn't such a person already receive the Christ of flour? Thus, there go the deceased and the flour Christ, both to purgatory.

What is this, gentlemen? How many conclusions could be drawn from such a Roman system?

It is a Roman idea that it is necessary for the priest to have the intention to consecrate. How can we know that this is the priest's intention when we often see him leave the place in a filthy, disapproved, immoral and ridiculous way?! In a city in my province a priest partied among many women on Christmas Eve. When the time for the midnight mass came, the sacristan took him out of the middle of the orgy to give the first mass and . . . he . . . did! Another priest was going to do a mass far from Maceio. Passing by a place accompanied by his sacristan [sexton]—who faithfully told us [the story]—he came across a mocotó lunch meal, and the priest, who likes mocotó, did not refuse it. Instead, he swallowed it with brandy . . . he then went on to the place for the mass. But . . . while doing the mass, and drinking the wine, not being able to reconcile in his stomach the wine with the brandy, there went the mocotó, brandy, the wine and . . . what's more, the wafer! The rest I cannot tell, as well as many other shameful facts, about which modesty tells me to be silent. And who doesn't know them, and who doesn't see them? Christ, when he instituted this sacrament, was looking and conversing with his disciples; could they eat it? "Neither will you allow your Holy One to see corruption" (Acts 2:27, 31; and Ps. 1[6]:10).

When the priest swallows the wafer, will it remain uncorrupted? The wafer and wine, after swallowing, go to the stomach. Then, from stomach to belly and from the belly, after being digested, they end up in the filthy place, and consequently, that god becomes corrupted!

Dear readers, such a wafer is not Jesus Christ, but an illusion, a sinful teaching, contrary to the Word of God. But I must make the point clear to you, because you, like me, were mistaken. Christ himself explained the great mystery to Romanism, and gave the infallible interpretation that closes the mouth of the entire clergy: "If you do not eat the flesh of the Son of man, and drink his blood, you will have no life in yourselves" (John 6:53). His disciples said to him, "This speech is hard, and who can hear it?" (John 6:61). Jesus said, "The spirit quickens, the flesh avails nothing; the words that I spoke to you are spirit and life" (John 6:63).

Priests devour the god they adore and, also, the people with them. They are, therefore, (in the second doctrine) deicides! Oh! What blasphemy, what blindness!

This doctrine of the wafer transforming into the body of Christ is contrary in itself, as well as absurd. They say it is a dogma of Roman faith that, after consecrated, the wine became blood.

Oh! Dear reader! Is it blood or not? Why these papal subtleties? If it is not blood, it cannot be "propitiatory for the remission of the sins of the living and the dead." What an annoyance! If it's blood, then it's not bloodless. Now, according to Christ, the bread and wine of the Lord's Supper are the memorial of his death; therefore, you cannot give transubstantiation or mass; therefore, it cannot remit sins. "Christ shed his blood for many, for the remission of sins" (Matt. 26:28).

The Lord's Supper is a true ordinance. The purpose for which Jesus Christ instituted it was not so that his body and his blood could be reproduced, or that his sacrifice on the cross of Calvary could be repeated; no, but to commemorate his death. "For as often as you eat this bread and drink this cup, ye shall proclaim the Lord's death, until he comes" (1 Cor. 11:26).

Christ himself is the propitiation "for our sins" (John 2:2). And this reconciliation is "by the blood of his cross" (Col. 1:20). "Here is the Lamb of God, here is the same One who bore our sins in his body on the tree" (1 Peter 2:24). Therefore, mass is worth nothing.

Now, dear reader, who is it that saves? Is it Christ, or the bread and the wine? Your conscience will tell you: Christ is the only one who can save. "This is a faithful word, worthy of all acceptance, that Christ came into the world to save sinners" (1 Tim. 1:15). So, Jesus is the one who has the power to forgive and save sinners and not the mass or the priests, who make the mass. "And Jesus came and spoke to them, saying, 'All power is given me in heaven and on earth'" (Matt. 28:18).

In Jesus we have the redemption of our sins: "In which we have the redemption through his blood, the remission of sins" (Eph. 1:7).

After all, it all ends in Jesus. So what are they trusting men for? "Search the Scriptures and they themselves are they which testify of me" (John 5:39).

The law of priests and sacrifices has passed, as they were types of Christ—figures and shadows of the Supreme Pontiff (Christ) who came to rescue the world. Animal sacrifices were figurative. Today the Christ who has come accomplished all this, giving us an eternal redemption, to all who believe.

No more sacrifices, bloody or unbloody; they are worthless; only that of Jesus Christ, "made once." There are not more sacrifices, "but a broken and contrite heart" (Ps. 51:17).

Christ commanded the apostles, and these the bishops, ministers, elders, and deacons, to preach the Gospel, not to do transubstantiations.

"Christ was once immolated to exhaust the sins of many" (Heb. 9:28).

Therefore, readers, trust only in Jesus Christ and in his sacrifice, made on the cross, as the only one who can save you.

II. Mandatory Celibacy

The ignorance in which the people live is the cause of the clergy to live as they wish, because they cannot be married!

Mandatory celibacy, or the priest not being able to be married, is not a divine institution, but only came forth from the papal brain.

I knew very well that the priest was obliged to keep celibacy because of what is said: "to be a purer, holier state; consonant with the priestly office," and also that they took this example of Christ pretending to be like him.

I regret that so many have been forced to imitate him in this sense, but they end up as *Le grenouille qui veut se faire aussi grosse que le boeuf.*

I knew and saw other things, however: I knew and saw how the priests around me guarded their supposed chastity—with impurity, each having his own family; some, hypocritically, hiding it a few leagues away; others, like my vicar, curate, and my Latin *et reliquia* lens, preferred to keep them in their own house!

In view of this, all young men know that the theory is chastity but the practice is concubinage. So that, in view of the practice, it is not much feared to be a priest, since they will console one another: they will do as they do, each one having, soon after being ordained, their family.

The state is beautiful, profitable, respectable, ostentatious. There is no civil law for those who do not want to obey celibacy (appeal to the public), unless the priest is too practical, because then the ordinary or the bishop suspend him from his orders for some time. For this reason, and to satisfy their parents more often than not, many young men decide to be ordained.

In this case I was thinking the same thing: be ordained and do as others do, to satisfy my parents' wishes.

How many young men, still in the seminary, said this to me, and are they doing so?

Ah! ecclesiastical justice!

When I arrived ordained in a city, I went to a colleague's house. Instead of rejoicing to see me like him, he was sad, and said to me: "Ah! my friend, you don't know what state you have chosen. It is the saddest, most miserable way of life in the world. I cannot say anything different because I consider myself as such. I would rather be a black in the mill than to wear a cassock, go up to the altar, dressed in gala, looking like a saint, when I am depraved, by necessity! I do this as a way of life and nothing else!"

Today it reminds me of what Jesus Christ used to say: "And they do all their works to be seen of men; for they bring broad phylacteries, and widen their fringes" . . . "And greetings in the squares, and being called by men—Rabbi, Rabbi" (Matt. 23:5, 7). This is the faithful portrait of the priest, of the entire Romanism: everything contrary to the teaching of Jesus Christ.

Their hypocrisy: "Woe to you, hypocritical scribes and Pharisees; for you are like white tombs, which outwardly really look beautiful, but inwardly they are full of dead bones and all filthiness. So also outwardly you seem righteous to men, but inwardly you are full of hypocrisy and iniquity" (Matt. 23:27, 28).

Since then I was also sad seeing, not without horror, the practice of celibacy for what it was! Soon doubts, fears and thoughts began to depress my spirit. I often sought relief from my sorrows, praying the breviary: but which! This devotion never had the power for anything. Here is the second doubt: is celibacy mandatory? My reasoning answered me: it is not possible. It was necessary to obey the voice of reason, of nature, and what more . . . the voice of God. "Therefore shall a man leave his father, and his mother, and be joined to his wife, and two shall be one flesh" (Gen. 2:24). Jesus Christ confirmed it (Matt. 9:4; Mark 10:7).

Dear reader, believe me: if I had known the goodness of God, and what he told me in the Holy Scriptures (1 Tim. 3:2), I would never have done what I did. No; rather I would look for an evangelical minister, and, informing myself with him, I would have married in accordance with the law of God.

Remorse, affliction, accompanied me everywhere. I was soon suspended; but (excuse me) the priest who brought me the order of suspension had two stolen girls; not in his house, but in the house across the street! I remained four years and a few months in this state, during which I was often urged to rehabilitate myself from the orders by friends, by priests, with advantageous promises. But I could not accept it, for they could not soothe my conscience. So I tried to study religion. An evangelical minister offered me a New Testament in the original Greek to read, and I also went to attend the evangelical service once. After living in a small town for three years, and quite poorly—I had no help from the priests, since they practiced like almost everyone, the same as I, so much so that it is said, "Wherever you see straws, cloths hanging in the window of the house, knock, for it is a canon's house"—I began to compare the book with a Bible in the Roman version. I did not attend the evangelical service anymore, nor the Roman Church. I was, in the case of the apostle's saying: "That you were at that time without Christ, apart from the fellowship of Israel, strangers to the covenant, having no hope of the promise, and without God in this world" (Eph. 2:12).

The majority of the priests have this same feeling!

I was reading the Holy Scriptures, which as the reader may already be aware, is the same divine book called the Bible. And I saw that the Old Testament narrated the marriages of the priests of the Old Law of grace. And I also read that the apostles were married. Here are the places in the Scriptures: "There was in the time of Herod king of Judea a priest named Zechariah of the class of Abijah, and his wife of the family of Aaron, whose name was Elizabeth" (Luke 1:5). We see from the passage mentioned that three priests were married, and we know from the Old Testament that all priests had the right to marry. Who can deny or who doesn't know that the mentioned couple was a saint? Let's see: "And both were righteous before God, walking without reproach in all the commandments and precepts of the Lord" (Luke 1:6). Now we see in the New Testament: "let the bishop be blameless, the husband of one wife . . ." (1 Tim. 3:2); and in verses 4 and 5, we read the following: "That he may know how to govern his own house well; let him have his (legitimate) children in subjection, in all honesty. Because who does not know how to govern his house, how will he take care of the church of God?" (See the difference between "house" of residence, and "church" of God.) V. 12: "Let deacons be the husband of one wife, that they govern their children and their houses well." "For this reason I am going to tell you is that I left you in Crete, that you might regulate what is lacking, and establish elders in the cities, as I sent you. He who is blameless, the husband of one wife, who has faithful children, who cannot be accused of dissolution or disobedience" (Titus 1:5–7).

How can it be interpreted from here that priests should not and cannot be married? But the priests say: the wife of which the apostle speaks is the church. What a falsehood! The apostle says, "For who does not know how to govern his house well, how will he care for God's church?"

Right here there are two houses: the family house and the house of God; there are also two wives: the wife, wife of the bishop, and the wife, church of Christ.

The priests say more, that my marriage is not valid, because it was made in the evangelical church and because it is forbidden by the pontiff.

All right; answer me: in which Church have you priests married? Because I see you all living with women! If I have legitimately married according to the Gospel, leaving the yoke of the pope, and they say that I live in fornication, what right do priests, wives and their children have? This is the illusion and blindness of Babylon the great (Rome), which "has the seven heads, which are the seven mountains on which the woman sits" (Rev. 17:9).

Ah, reader, I have lost faith in the church of Rome; I preferred to be married according to the Gospel of Jesus Christ than to live in fornication according to the Pope's law.

"By faith Moses, when he was old, said that he was not the son of Pharaoh, choosing rather to be afflicted with the people of God, than to enjoy the transient complacency of sin; having the reproach of Christ for greater riches than the treasures of the Egyptians" (Heb. 11:24–26).

But I continued to read the Bible, "Now the spirit clearly says that in the latter times some will fall away from the faith, giving heed to spirits of error, and the doctrine of demons, who will speak a lie in hypocrisy, and who will have cauterized their conscience, they will forbid marriage, and order them to abstai`n from certain foods that God created . . ." (1 Tim. 4:1–3). Reading this passage shook me a lot. I saw clearly in Romanism the reality of this prophecy: the Pope forbidding marriage and also the eating of meat on Good Friday and Saturday, and Lent.

But what more does the word of God say: "Let marriage be treated with honor among all, and the bed undefiled: but fornicators and adulterers God will judge" (Heb. 13:4). Therefore, it is not a sin. And if it is not sin, a minister like any other person can be married and live holy, just, and righteously in the Lord's commandments, as walked the holy prophets and ministers of the Bible, who were married. Therefore, it is not necessary, nor should it—or, to put it better, it cannot—be forced to live celibate, to be holy, just and upright. Clerical celibacy, far from producing holiness, has opened a wide door to immorality, disobedience and prostitution.

What is the known religion that has forced its ministers not to marry, and the people not to eat meat on certain days? Just the Roman religion, the Pope's religion.

I read the following in the word of God: "And when Jesus came to Peter's house, he saw that his mother-in-law was in bed with a fever" (Matt. 8:14). Indeed! Peter, the apostle upon whom the priests wrongly presume, Jesus founded his church, did he have a mother-in-law? Well, if he had a mother-in-law, he was married.

And more: if Jesus did not approve of a married man, or if he did not consider marriage as holy, he would not want to call Peter to the apostleship. But we see the opposite here; after Jesus having called Peter, he went with Peter to the house where his mother-in-law was.

But the priests say: Since Peter became an apostle, he abandoned his wife. This reveals two things: the priests' ignorance of the Holy Scriptures, or their bad faith to deceive the people. Let's look at the proof given by Paul, more than twenty-five years later: "Do we have no right to take along a believing wife, as do also the other apostles, the brothers of the Lord, and Cephas?" (1 Cor. 9:5). You should know that Cephas was the same Peter the apostle, who lived more than twenty-five years married, after becoming an apostle, so much so that Paul mentions him.

Dear reader, in view of this, you can already know that not only can the minister be married, but that he can also live in this state just, holy and righteously.

Nothing is clearer than these statements, in view of which, I was willing to marry and also to abandon forever the iron law that only produces immorality, which had so long held me back in sin!

Not only this: I looked for Jesus Christ, the only refuge of sinners and perfect Savior, all sufficient and eternal, whom I knew only by name, in order to know him with my heart.

I implored God's mercy and his Holy Spirit; I found him, adored him in spirit and in truth. Accept him yourself. Yes, I tell you, dear reader, that at that time, the happiest of my life, I felt the effluvium of God's grace and the work of the Holy Spirit giving me what I didn't yet have—the regeneration of my soul.

Since then I have felt peace, relief and joy in the Lord.

On September 7, 1878, in the city of Recife, after the wedding banns had been concluded, in accordance with the law of this Empire, I was married, at 7:00 pm, by Rev. Smith [John Rockwell Smith, Presbyterian] evangelical minister, in the presence of more than a hundred people, with all attention and calm. I was legitimately married, as were the apostles, bishops and deacons in the New Testament, although without the presence of the Roman priest, because then in the time of the apostles there were none.

Indeed, reader, we do not have a single passage in the Holy Scriptures from which mandatory celibacy can be inferred. Everything has been forged in Rome to form a militia, ready and prepared for combat, not that of the faith, but that of the pope's political-ecclesiastical interests! What disastrous consequences have not been produced by mandatory celibacy! It's no secret: convents have often become the hiding place for the results of such celibacy. Why is it that the iron bars in these convents are stronger than the bars in prisons? Does innocence need such strong restrictions?

The effects of celibacy are so well known that I refrain from listing them; suffice it to say that at balls, theaters, carnivals, sambas, games, brothels and . . . you will see them. How many times have you heard, dear reader, of prostitution produced by priests? And still can you not persuade yourselves that such a class is prejudicial to the morality that our country should have?! Oh, Brazilians, let us no longer sleep in the sleep of indifference, in the face of so much evil caused by a religion that does not bring goodness, morality, the salvation of souls, but yet, and only, the perdition and condemnation of our patricians.

Ah, my dear former colleagues, if you would concentrate for a little while reading the Holy Scriptures, you would be persuaded that your condition before God is terrible. A very respected man told me: "I only live for this world, and I know very well that there in heaven, I will not enter." How many of you are not in this case?!

Trust not in your state, nor in the ceremonies or sacraments imposed upon you; trust in only one Savior—Jesus Christ. See what he says: "Repent and believe in the Gospel" (Mark 1:15).

After having thus studied the Holy Scriptures, I could not possibly follow Romanism.

But someone told me, "Don't be silly, this is a way of life like any other." And I answered: "What good is it for me to acquire all the treasures of this world if I later lose my soul."

Therefore, clerical celibacy was a burden to me, and I could no longer bear it. Since then I became convinced that I should no longer continue to belong to a church that forced me to live, not only against the Holy Scriptures, but also against morality, society and reason.

III. Auricular Confession and Absolution

Confession made in the ear of the priest is a dangerous invention, which has no foundation in the Holy Scriptures. Romanism has invented things that are harmful and have ungodly effects. Auricular confession is the key that often opens the treasure of iniquities; like a seductive serpent in Eden, so does the priest hissing in the ear of the unwary young woman.

How many sad, black and horrible cases did I have to narrate, effects of confession? The penitent, the priest, the secret!

Oh! fathers of families, have care and compassion for your children! Give them the faith and morals of the Gospel, and you will have opened for them an inexhaustible treasure of the ineffable riches of Christ! In the Gospel you will find for yourselves and for them all the remedies capable of curing your infirmities, which are your sins, and it shall be given to you a perfect and complete absolution for them, without the need for the priest's intervention: "Who can forgive sins but only God?" (Mark 2:7).

In a certain city, at least five individuals were murdered because of a confession, or because of a secret revealed in the confessional. A rich man, knowing that his daughter had been betrayed some time ago, yet not knowing by whom, in order that he might come to that knowledge, called the vicar and declared his intention to him, and asked him to confess his daughter and . . . more . . . to demand of her to tell him the author of the tragedy of the occurred fact. After the act, the priest revealed everything to the rich man. He, incontinent, had the young accomplice killed, but finding himself surrounded by some friends, the accomplice resisted. A fight broke out dropping five people dead at last! How horrible is that! It is the consequence of a false institution! I say one thing: that there is no better opportunity for the priest to do whatever he wants than during the time when he is in confession. A vicar in a city was hearing the confession of a girl when she suddenly got up, shouting: "This priest is seducing me, asking me where my house is, if it has a yard and a gate!" I can't share more stories: how many prostitutions, daughters of such confession! Such facts greatly shook my spirit to no longer give credit to Romanism. I had already read that this institution had been made in the century of the famous and tenebrous Inquisition; how impious and damned, how fierce monsters that swallow up the living flesh, so such priests did to those who did not want to worship their crucifixes. In order to know the secrets of the cities, they invented this confession. The desire for gold, power, greed, and more . . . concupiscence, intoxicated the brains of those friars!

A married woman often reveals secrets to the priest that she would not tell her husband. In this way, she establishes the priest as most well informed and thus superior in the family, destroying the art of marital love and the trust that must exist between husband and wife. And what is more . . . it plants dissension in the household, as did the Jesuits in Pernambuco (1873) with several important families in Recife, so that married ladies were already preferring to obey and submit themselves more to the Jesuits than to their own husbands. "Women are subject to their husbands as to the Lord" and not to priests (Eph. 5:22).

The people of Pernambuco have placed themselves at the height they should. They asked for the permanent expulsion of the Jesuits from that province, which was granted by order of the current president. Honor to a people who know how to guard their pride. The strongest link in corruption in Brazil is Romanism.

I appeal to wise men to tell me whether it is accurate or not? The river in its current carries rot and offal. So Romanism, in the course it has taken, takes honors and infanticide. Evangelical Christians pray and confess daily to God, having only as their only perfect Mediator, Intercessor and Advocate, Jesus Christ, "whose blood cleanses from all sin" ([1] John 1:7).

"And so each one of us will give to God an account of himself" (Rom. 14:12). "Who can forgive sins but only God?" (Mark 2:7). "Here is the Lamb of God, here is he who takes away the sin of the world" (John 1:29). This is the true absolution—Christ.

The priest is a sinner like other men. Certain of this, how can he forgive, if he also needs forgiveness?

They say that they have power because they are the successors of the apostles. Ah! Ungrateful! Successors have the same right as the predecessor, and if the apostles were like the priests . . . oh! Blasphemy! Read the scriptures and see if there is the smallest comparison between the apostles and the priests. Priests have been successors of others (John 8:44); this yes, but of the apostles, no.

The apostles, dear readers, had no successors in this respect of working miracles, speaking different languages, and drinking any poison without harming them; no, because no priest can do that. I just wanted some priest to want to give me his proof of succession—by performing some miracle, or drinking poison, or getting bitten by some snake. Anyone! Everything is guesswork. Everything ceased with John the evangelist, or with the introduction of the Gospel (Mark 16:17, 18). These were the distinguishing signs of the apostles. The Bible, dear reader, is only false for priests. And it cannot only be the rule of faith and doctrine, when it fights and condemns the errors and scandals of Romanism.

"And so every priest presents himself each day to exercise his ministry, and to offer many times the same wafer (sacrifices), which can never take away sins. But this one (Christ), having offered only one wafer (sacrifice of his body) for sins, is forever seated at the right hand of God" (Heb. 10:11–12). The true ministers of God, who are only ministers of the Gospel, are the legitimate successors of the apostles: as to preaching the Gospel, administering the two ordinances (Baptism and the Lord's Supper), and practicing the same duties. They don't do miracles or confess, because there is no commandment to do this.

To submit to men is to trust in the matter. To reject God is to despise heaven. God wants to save, men want to lose. Human pride has come to the point of forgetting the power of God, if they make themselves God: "who opposes and exalts himself above all that is called God or that is worshiped, so that he sits as God in the temple of God, showing himself that he is God" (2 Thess. 2:4).

"For I bear them witness that they have a zeal for God, but not according to knowledge. For they being ignorant of God's righteousness, and seeking to establish their own righteousness, have not submitted to the righteousness of God. For Christ is the end of the law for righteousness to everyone who believes" (Rom. 10:2–4).

God does not refuse anyone who comes to him, asking for forgiveness, since we are all sinners.

"If we say that we have no sin, we ourselves are deceived, and there is no truth in us. However, if we confess our sins, He is faithful and just to forgive us our sins and to cleanse us from all iniquity" (1 John 1:8, 9). "There is just one Legislator, a Judge, who can condemn and who can save" (James 4:12).

The Babylon of the Apocalypse (Rome), the throne of the popes, fell to the ground before the Word of God!

"Bless the Lord, oh my soul, and do not forget all of his benefits. It is he who forgives all your iniquities, and heals all your infirmities" (Ps. 103:2, 3).

James says the following: "Confess *your* sins one for another" (James 5:16).

However, how should it be done? Men are evil by their own nature: There is, therefore, public, private, and secret confession, according to the word of God, and these are what evangelical Christians practice.

John Baptist and the apostles received many people to be baptized, people who confess, "repenting of their sins." They did not confess in the ear of the priest at the confessional!

Romanism is so cunning, like the devil in the serpent in paradise, which disguises, deceives, and seduces, saying: "My ministers have the power to absolve or forgive" the sins of anyone who comes "to their ears"!!! And they say they rely on the Holy Scriptures. The apostle says, "Confess to one another." If I offend John, I won't ask Samuel or Manuel for forgiveness. In this case I must confess to whom I offend.

The devil also mentioned the scriptures when he tempted Christ (Matt. 4:6). Why don't priests also confess to the people, as James commands? If anyone has done anything against the priest, then he must ask his forgiveness; and likewise, he must ask our forgiveness if he offends us! And how many have not offended us!!! When, however, we offend God, only God should we ask for forgiveness, because we have not offended the priest. It is a wonder that a people like this still delude themselves with such men! But why does this happen? Because it is a people without a Bible.

When the Gospel is freely preached, then the Brazilian people will be able to count on God's blessings, and a new hope of true religion will dawn, which will rescue these people from the power of prostitute Rome, mother of condemnations—"with whom the kings of the earth fornicated, and who has made the population of the land drunk with the wine of their prostitution" (Rev. 17:9). "And the woman you saw is the great city (Rome), which reigns over the kings of the earth" (Rev. 17:16).

"Woe, woe to that great city, in which all who had a ship at sea got rich, from her prisoners: which in one hour was desolated" (Rev. 18:19).

What city has seven hills? Rome. And Rome only. So it's clear that Rome is close to damnation.

Finally, I say to you: run away from those, and hear the voice of the Holy Spirit: "And what consent does the temple of God have with idols? For you are the temple of the living God as God said: In them I will dwell, and I will walk among them; and I will be their God, and they will be my people. Come out from among them, and depart, says the Lord; and touch nothing unclean, and I will receive you; and I will be a Father to you, and you will be sons and daughters to me, says the Lord Almighty" (2 Cor. 6:16–18).

And the angel's voice: "Come out of her, my people, that you may not be participants of her sins, so that you may not fall in her plagues" (Rev. 18:4).

I reflected on my state, my condition, not in front of any authority above myself, but before God. I solved the difficult problem for many, yet easy for me, according to the word of God: to leave the church of Rome was my duty, and to embrace the eternal holy Gospel of the Son of God, Jesus Christ, that I might find in it peace and tranquility of mind in this world, and eternal salvation in the next, the only happiness to which man should aspire.

Vanished completely, entirely and perpetually, the darkness of error, ignorance, superstition, idolatry and sins that existed in me from my childhood, with all the circumstances, prejudices, family, politics and well-being.

I wanted nothing more than to hear the gentle, infallible, comforting voice of the Son of God—"Come unto me, all you that labor and are heavy laden, and I will give you rest. Take my yoke upon you, and learn from me, for I am gentle and humble in heart, and you will find rest for your souls. For my yoke is easy and my burden is light" (Matt. 11:28–30).

Happy day! When I was able to say: my soul rests in Jesus, and he in me. Oh! dear reader, I do not have expressions that are clear enough to signify the joy that my soul has found itself possessed by since the moment I accepted my Savior, Jesus Christ: when I opened the doors of my heart for him to come in, and for the Holy Spirit to do the great work of regeneration of my soul.

Like Nicodemus, I was looking for and really desiring the salvation of my soul: but how? Men, priests, the church of Rome, everything incapable of it; sinners like me could not give me what I longed for the most—the salvation of my soul—for they also needed it.

But I didn't stay like Nicodemus—scared, afraid of the world, like many today, who fully know that the only religion that shows us the only way of salvation is the Gospel of Jesus Christ, and yet they hide in fear of losing friends, jobs and political conveniences. No, I did not tremble; without further delay I fell at the Saviour's feet: "Oh God, have mercy on me, a sinner."

"In my despondency I knew the Lord." I heard that voice: "Verily, verily I say unto you, whoever is not born of water and the Spirit cannot enter the kingdom of God" (John 3:5).

This is the new birth, not of the flesh, but of the Spirit—a new nature—that it takes to save our souls, filled with sin by our old nature, inherited from our parents.

From the happy moment I left the burden, not only of Rome, but of sin, having cast myself upon the mercy of God, that "my spirit rejoiced in God my Saviour." My soul felt peace and joy, and shadows and darkness vanished forever.

From the exposition above, it is clearly seen that auricular confession does not satisfy the spirit; it does not benefit man. It is entirely unable to save or forgive the sinner. It only enables you to commit more and more sins.

"I am the way, the truth and the life: no one comes to the Father except through me" (John 14:6). "For there is only one Mediator between God and men, and that is Jesus Christ the man" (1 Tim. 2:5).

Conclusion

The three reasons that are explained here were those that made me leave the church of Rome; but, soon after reading the Holy Scriptures, I was assured of many others, so I should not continue to belong to the church of Rome, as I do not intend, and I never will.

For now, I am content to publicize just these three, hoping that they will serve as a useful example to the people and to my former colleagues, to whom I recommend the meditation on these truths, comparing them with the Holy Scriptures, the only standard by which we are to justify our faith in this life.

I close this booklet by declaring that I am very happy and fully satisfied not only to have left Romanism, but to have embraced the one true religion of Jesus Christ, as contained in the Gospel, which I profess, preach and will preach until that day that God "unties me from this flesh to go to dwell with my Lord Jesus forever."

Jesus said, "Search the Scriptures, for in them you will have eternal life, and they are the ones which testify of me" (John 5:39).

The priests tell us that the people cannot understand the Bible, but everyone who has read it understands it very well. You have already seen the counsel of Jesus, now also read what is said about the Christians of Berea: "Now these were nobler than those in Thessalonica, for they gladly received the word, examining each day in the Scriptures whether these things were so" (Acts 17:11).

Here I end waiting for God to bless you and lead you to the path of truth, enlightening you with the Holy Spirit.

Appendix 2

The Testimony of Antônia Teixeira:
A Synopsis

This synopsis is based on two accounts given by Antônia Teixeira about her assaults by Steen Morris. The middle column is taken from an interview with a journalist published in the *Waco Morning News* on June 16, 1895. The testimonies in the first and third columns are based on Antônia's court testimony given on July 24, 1895. The first column (on the left) is a transcription of the court stenographer's report that is housed in the McLennan County Archives for district 54. The third column (on the right) was published by the *Fort Worth Gazette* in the July 25, 1895, issue. Both accounts derive from the same testimony, though they vary at times both in wording and content. The analysis in the present volume depends heavily on the court stenographer's report as it is most likely a more accurate rendering of Antônia's testimony and the testimony itself is likely to be more reliable because Antônia is under oath, while the interview seems, at points, to be heavily filtered through the language and idiom of the reporter.

Antônia's Court Testimony Transcribed July 24, 1895	*Waco Morning News* June 16, 1895 Interview with Antônia Teixeira	*Fort Worth Gazette* July 25, 1895 Reported Testimony of Antônia Teixeira
	"In January, 1892, I landed in New York in company with Rev. Z. C. Taylor and family and went from thence to Philadelphia, where Mrs. Taylor was the subject of a surgical operation. I accompanied Mr. Taylor and the children to Belton, Texas, to the	

Antônia's Court Testimony	*Waco Morning News*	*Fort Worth Gazette*

Waco Morning News column:

home of Mrs. Taylor's parents.

"From Belton I came to Waco in July, 1892, and entered Baylor University, taking up my abode with the president and his wife. Mr. Taylor had promised me five years of schooling, etc., to fit me for missionary service on my return home.

Antônia's Court Testimony column:

My name is Antônia Teixeira. I am fifteen years old. I will be sixteen September 1895. I know the defendant H. S. Morris. I first met him at Mrs. Burleson's three years ago. I lived there at that time. He also lived there at that time and until about a year ago, I lived there. I helped work in the house and went to school at Baylor University. The first year I went six months all day and after that I just worked in the morning for the rest of the year. The next year I work half of the session in the morning and the balance for the rest of the year. The next year I work half of the session in the morning and the balance of the year I worked around the house. Last year I lived at the place and went to school when I had spare time. Mr. Morris did not live at Mrs. Burleson's but lived at his brother's just across the street.

Waco Morning News column:

"My father was at one time a Catholic priest, but was converted by a Baptist missionary and became a minister of that church before his death, which occurred eight years ago, my mother and five children surviving him.

"Stein Morris took his meals at the Burleson residence during the greater portion of my stay there, rooming in another house in the same yard.

Fort Worth Gazette column:

"My name is Antônia Teixeira. I am 15 years old; I will be 15 the 7th of September next. I know the defendant H. S. Morris. I first saw him at Mrs. Burleson's three years ago. I lived at Mrs. Burleson's. He also lived at Mrs. Burleson's. He quit living there almost one year ago. I was helping Mrs. Burleson doing the housework and going to school at Baylor University; I went to school six months all day the first year, and after that I went only in the afternoon and worked at the house the balance of the time; last year I lived with Mrs. Burleson and went to school when I could; last year Mr. Morris lived with his brother, S. L. Morris, a short distance away: he did not come over there very often.

Waco Morning News column (bottom):

"He always treated me with great freedom, taking certain liberties when we were alone, but ignored me when others were present. He, Morris, often entreated me to come to his room, and asked me to meet him at the

The Testimony of Antônia Teixeira: A Synopsis

Antônia's Court Testimony

I saw Mr. Morris in November of last year. It was about 9 o'clock p.m. I was in the kitchen at Mrs. Burleson's washing the dishes. No one was at the house except Grandma Jenkins who is 85 years old and she was in the front room of the house. There are three rooms between the front room and the kitchen where I was. At about 9 o'clock the defendant came to the kitchen door which was shut. I heard someone walking around outside and opened the door to see who it was and saw it was the defendant. He was about six feet from the door and asked me to come out then which I refused to do. He then took me by the arm and pulled me out there. He then threw me down on the ground and got on top of me. He said when he dragged me out there he was not going to hurt me.

Waco Morning News

barn, but I did not like him and was always afraid of him, hence did not go.

"The occasion of his first assault upon my person was in the early days of November, 1894, between 8:00 and 9:00 o'clock at night. He came to the kitchen door and asked me if I did not want something good to drink. He then opened the door, took me by the arm and forcibly drew me out into the yard. He had some whitish looking liquor in a bottle which he offered to me to drink. I said I did not want it, but was induced by him to drink it. I do not know what it was, the liquor tasted sweet.

"Whatever it was, the liquor affected me so that I became dizzy. He then threw me to the ground and took liberties with my person. I was held so closely by him that I could not utter a cry. On this occasion he let me go after a few moments, without fully accomplishing his purpose.

Fort Worth Gazette

"I saw Morris in November of last year. It was at 9 o'clock in the night, about the first of the month; I was in the kitchen at Mrs. Burleson's washing dishes; there was nobody by; Grandma Jenkins was at home at the time; she is 85 years old; she was in the front room of the house: there are three rooms between the front room and the kitchen where I was; he came to the kitchen door where I was; he came to the kitchen door in the back yard; the door was shut; I heard somebody walking around; opened the door to see who it was. It was Steen Morris; he called me out to him but I didn't go. He was about six or eight feet away; he then took me by the arm and pulled me out into the back yard; he forced me down on the ground; he said he was not going to hurt me."

After one or two further statements the witness said she could not explain further and a leading question brought an objection from the defense. The justice told her to proceed and explain the best she could.

Here the witness proceeded to tell in detail the manner and circumstances of the assault upon her and the physical injury it

He just got on top of me[,] pulled my clothes up and stayed on me about 10 minutes and when he quit I was all bleeding

Appendix 2

Antônia's Court Testimony

in my privates. He entered my private organ with his male member. He penetrated me.

He hurt me but did not hurt me very bad. It made me bleed, not a great deal. I had on a pair of drawers open at the side; he tore those open.

I tried to get away from him but I couldn't because he was holding me so tight. I tried to holler, but could not because he was holding me so tight. I could holler a little but not loud which I did. He kept telling me not to holler that he was not going to hurt me.

I went in the house and did not say anything that night. There was no one there but Mrs. Jenkins. She was in bed and I think she was asleep.

The next morning I told Mrs. Burleson I did not consent but resisted.

About 2 weeks after that I saw Mr. Morris at the same place at about the same time at about the same hour of the night. I was washing dishes and no one was at home but Mrs. Jenkins. The door was shut and the defendant pushed it open and caught me by the arm and pulled me out and started to throw me down.

Waco Morning News

"At the time of this assault I was alone in the house with Grandma Jenkins, who is 83 years old [Georgia's mother]. I was not very badly injured by Morris on this occasion and was able to attend school the next day.

"The morning following the first assault I spoke to Mrs. Burleson and told her that Mr. Morris had been bothering me, but did not tell her what he had done. Mrs. Burleson repeated my statement to Mrs. S. L. Morris, Stein's sister-in-law, who spoke to Stein Morris about it and he denied having seen me at all on the occasion.

"It was some weeks later, November 20, I think, he accosted me the second time at about the same hour of the evening. I shut the door on him but he pushed it open[,] took hold of me and dragged me out as before. After getting me out in the yard he repeated his treatment of me, as on the former occasion.

Fort Worth Gazette

inflicted upon her. Continuing, she said:

"I could not cry out because he held me so tight; I did holler, but I could not cry out loud. He told me not to cry out, and said he would not hurt me. I tried to get away from him, when he threw me down, but I could not.

"When he got through he went home, and I went into the house.

"I did not say anything to anyone that night, because there was no one there; Mrs. Jenkins was on the bed and I supposed she was asleep;

"the next morning I talked to Mrs. Burleson about it. I did not give my consent to Mr. Morris;

"it was at the same place and about the same time, I was again washing dishes; no one was at the house but Mrs. Jenkins; I had the door closed but it was pushed open and Mr. Morris pulled me out the door and threw me down,

The Testimony of Antônia Teixeira: A Synopsis

Antônia's Court Testimony

At that time he turned me aloose and ran. I did not hear anyone in the front hall. When I went in the house, I did not see any one. I did not know anything about anything of that kind and did not know that people did things of that sort.

I next saw the defendant about the first of December 1894 which was about 2 weeks after he had run away. I saw him at the same place and about the same hour. I was again washing dishes. I did not see him at all until he opened the door and pulled me out. He threw me down on the ground [and] pulled up my clothes. [He] got on top of me and that hurt me. He kept me down about 10 minutes. He penetrated me and it hurt my private organ. It lacerated me and made me bleed more than it did the first time. I could not hardly walk and couldn't go to school the next day.

No one was at home but Grandma Jenkins.

I complained next morning to Mrs. Burleson. I did not know what it was called or really was. I did not see him any more. There was a great deal of soreness and laceration produced from each time and I did not recover from it until about a month ago. I first had my monthly sickness about several months before the first assault. The first time he came he gave me something in a little

Waco Morning News

"But this time he was frightened away by a noise as of someone approaching.

"I again spoke to Mrs. Burleson that he kept after me and she again spoke to Mrs. Morris, but nothing was done.

"The last of November Stein Morris made his third and last assault upon me in practically the same manner and at the same hour as before.

"This time he accomplished his purpose. The next day I was unable to attend school, owing to my injuries, he having lacerated me badly.

"I said nothing of this last assault to anyone, as before my statements were denied by Morris and disbelieved by others.

Fort Worth Gazette

"but just then he heard some one walking in the house and he left me and ran away; I did not hear anyone in the front hall, but I think he did; I did not think anyone was there, as I did not [see] any one later. The first time he came to me I did not know what he was doing or trying to do.

"After he ran away the next time I saw him was about the first of December. It was at the same place. I was washing dishes; I did not see him at all until he opened the door and pulled me out of the house; he threw me down on the ground."

Here the witness described the assault in detail:

"I could hardly walk after he left me; I could not go to school the next day;

"no one was at home but Mrs. Jenkins at this time.

"I told Mrs. Burleson about it the next morning. I did not know what it meant, by his actions. I did not see Mr. Morris any more at that place; the laceration or soreness produced lasted all the time. The first time Mr. Morris came to me he gave me something to drink out of a small glass; he was standing at the door at the time he gave me the drink, and he was on the outside; I do

Antônia's Court Testimony

glass and told me to drink it, that it was good. This was before he had dragged me out. I was on the inside and he on the outside. He got the glass and bottle out of his pocket. It was a little flat vial. It was white fluid. The only effect I noticed was it made me dizzy. It made me sleepy. I went to bed and was still dizzy when I went to sleep. I don't know exactly how it tasted. It did not taste like anything I have ever tasted before. All that I have shared occurred in this county and state.

In April of this year, the defendant and his brother S.L. Morris and Dr. Burleson were present. The defendant was on the front porch.

At first, Dr. Burleson asked me if I would swear it before the defendant. I said yes and he went after him. And his brother said he was on the front porch already. The defendant came right in with Dr. Burleson and Dr. Burleson asked me would I say before the defendant what he had done to me.

Waco Morning News

"On or about December 1st Mr. Morris went to Louisiana, and three weeks later returned with a bride. I was glad that he was married and said so, because I thought I would escape further ill usage at his hands.

"Knowledge of my condition was first gained in the Burleson household some months after I, myself, had discovered that I was enceinte [pregnant]. It was at first suspected from certain evidence and a physician called in who confirmed the fact.

"The above confirmation came four and one-half months after pregnancy. I was then removed to the home of Mrs. O. W. Jenkins, whose husband is a nephew of Mrs. Dr. Burleson.

Fort Worth Gazette

not know where he got the stuff he gave me to drink; it was in a small flat bottle; it was a white fluid, it made me dizzy; it made me sleepy; I went straight to bed and do not know how long the dizziness lasted; the stuff in the bottle tasted like water, or did not have any taste at all. All this occurred in McLennan County, and the State of Texas.

"I had a conversation with Dr. Burleson and S. L. Morris. This conversation occurred in the house; the defendant was on the front gallery and Dr. Burleson brought him in.

"I was asked if I would swear the child was Steen's and I said I would. I told Steen Morris he was the cause of it; he looked pale and did not say anything. Mr. S. L. Morris kept asking me questions. He asked me how Steen came and when he came to the house."

An exception was here taken

The Testimony of Antônia Teixeira: A Synopsis

Antônia's Court Testimony

I then accused him to his face of it. He looked pale and excited and trembled. He just looked at me. He said he didn't do it. The defendant's brother kept asking me questions and told him all about it.

When the defendant denied it there in my presence, I said to him, "You did it. You know you did it, and if you didn't what are you so pale and trembling for."

Dr. Burleson had asked the defendant if he wanted to ask me any questions. He said yes and asked me what kind of drug that was he had given me. I told him he had it and gave it to me and he ought to know himself. The defendant then said he wasn't there at all and I then asked him why he was so pale and trembling if he was innocent.

I did not say so very much because everything I would say S. L. Morris would call me a liar and tell Dr. Burleson that I was lying and that his brother had never told a lie.

Mr. S. L. Morris asked me in that conversation if it wasn't a little Negro boy around the house that did it and asked me if I didn't know it was. I said no. He then asked me if it wasn't a school boy named Ola Leesburg. It was then known that I was pregnant. Dr. O. I. Halbert had examined me about a week before.

The last time I had monthly sickness was Nov. 12th, which was about one week after the first time he assaulted me.

Waco Morning News

Fort Worth Gazette

to a question as to what the witness said to Steen Morris in the presence of Dr. Burleson and S. L. Morris.

The question was, "Did you say to Steen Morris, 'you did it, you know you did it. If you did not, why do you tremble so?'"

The justice told the witness to state what she said to the defendant. The answer was, "I did accuse Steen of assaulting me; he denied it, and

"S. L. Morris every time I spoke said it was a lie, and said to Dr. Burleson that I have told several lies already."

Continuing the witness said:

"S. L. Morris asked me if it was not a little colored boy that ran about the house who assaulted me. I told him no it was not. I gave a school boy my ring to wear, but did not mean any harm by it. It was known at this time that I was pregnant. Dr. Halbert had examined me almost one week previous.

"My home is in Bahia, Brazil. I have been in this country three years. I gave birth to a girl baby on June 18. It is a white baby.

Appendix 2

Antônia's Court Testimony

My home is Bahia, Brazil. I have been in Texas about three years. I gave birth to a girl June the 18th. It is white.

The laceration and wounds caused from the assaults continued until about the time I was confined.

Defendant Steen Morris is the father of my child.

Cross examination

I was born in 1880 Sept 7th and came to Texas in 1892 with Mr. Taylor and have been in Waco ever since at Mrs. Burleson's and went to school at Baylor University. When I first went there Mr. S. L. Morris and his wife and Steen Morris and Mrs. Jenkins and Mrs. Burleson and Dr. Burleson and their son and his wife, all were living there in his house. About two years after I came Steen Morris left there but up to that time he lived there as one of the family and I saw him frequently. It think he had been away about six months from the time he left there until he came back and called me out as detailed. I had seen him but had not talked with him from the time he left until he called me out the first time. I used to go over to Mrs.

Waco Morning News

Fort Worth Gazette

"The laceration or soreness continued up to the time I was confined."

Court then adjourned until 2 o'clock this afternoon.

Court was called to order after 2 o'clock, with Antônia Teixeira still on the stand. The state continued its testimony, which was as follows:

"Steen Morris is the father of the child that was born to me in June."

The witness was then turned over to the defense and the cross examination was conducted by T. A. Blair, Esq. The testimony was substantially the same as the direct evidence.

Antônia's Court Testimony	*Waco Morning News*	*Fort Worth Gazette*

Morris' and would see him but never talked to him. From the time he left up to the time of this first assault he never spoke to me and I never to him. During the two years he lived there he never said anything to me where any one was but always did when there was no one present. He never said anything to me but called me to go out with him. He was always calling me to go out with him. I had been I think about six months when he wanted me to go out with him. He called me to come to him late in the evening. He would call me and tell me to come out there and did so every time he had a chance to. During the time he was living at the same place with me he never took hold of me. He called me out that way about a month or two before he left. About six months after he came and dragged me out as I have detailed I think that it was about the 6th of November 1894, he made the first assault. Mrs. Jenkins is very old being 85 years old. When he came the first time it was dark. He never came inside: He was about six feet from the house when he called me and I was in the kitchen with a lamp light. When he first came I was in the room by the table washing dishes and never stopped when he called to me, but he stood at the foot of the steps on the ground, there being two, and reached up to me and caught me

| **Antônia's Court Testimony** | *Waco Morning News* | *Fort Worth Gazette* |

by the arm, I can't say which one, and pulled me out. When he caught hold of me I had not changed my position at all. He standing at the foot of the steps, I was facing the table and my side to the door. I didn't turn to see him when he called me and there had been no trouble up to that time and he had not hurt my feelings up to that time. He told me to come there and I didn't answer. He called me only once or twice. I didn't love anything about the defendant. He never said what he wanted and I didn't know. I know his voice and I could see his face. I fell to the ground when he pulled me out and then he got on top of me and had illicit intercourse with me. I was there about ten minutes and when I got up I went into the house. I was bloody but can't say just how much. I saw the blood on my clothes. It hurt me and as soon as I got in the house I examined myself and found blood on my clothes. I don't know what became of the defendant. I had said nothing to him. I wore a light dress of wool. I said he tore my drawers. I remained in the kitchen only a little while before going to bed. I don't know where the Burlesons were, but know they were not in the house. It was the first time he came that he gave me the drug and before he pulled me out that he gave me the drug. . . . He gave me the drug

Antônia's Court Testimony	Waco Morning News	Fort Worth Gazette

pulled me and told me that there was something to drink from a glass he took out from his pocket. I think when he was holding me. He had hold of me with one hand and the glass in the other. I told him I didn't want it and he said it was good and to drink it. And I did so and it made me dizzy by the time I got back in the house and not before. The pain didn't keep me awake. I said in direct examination that he never hurt me as much the first time as the last. The next morning I told Mrs. Burleson that Steen Morris was bothering me. I didn't tell her that he threw me down and had connection with me—she never asked and I didn't know how to tell her. When I told her about it she said she was going to ask him about it. That is all that I did tell her.

It was before breakfast out in the kitchen that I told her about it. I don't know what kind of liquid it was I took, but as well as I could see it was white. I didn't see him during this interval that I have told of about the assaults. Only Mrs. Jenkins was there. I don't know how he came to know there was no one else there. He came to the same place and at about the same hour the second time as the first. I told him that I didn't want to go out with him and was standing in about the same positions and I was washing the dishes as before.

"I have been here since April and have only left the premises once, that being to appear in court today.

"Yes, I was kindly treated by Mrs. Burleson and all the family, but, of course, I assisted in the household work.

"No, I did not prefer any charge against Stein Morris until brought into court on a subpoena from the Justice. There I made the same statement that I am

Appendix 2

Antônia's Court Testimony

I tried to holler but couldn't. He had me around the waist. I hollered as loud as I could but I couldn't very loud. He pulled me out but didn't get me on the ground, when I suppose he heard someone coming and left. I tried to get away from him but could not until he turned me loose. I told Mrs. Burleson the second time he came in the same way that I told of the first. It was I think about two weeks later. The last time was about the same time of night at about the first of December. I was engaged the same way in the same place and occupied the same position as before. He told me to come out as he had the previous times and took hold of my arm and pulled me out. I don't remember anything about which arm it caught me by but think the same one each time and when he got me out there he did the same thing he had done on the first time and when I tried to holler, I couldn't very loud as he had hold of me. I hollered as soon as he caught me and while he was pulling me down the steps. The nearest neighbors are across the street. He hurt me a great deal this last time and I bled a great deal. Mrs. Powers was living there in the yard and was the nearest person, but she was not living there then as she was off with her niece.

Mrs. Powers was living there on the 6th of November. I don't know whether she was at home

Waco Morning News

making now and the same I made to you a week or ten days ago, when you first interviewed me for the News, only you did not ask me and I did not tell you how my ruin was accomplished.

"I have been kindly treated, indeed by Mrs. Jenkins, who has done all that a mother could have done for me, and I shall remain with her as long as I am permitted, because I shall never feel as though I could face my own mother again, after this."

Fort Worth Gazette

The Testimony of Antônia Teixeira: A Synopsis

Antônia's Court Testimony	*Waco Morning News*	*Fort Worth Gazette*

or not but do know that she had been gone about a week when the last assault was made. Mr. Powers lived as far as across the house from where we were but I don't know if there was anybody at home or not.

I remember the time Dr. Halbert examined me and I told Mrs. Burleson that I didn't know what was the matter with me. She did not charge me with being pregnant and I told her that nobody but Steen Morris had ever touched me and I would swear to it. I told her before that Steen Morris was bothering me. I never did tell her that Steen Morris had had connection with me. I never told that to anybody.

I did not tell Mrs. Burleson that I would put my hand on a Bible and swear that no one had ever had connection with me. I did tell her that no one but Steen Morris had ever had connection with me.

I know Mrs. Sam Johnson. I did not tell her that a man whom I didn't know had on two occasions come to the house where I was working and tried to get me out of the house. I never told anyone before Dr. Halbert examined me that I was in a family way and didn't know it. I didn't tell anyone that Steen Morris had had connection with me, except I stated to Mrs. Burleson that he had been bothering me. I used to know a boy by the name of Ora Leesburg there at school this last

Antônia's Court Testimony	*Waco Morning News*	*Fort Worth Gazette*

session and also knew a negro boy who worked there named John.

Re Direct Examination

At that time all this come up I did not know what the term illicit intercourse or connection meant. I did not know what was to be pregnant or what pregnancy was until the doctor informed me.

[signed] *Antônia Teixeira*

Appendix 3

Medical Reviews

Drs. Ann Sims and Craig Keathley reviewed the testimony in the trial of Steen Morris and submitted their reports independently. While the conclusions they reached regarding the sexual assault of Antônia Teixeira are similar, they did not collaborate with each other on their reports.

1. Comments by Ann Sims, MD

As a retired obstetrician/gynecologist who spent the last twenty years in practice as medical advisor and child sexual abuse examiner for a nonprofit that offers services to survivors of child sexual abuse and adult sexual assault, I found the testimony of Antônia and the doctors who were involved in her care fascinating. Having performed more than one thousand medical histories and physicals on these children, and having testified in court more than eighty times about these exams, I was surprised to discover that the medical history given by Antônia reflected the same childlike detail and simple perception of the events that I heard when talking with the children I examined in recent years. Her straightforward responses to questions about events that she had

Dr. Ann Sims is a retired obstetrics and gynecology physician. She holds degrees from East Texas Baptist University (BS) and University of Texas Medical School at Galveston, TX (MD). From 1987 to 2019, Dr. Sims served as medical advisor to the Waco/McLennan County Advocacy Center for Crime Victims and Children. In that role, she conducted more than one thousand medical forensic exams on children for possible sexual abuse and testified in court on more than eighty cases of child sexual abuse.

no experience by which to understand was something I had heard many times. As with the children I had examined who were required to testify in court and were prepared for this by the prosecuting attorneys, Antônia's vocabulary and description of the events became more precise in the court testimony as opposed to the testimony she initially gave to the newspaper (e.g., "took liberties with my person" in the newspaper testimony, "entered my private organ with his male member" in the court testimony). But the childlike detail and consistency remained the same without any attempt to add information that she wasn't sure about (e.g., she said she didn't know which arm he grabbed, and she was not sure how much she bled). These are very important things to notice when attempting to get medical information from a child without asking leading questions and attempting to assure as much as possible that the child is being truthful and has not been coached ahead of time. Antônia's maturity in responding calmly and precisely to questions that were accusatory was really quite admirable (e.g., "You did it. You know you did it, and if you didn't what are you so pale and trembling for?"). Antônia's description of the events was consistent with either sexual assault or abuse, depending on her actual age and the standards of the time. She repeatedly testified that her assailant forced her outside and held her down so tightly that she couldn't scream. She testified in court that she didn't want this and that she didn't love him, both answers to questions commonly asked by defense teams in court. Although laceration and bleeding do not always occur in sexual assault/sexual abuse cases, her description of these was consistent with possible injuries sustained from these events. "Drugging" a child or adult prior to sexual assault/abuse, as happened in the first encounter, is common today and used by perpetrators of both children and adults. Antônia's description of the degree of injury ("he did not hurt me bad" after the first assault and "made me bleed more than the first time" and "I could hardly walk" after the third assault) again add to the detail that makes Antônia's testimony so credible. The descriptions of the physical findings given in testimony by the two physicians who examined Antônia were a bit puzzling. The medical field of child sexual abuse was not established until after the 1970s. Since then there have been numerous studies conducted and information reviewed, and our understanding of the physical exam characteristics, descriptions, and findings associated with sexual abuse/ sexual assault, as well as the normal anatomy, have advanced significantly. In examining survivors of sexual abuse/sexual assault today, colposcopy is gener-

ally used, which magnifies the field being examined, making physical description of normal anatomy as well as injury much more precise. These physicians'
lack of basic anatomical knowledge and their descriptions about the findings
in Antônia's case need some clarification. Dr. Halbert testified that in his exam
of Antônia in April 1895, he found no abrasions or tears and no soreness. He
went on to say that the hymen was "not there," that the "parts had been used
more than once. . . . the parts had been used a great deal," and "the parts were
relaxed . . . from use in sexual intercourse." On cross examination, Dr. Halbert
admitted that he had not looked at Antônia's genital area ("no ocular") so
that his findings "might be fallacious." It would have been impossible for him
to rule out abrasions or tears without visualizing the genital area. The hymen
of a postmenarchal female is a narrow collar of tissue recessed ½–1 cm inside
the vagina, and except in cases where there is a congenital abnormality, there
is always an opening in the hymen. Visual exam is the only accurate way to
evaluate the hymen, and without magnification it can be difficult to see. The
hormones of pregnancy make the genital organs relaxed, especially the vagina,
so the relaxation described by Dr. Halbert could reflect the hormonal state of
Antônia's being pregnant, not necessarily her sexual activity. The exam done
in the latter part of May 1895 by Dr. Young was more decipherable. Dr. Young
testified that he found an "ulceration in the lower part of the vulva. It was an
old ulcer due to laceration." He said it was "a tear of the lower portion or back
portion of the vulva," and that "it might have been produced by the insertion
of the male member of a man." He went on to say that he couldn't say how
long it had been there, but that it could have been there for some time, "several
months." "It was the result of laceration." He said, possibly in response to the
testimony from Dr. Halbert, that he would not have noticed the laceration
on just digital exam ("with the finger") unless it was extensive. This is all very
consistent with evaluation results that might be described today, and I applaud
him for his diligence. The term "vulva" today refers to the outside genital parts
of female anatomy, including the labia, clitoris, vaginal opening, and urethral
opening. When Dr. Young speaks of the lower part of the vulva, he is probably
referring to the posterior fourchette (child) or perineum (adult), which are
the areas most frequently injured in sexual abuse and sexual assault, as well
as occasionally in consensual sexual activity. Those areas usually heal quickly,
depending on the degree of injury, but can create a scar, usually of white col-
oration, which Dr. Young might have referred to as an ulceration. The findings

testified to by these doctors, especially Dr. Young, are very consistent with the history that Antônia gave. The pain and bleeding created by the events Antônia described are consistent with forceful entry of some object into the female genital organ (which by definition is all the genital organs proximal to or closer to the body than the plane formed by the outmost surface of the labia majora). Together, Antônia's description and the physicians' findings are consistent with sexual abuse/sexual assault.

2. Comments by Craig Keathley, MD

In reviewing the medical testimony of Drs. Halbert and Young, there are consistencies in both testimonies that support physical-exam evidence of vaginal injury consistent with rape. Dr. Halbert describes a digital vaginal exam with a finding of "laxity" and the impression that "the parts had been used a great deal," suggesting sexual promiscuity. This is an unsupported inference on his part and is just as easily explained by the more detailed findings of Dr. Young, who describes a visual inspection with a finding of an "ulcer due to laceration." The presence of a laceration is further supported in Antônia's own description of an encounter in late November in which she was badly "lacerated," causing her to miss school the next day.

A laceration that is left untended will heal by a process called second intention with formation of granulation tissue that would have a similar appearance to an ulcer. The lack of a primary repair and approximation of the edges of the laceration would also contribute to an enlargement of the opening that Dr. Halbert would perceive on digital examination as laxity. Both doctors describe findings that would be consistent with traumatic laceration despite Dr. Halbert's suggestion otherwise. My impression of the medical testimony is that this young woman suffered a traumatic genital injury consistent with that of a rape victim.

The description in the testimony suggests a preterm delivery that would support a conception date about November 1894. A conception occurring late November or early December would have put the gestational age at de-

Dr. Craig Keathley is an obstetrics and gynecology physician in Fort Worth, Texas. He holds degrees from Baylor University (BS) and the University of Texas Medical School at Galveston (MD). Dr. Keathley is a practicing physician specializing in women's health. He has provided written medical opinions for a number of sexual assault cases.

livery (6/18/1895) at approximately thirty weeks. Normal gestation is forty weeks dated from the first day of the last menstrual period. A term delivery is a delivery that occurs at or beyond thirty-seven weeks. A baby born at thirty weeks in the late nineteenth century would most likely not survive and die shortly after birth. The fact that this child did survive until spring of 1896 would suggest a somewhat later gestational age consistent with a conception in the early part of November. This would correlate with a gestational age closer to thirty-four weeks. A child born at this gestational age in the late nineteenth century would still be considered significantly premature but would be much more likely than a thirty-week delivery to survive for the several months that this child apparently survived. The trial testimony mentions an encounter on November 6, 1894, and a comment that a menstrual period ensued afterward about November 12. An episode of vaginal bleeding (whether it was truly a menstrual period is unknown) following a sexual encounter does not necessarily eliminate that encounter as a potential conception date. Dr. Halbert in his testimony suggested "the probability would be against a girl like this conceiving when she was raped on the 6th of November, but such cases have been known." This is a statement that lacks support, and certainly any woman or young girl that ovulates can conceive during any sexual encounter as was pointed out by Dr. Young in his testimony.

The physical exam findings of both physicians are consistent with injuries as a result of rape. The baby was clearly premature based on the testimony, and survival of the child beyond the immediate neonatal period suggests a date of conception earlier in the sequence of events rather than later.

Bibliography

Archives Consulted

Public and University Archives

Arquivos Públicos de Maceió.

B. H. Carroll Papers. Texas Collection. Baylor University.

Baptist General Convention of Texas Annuals. Religious Collections. Baylor University Digital Collections. https://digitalcollections-baylor.quartexcollections .com/religious-collections/baptist-general-convention-of-texas-annuals.

Central Library. Memphis, TN.

Fifty-Fourth District Court in McLennan County. McLennan County Archives.

Livraria da Pontífica Universidade Católica de Pernambuco.

Livraria da Universidade Católica de Petrópolis.

Luther Bagby Collection. Texas Collection. Baylor University.

McLennan County Archives.

Rufus Burleson Correspondence. Texas Collection. Baylor University.

Seminário Teológico Batista do Norte do Brasil.

Texas Collection. Baylor University.

University Catalogues. Baylor University Archives. Baylor University Digital Collections. https://digitalcollections-baylor.quartexcollections.com/explore -the-collections/list/collections/51.

Waco City Directories. Texas Collection. Baylor University Digital Collections.

https://digitalcollections-baylor.quartexcollections.com/explore-the-col
lections/list/collections/12.

William Cowper Brann Collection. Texas Collection. Baylor University.

Wright Library. Princeton Theological Seminary. Princeton, NJ.

Wright Learning and Information Center. Austin Presbyterian Theological Seminary. Austin, Texas.

Zachary Taylor Papers. Texas Collection. Baylor University.

Church and Denominational Archives

Arquivos da Cúria de Maceió.

Arquivos Dom Lamartine, Arquidiocese de Olinda.

Catedral Metodista do Rio de Janeiro.

Foreign Mission Board Archives.

International Mission Board Archives.

Primeira Igreja Evangélica Batista de Maceió.

Primeira Igreja Presbiteriana do Recife.

Southern Baptist Convention Library and Archives.

Primary Sources

Journals and Periodicals

"A Lei." *Diario de Minas* 1, no. 62 (August 31, 1888): 2.

A Reforma 2, no. 95 (November 4, 1888).

"Alagôas." *Diario de Pernambuco* 48, no. 273 (November 27, 1872): 3.

Bagby, William B. "Brother Bagby on Brazil and Its People." *FMJ* 13, no 12 (1882): 3.

———. "Change of Base." *FMJ* 14, no. 4 (November 1882): 3.

———. "Christmas at Bahia (26 December 1884)." *FMJ* 16 (March 1885): 2.

———. "The Death of Antonio Teixeira d'Albuquerque." *FMJ* 18, no. 17 (June 1887): 1.

———. "Discurso Histórico." *Jornal Batista* 26, no. 12 (1926): 4.

———. "From Brother Bagby." *FMJ* 14 (July 1883): 2.

———. "Further from Bahia." *FMJ* 15, no. 2 (September 1883): 4.

———. "Our Cause in Brazil." *FMJ* 15, no. 4 (November 1883): 4.

Baptist Standard, July 25, 1895.

Baptist Standard, August 19, 1897.

Barros, A. L. "Parabens ao Padre." *Jornal do Recife* 21, no. 106 (May 9, 1878): 2.

"Board of Domestic Missions: From Our Missionaries." *Southern Baptist Missionary Journal* 4, no. 12 (May 1850): 310.

Bowen, Thomas J. "Yoruba-Central Africa: Letter from Rev. T. J. Bowen." *Home and Foreign Fields* 4, no. 10 (April 1855): 39.

Bratcher, Robert G. "A Well-Favored Land." *The Commission* 17, no. 8 (September 1954): 2–5.

"Brazil Mission." *The Commission* 4, no. 5 (November 1859): 148.

"The Brazil Mission." *The Commission* 4, no. 8 (February 1860): 249.

"Brazilian Notes." *The British and American Mail* 5, no. 10 (May 24, 1878): 4.

Brooks, S. P. "A Story of the Corpus Christi Storm." *Baptist Standard*, October 16, 1919.

"Chronica." *A Família* 1, no. 15 (December 12, 1872): 4.

"Collegio Albuquerque." *A Alvorada* 1, no. 22 (November 28, 1880): 4.

"Collegio Nacional." *A Alvorada* 1, no. 3 (June 23, 1880): 3.

Commercial Appeal (Memphis, TN), August 14, 1896.

Dallas Morning News, July 9, 1895.

"Deplorable Indeed." *Waco Morning News*, June 6, 1895.

Duclerk, C. C. "O Evangelho em Alagoas." *Jornal Batista* 27, no. 32 (August 11, 1927): 13–14.

"Falleceu." *Gutenberg* 6, no. 77 (April 12, 1887): 3.

Fort Worth Gazette, July 25, 1895.

Galveston Daily News, June 16, 1895.

Galveston Daily News, June 17, 1895.

Galveston Daily News, July 25, 1895.

Galveston Daily News, July 26, 1895.

Galveston Daily News, July 27, 1895.

Galveston Daily News, May 22, 1896.

Galveston Daily News, May 15, 1901.

Gazeta de Notícias 5, no. 79 (March 21, 1879): 2.

Gazeta de Notícias 5, no. 113 (April 25, 1879): 1.

Gazeta de Notícias 13, no. 111 (April 27, 1887): 1.

Ginsburg, Solomon L. "Some Achievements and Prospects After Forty Years." *Home and Foreign Fields* 8, no. 5 (May 1924): 12–13.

Hampton, Roberta. "American Settlers in Brazil." *The Commission* 30, no. 4 (April 1967): 8.

"Imprensa." *Gazeta do Norte* 7, no. 236 (October 18, 1886): 1.

"Imprensa." *Jornal de Recife* 29, no. 228 (October 5, 1886): 1.

"In Memoriam." *The Commission* 21, no. 1 (January 1958): 21.

"Instituto Litterario Olindense." *Diario de Pernambuco* 52, no. 283 (December 12, 1876): 1.

"Instituto Litterario Olindense." *Diario de Pernambuco* 53, no. 10 (January 13, 1877): 2.

The Lagrange Journal 16, no. 31 (August 1895). https://texashistory.unt.edu/explore /collections/TDNP/.

Manly, Basil, Jr. "Is Brazil Missionary Ground?" *Home and Foreign Journal* 8, no. 10 (April 1859): 39.

"Missions to South America." *The Commission* 3, no. 5 (May 1851): 1.

"Mudou de Culto." *Jornal do Recife* 21, no. 102 (May 4, 1878): 1.

"New Missionaries Under Appointment." *The Commission* 3, no. 9 (March 1859): 286.

"Notas Religiosas." *O Libertador* 6, no. 85 (April 17, 1886): 3.

O Apostolo 18, no. 24 (March 2, 1883).

O Orbe 6, no. 130 (November 9, 1884).

"O Protestantismo." *Pacotinlha* 8, no. 54 (February 24, 1888): 2.

O Reporter 1, no. 74 (March 21, 1879).

"Onde Foram se Animar." *Correio do Brazil* 1, no. 387 (December 8, 1872): 2.

"Ordenação." *A Constituição* 9, no. 174 (December 1, 1871): 2.

"Our Missionaries." *FMJ* 16 (September 1884): 2.

"Our Missionaries." *FMJ* 17 (October 1885): 2.

"Padres Reformados." *Diario de Minas* 1, no. 250 (March 3, 1889): 2.

"Passageiros." *Diario de Pernambuco* 47, no. 281 (December 9, 1871): 3.

"Protestos." *O Apóstolo* 9, no. 9 (January 22, 1874): 4.

"Que Bello Exemplo!" *O Pelicano* 1, no. 56 (January 2, 1873): 2.

Quillin, E. H. "A Roman Priest in Search of the Primitive Church." *FMJ* 7 (October 1880): 4.

"Rapto por um Padre." *O Santo Officio* 3, no. 1 (January 6, 1873): 3.

"Rapto." *O Espirito-Santense* 3, no. 161 (January 10, 1973): 3.

"Recebemos." *O Orbe* 8, no. 146 (October 29, 1886): 1.

"Refutação as Conferencias do Sacerdote Apostata, Antonio Teixeira de Albuquer-que." *O Orbe* 6, no. 134 (November 19, 1884): 2.

"Revista do Interior." *Jornal do Recife* 30, no. 251 (November 4, 1887): 2.

Ribeiro, Mario. "Rio Largo: Berço e Túmulo de dois pioneiros Batistas (Mello Lins e Teixeira de Albuquerque)." *Jornal Batista* 75, no. 6 (February 9, 1975): 4–5.

"Sociedade Propagadora da Instrução Publica." *Diario de Pernambuco* 54, no. 55 (March 7, 1878): 3.

Soper, E. H. "Rio De Janeiro-Brazil." *FMJ* 18, no. 12 (July 1887): 2.

The Sunday Gazetteer (Denison, TX), October 6, 1895.

The Sunday Gazetteer (Denison, TX), May 24, 1896.

Taylor, Z. C. "Bright Prospects (10 September 1884)." *FMJ* 16 (November 1884): 3.

———. "From Brazil." *FMJ* 14 (June 1883): 3.

———. "Incidents in Bahia." *FMJ* 14, no. 10 (May 1883): 4.

———. "Later." *FMJ* 16 (March 1885): 2.

———. "Letter from Z. C. Taylor." *FMJ* 18, no. 4 (November 1886): 3.

———. "One Hundred Baptized into the Church at Bahia." *FMJ* 19, no. 2 (September 1887): 2.

———. "Persecution and Progress (May 24, 1884)." *FMJ* 15 (July 1884): 2.

———. "Quarterly Report (12 July 1884)." *FMJ* 16 (October 1884): 3

———. "Quarterly Report (31 October 1884)." *FMJ* 16 (January 1885): 3

———. "Quarterly Report." *FMJ* 17 (August 1885): 2.

———. "Quarterly Report of Bro. Z. C. Taylor." *FMJ* 18, no. 3 (October 1886): 3.

Teixeira de Albuquerque, Antônio. "Abjuração." *Jornal do Recife* 21, no. 104 (May 7, 1878): 2.

———. "Abjuração." *Jornal do Recife* 21, no. 107 (May 10, 1878): 2.

———. "A Educação." *A Alvorada* 1, no. 7 (July 23, 1880): 2.

———. "A Educação." *A Alvorada* 1, no. 11 (August 25, 1880): 3.

———. "A Educação." *A Alvorada* 1, no. 12 (August 31, 1880): 2–3.

The Temple Times, August 30, 1895.

Texas Baptist and Herald, August 5, 1897.

Theophilus. "Brazil as a Missionary Field: No 1." *The Commission* 4, no. 1 (July 1859): 10–12.

———. "Brazil as a Missionary Field: No 2." *The Commission* 4, no. 2 (August 1859): 39–40.

———. "Brazil as a Missionary Field: No 3." *The Commission* 4, no. 4 (October 1859): 102.

"Um passeio por Terra até a Cidade do Pillar da Provincia de Alagoas Partindo-se da Cidade da Escada em "Pernambuco." *Diario de Pernambuco* 65, no. 99 (May 3, 1889): 3.

"Um Santo Exemplo." *O Liberal do Pará* 5, no. 6 (January 9, 1873): 1.

"Um Voto Eterno de Agradecimento." *Diario de Pernambuco* 49, no. 283 (December 10, 1873): 3.

Waco Morning News, June 16, 1895.

Waco Morning News, June 18, 1895.

Waco Morning News, September 29, 1895.

Waco Morning News, May 19, 1896.

Waco Morning News, May 20, 1896.

Waco Tribune-Herald, April 24, 1912.

Waco Tribune-Herald, May 21, 2022.

"The Year of 1860." *The Commission* 4, no. 7 (January 1860): 217–18.

Other Journals and Periodicals Consulted

Diario de São Paulo

Gazeta de Joinville

Gazeta de Notícias

Jornal de Alagoas

Monitor Campista

Noticiador de Minas

A Regeneração

Manuscripts and Books

Almanak da Provincia das Alagoas para o Anno de 1873, Anno II. Maceió: Typ. Social de Amintas & Soares, 1873.

An American Commentary on the New Testament. Philadelphia: American Baptist Publication Society, 1881.

Bagby, W. B. *Brazil and the Brazilians.* Baltimore: Maryland Baptist Mission Rooms, 1889.

———. "*O Gigante que Dome.*" Rio de Janeiro: Casa Publicadora, 1947.

Bagby, W. B., Z. C. Taylor, and J. A. Baker. *Missionary Catechism on Brazil.* Baltimore: Maryland Baptist Mission Rooms, 1899.

Brann, William Cowper. *The Complete Works of Brann, The Iconoclast.* 12 vols. Brann Publishers, 1919.

Burleson, Georgia, ed. *The Life and Writings of Rufus C. Burleson, Containing a Biography of Dr. Burleson by Hon. Harry Haynes.* Texas: Compiled and Published by Georgia J. Burleson, 1901.

Bibliography

Catalogue of Baylor University, Waco Texas, 1893–94. Waco: Kellner Printing Company, 1894. Accessed January 4, 2022. https://digitalcollections-baylor.quar texcollections.com/Documents/Detail/catalogue-of-baylor-university-at -waco-texas-1893-1894/843719?item=843731.

Carvalho, Alfredo de. *Recife: Cultura Academica.* Recife: Imprensa Industrial, 1907.

Crabtree, A. R. *História dos Baptistas do Brasil.* Vol. 1. Rio de Janeiro: Casa Publicadora Baptista, 1937.

Mein, John. *A Causa Baptista em Alagôas.* Recife: STBNB, 1929.

Mesquita, Antônio Neves de. *História dos Baptistas do Brasil.* Vol. 2. Rio de Janeiro: Casa Publicadora Baptista, 1940.

O Padre Antônio Teixeira de Albuquerque e as Razões de Sua Apostasia. Recife: Typographia Industrial, 1886.

Ray, T. B. *Brazilian Sketches.* Louisville: Baptist World Pub. Co., 1912.

Taylor, Zachary Clay. "The Rise and Progress of Baptist Missions in Brazil: An Autobiography." Unpublished manuscript, c. 1916.

Teixeira de Albuquerque, Antônio. *Três Razões Porque Deixei a Igreja de Roma.* Casa Publicadora Baptista, 1951.

Tupper, H. Allen. *Armenia: Its Present Crisis and Past History.* New York: John Murphy & Company, 1896.

Secondary Sources

Albanese, Catherine L. *American Religious History: A Bibliographical Essay.* Currents in American Scholarship Series. Washington, DC: US Department of State, 2002.

"Allianca, List of Passengers, January 26, 1892." The Statue of Liberty—Ellis Island Foundation, Inc. Accessed October 23, 2021. https://heritage.statueofliberty .org/.

Almeida, Argus Vaconcelos de, Francisco de Oliveira Magalhães, Cláudio Augusto Gomes da Câmara, and Jadson Augusto de Almeida da Silva. "Pressupostos do Ensino da Filosofia Natural no Seminário de Olinda (1800–1817)." *Revista Eletrónica de Enseñanza de las Ciencias* 7, no. 2 (2008): 480–505.

Almeida, Bianca Daéb's Seixas. *Uma História das Mulheres Batistas Soterapolitanas.* Salvador: Sagga Editora, 2017.

Alves, Pedro Henrique. "Primórdios Batistas no Brasil: Abertura de Igrejas e Formação da Equipe Missionária (1881–1886)." *Mosaico* 12, no. 18 (2020): 162–83.

Ames, Eric S. *Hidden History of Waco.* Charleston, SC: The History Press, 2020.

Bibliography

Anderson, Gary A. *The Genesis of Perfection: Adam and Eve in Jewish and Christian Imagination*. Louisville: Westminster John Knox, 2001.

Araújo, Maria Paula Nascimento and Myrian Sepúlveda dos Santos. "History, Memory and Forgetting: Political Implications." *RCCS Annual Review* 1, no. 1 (September 2009): 77–94.

The Associated Press. "Key Dates and Developments in the Baylor Assault Scandal." *AP News*, August 11, 2021. https://apnews.com/article/sports-college-foot ball-violence-lawsuits-sexual-assault-9fe035761dc3d1f3d42c714a87c78a10.

Bakker, Janel Kragt. *Sister Churches: American Congregations and Their Partners Abroad*. New York: Oxford University Press, 2014.

Barbosa, José Carlos. *Slavery and Protestant Missions in Imperial Brazil: "The Black Does Not Enter the Church, He Peeks in from Outside."* Translated by Fraser G. MacHaffie and Richard K. Danford. Lanham, MD: University Press of America, 2008.

Baylor University. "Rufus C. Burleson, Baylor President (1886–1897)." About Baylor. Accessed December 29, 2021. https://www.baylor.edu/about/index.php?id =89259.

"Baylor University Announces Members, Charges for Commission on Historic Campus Representations." Baylor University: Media and Public Relations. July 6, 2020. https://www.baylor.edu/mediacommunications/news.php?ac tion=story&story=219486.

Baylor University Board of Regents. *Findings of Fact*. Baylor University: Our Commitment. Our Response. May 26, 2016. https://www.baylor.edu/thefacts /doc.php/266596.pdf.

"Baylor University Board of Regents Acknowledges University's History, Ties to Slavery and Confederacy; Unanimously Passes Resolution on Racial Healing and Justice." Baylor University: Media and Public Relations. June 26, 2020. https://www.baylor.edu/mediacommunications/news.php?action=story &story=219405.

Baylor University Commission on Historic Representation. *Final Report*. December 2020. https://www.baylor.edu/diversity/commission/doc.php/372287.pdf.

Bebbington, David. *Baptists through the Centuries: A History of a Global People*. 2nd ed. Waco, TX: Baylor University Press, 2018.

Beckert, Sven. *Empire of Cotton: A Global History*. New York: Alfred A. Knopf, 2014.

Blight, David W. *Race and Reunion: The Civil War in American Memory*. Cambridge, MA: Belknap Press, 2002.

Bibliography

Brackney, William H. *Baptists in North America: An Historical Perspective*. Oxford: Blackwell Publishing, 2006.

Braga, Erasmo, and Kenneth G. Grubb. *The Republic of Brazil: A Survey of the Religious Situation*. New York: World Dominion Press, 1932.

Brinsfield, John Wesley, Jr. *The Spirit Divided: Memoirs of Civil War Chaplains*. Macon, GA: Mercer University Press, 2006.

Brundage, W. Fitzhugh. *The Southern Past: A Clash of Race and Memory*. Cambridge, MA: Belknap Press, 2005.

Burkhalter, Frank E. *A World-Visioned Church: The Story of the First Baptist Church Waco, Texas*. Nashville: Broadman, 1946.

Burleson, Blake, and Burt Burleson. "Our Letter to Uncle Rufus, Confronting Baylor's Racist Past." *Waco Tribune-Herald*, April 24, 2021. https://wacotrib.com /opinion/columnists/blake-and-burt-burleson-our-letter-to-uncle-rufus -confronting-baylors-racist-past/article_0d91ee96-a3b4-11eb-a1e3-3b5b 9b3a5c8f.html.

Burleson, James D., ed. *The Burlesons of the Texas Frontier*. Texas: Compiled and Published by James D. Burleson, 2006.

Butler, Anthea. *White Evangelical Racism: The Politics of Morality in America*. Chapel Hill: University of North Carolina Press, 2021.

Cameron, David J. "Race and Religion in the Bayou City: Latino/a, African-American, and Anglo Baptists in Houston's Long Civil Rights Movement." PhD diss., Texas A&M University, 2017.

Campbell-Reed, Eileen. *Anatomy of a Schism: How Clergywomen's Narratives Reinterpret the Fracturing of the Southern Baptist Convention*. Knoxville: University of Tennessee Press, 2016.

Carver, Charles. *Brann and the Iconoclast*. London: T. Nelson, 1958.

Cathcart, William. *The Baptist Encyclopædia*. Philadelphia: L. H. Everts, 1881.

Cavalcanti, Daniel Augusto. *Protestantismo e Ditadura Militar no Brasil*. São Paulo: Editora Reflexão, 2015.

Cavalcanti, H. B. "Southern Baptists Abroad: Sharing the Faith in Nineteenth Century Brazil." *Baptist History and Heritage* 38, no. 2 (2003): 52–67.

Chang, Derek. *Citizens of a Christian Nation: Evangelical Missions and the Problem of Race in the Nineteenth Century*. Philadelphia: University of Pennsylvania Press, 2010.

Chaves, João B. "Expanding the Fear of the Mongrel: Baptist Missions in Latin

America and Transnational Racist Cross-Pollination." *Baptist History and Heritage* 54, no. 2 (2019): 81–91.

———. *The Global Mission of the Jim Crow South: Southern Baptist Missionaries and the Shaping of Latin American Evangelicalism.* Macon, GA: Mercer University Press, 2022.

———. *Migrational Religion: Context and Creativity in the Latinx Diaspora.* Waco, TX: Baylor University Press, 2021.

———. *O Racismo na História Batista Brasileira.* Brasília: Novos Diálogos, 2021.

Chaves, João B., and C. Douglas Weaver. "Baptists and Their Polarizing Ways: Transnational Polarization Between Southern Baptist Missionaries and Brazilian Baptists." *Review and Expositor* 116, no. 2 (2019): 160–74.

Chute, Anthony L., Nathan A. Finn, and Michael A. G. Haykin. *The Baptist Story: From English Sect to Global Movement.* Nashville: B&H Academic, 2015.

"City Population History from 1850–2000." In *Texas Almanac.* Accessed January 26, 2022. https://texasalmanac.com/sites/default/files/images/CityPopHist%20web.pdf.

Conger, Roger N. "Cotton Palace." In *Handbook of Texas Online.* Texas State Historical Society, 1954. Updated December 1, 1994. https://www.tshaonline.org/handbook/entries/cotton-palace.

Costa, Jovesi de Almeida. *O Evangelho Chega à Terra de Alagoas: Primeira Igreja Evangélica Batista de Maceió.* Maceió: Poligraf, 2017.

Cowan, Benjamin A. *Moral Majorities Across the Americas: Brazil, the United States, and the Creation of the Religious Right.* Chapel Hill: University of North Carolina Press, 2021.

Cox, Karen L. *No Common Ground: Confederate Monuments and the Ongoing Fight for Racial Justice.* Chapel Hill: University of North Carolina Press, 2021.

D'Andrea, Anthony. *Reflexive Religion: The New Age in Brazil and Beyond.* Leiden: Brill, 2018.

Dantas, Leandro. "Seminario de Olinda e a República." *Revista Algomais,* April 8, 2017.

Dawsey, Cyrus B., and James M. Dawsey. "Leaving: The Context of Southern Emigration to Brazil." In *The Confederados: Old South Immigrants in Brazil,* edited by Cyrus B. Dawsey and James M. Dawsey, 11–23. Tuscaloosa: University of Alabama Press, 1998.

Dawson, Joseph Martin. *Rufus C. Burleson: Pro Ecclesia, Pro Texana.* Dallas: Baptist Standard Pub. Co., 1956.

DeMatteo, David, Meghann Galloway, Shelby Arnold, and Unnati Patel. "Sexual

Bibliography

Assault on College Campuses: A 50-State Survey of Criminal Sexual Assault Statutes and Their Relevance to Campus Sexual Assault." *Psychology, Public Policy, and Law* 21, no. 3 (August 2015): 227–38.

Denson, Andrew. *Monuments to Absence: Cherokee Removal and the Contest over Southern Memory*. Chapel Hill: University of North Carolina Press, 2017.

Dochuk, Darren. *Anointed with Oil: How Christianity and Crude Made Modern America*. New York: Basic Books, 2019.

———. *From Bible Belt to Sunbelt: Plain-Folk Religion, Grassroots Politics, and the Rise of Evangelical Conservatism*. New York: W. W. Norton, 2012.

Dusilek, Sérgio, Clemir Fernandes, and Alexandre Carvalho. "A Igreja e a Farda: Batistas e a Ditadura Militar." *Estudos Teológicos* 57, no. 1 (January/June 2017), 192–212.

Early, Joseph E., Jr. *A Texas Baptist Power Struggle: The Hayden Controversy*. Denton, TX: University of North Texas Press, 2005.

Eighmy, John Lee, and Samuel S. Hill. *Churches in Cultural Captivity: A History of the Social Attitudes of Southern Baptists*. Knoxville: University of Tennessee Press, 1987.

Ferreira, Ebenézer Soares. *História Dos Batistas Fluminenses, 1891–1991*. Rio de Janeiro: JUERP, 1991.

Flemmons, Jerry. "Truth: The Life and Death of the Iconoclast, W. C. Brann." *Heritage* 3 (1999): 14–16.

Flowers, Elizabeth H. *Into the Pulpit: Southern Baptist Women and Power since World War II*. Chapel Hill: University of North Carolina Press, 2012.

Flowers, Elizabeth H., and Karen K. Seat, eds. *A Marginal Majority: Women, Gender, and a Reimagining of Southern Baptists*. Knoxville: University of Tennessee Press, 2020.

Foley, Neil. *The White Scourge: Mexicans, Blacks, and Poor Whites in Texas Cotton Culture*. Berkeley: University of California Press, 1997.

Fuller, A. James. *Chaplain to the Confederacy: Basil Manly and Baptist Life in the Old South*. Baton Rouge: LSU Press, 2000.

Goldman, Frank. *Os pioneiros Americanos no Brasil: Educadores, Sacerdotes, Covos e Reis*. São Paulo: Pioneira, 1972.

Gomes, César Leandro Santos. "O Veneno da Heresia deve ser Queimado: O Antiprotestantismo Católico da Imprensa Pernambucana (1895–1910)." *PLURA— Revista de Estudoes de Religião* 11, no. 2 (2020): 90–124.

Gomes, Laurentino. *Do Primeiro Leilão de Cativos em Portugal até a Morte de Zumbi dos Palmares*. Vol. 1 of *Escravidão*. Rio de Janeiro: Globo Livros, 2019.

Griggs, William Clark. *The Elusive Eden: Frank McMullan's Confederate Colony in Brazil.* Austin: University of Texas Press, 1987.

Grober, Glendon Donal. "An Introduction to and Critical Reproduction of the Z. C. Taylor Manuscript: The Rise and Progress of Baptist Missions in Brazil." Master's thesis, Ouachita Baptist University, 1969.

Gunn, Jack Winton. "The Life of Rufus C. Burleson." PhD diss., University of Texas, 1951.

Hankins, Barry. *God's Rascal: J. Frank Norris and the Beginnings of Southern Fundamentalism.* Lexington: University Press of Kentucky, 1996.

Harris, Jessica C. "Women of Color Undergraduate Students' Experiences with Campus Sexual Assault: An Intersectional Analysis." *Review of Higher Education* 44, no. 1 (Fall 2020): 1–30.

Harrison, Helen Bagby. *The Bagbys of Brazil.* Nashville: Broadman Press, 1954.

Harter, Eugene. *The Lost Colony of the Confederacy.* College Station: Texas A&M University Press, 2006.

Harvey, Paul. *Redeeming the South: Religious Cultures and Racial Identities Among Southern Baptists, 1865–1925.* Chapel Hill: University of North Carolina Press, 1997.

Hawkins, J. Russell. *The Bible Told Them So: How Southern Evangelicals Fought to Preserve White Supremacy.* New York: Oxford University Press, 2021.

Haynes, Harry. "Dr. Rufus C. Burleson." *The Quarterly of the Texas State Historical Association* 5, no. 1 (1901): 60.

Helgen, Erika. *Religious Conflict in Brazil: Protestants, Catholics, and the Rise of Religious Pluralism in the Early Twentieth Century.* New Haven, CT: Yale University Press, 2020.

Hollinger, David A. *Protestants Abroad: How Missionaries Tried to Change the World but Changed America.* Illustrated ed. Princeton: Princeton University Press, 2017.

Horne, Gerald. *The Deepest South: The United States, Brazil, and the African Slave Trade.* New York: NYU Press, 2007.

"How Fast Did Early Trains Go?" World Wide Rails. Accessed January 26, 2021. https://worldwiderails.com/how-fast-did-early-trains-go/.

Hunt, Geof. "Texas over Time: Waco's Provident Building—Once the Biggest Office Building in Central Texas and Beyond." *The Texas Collections* (blog). Baylor University, June 19, 2019. https://blogs.baylor.edu/texascollection/2019/06/19/wacos-provident-building/.

Jarnagin, Laura. *A Confluence of Transatlantic Networks: Elites, Capitalism and Confederate Immigration to Brazil.* Tuscaloosa: University of Alabama Press, 2008.

Johnson, Robert E. *A Global Introduction to Baptist Churches*. Introduction to Religion. New York: Cambridge University Press, 2010.

Jones, Judith Mac. *Soldado Descansa! Uma Epopéia Norte-Americana sob os Céus do Brasil*. São Paulo: Fraternidade Descendência Americana, 1998.

Jones, Robert P. *White Too Long: The Legacy of White Supremacy in American Christianity*. New York: Simon & Schuster, 2020.

Julio, Kelly, and Edriana Nolasco. "Entre Famílias: Alianças Matrimoniais Vinculadas a Relações de Poder—Padres e Filhos, Minas Gerais (Século XVIII e XIX)." *Notandum* 21, no. 47 (May–August 2018): 132–53.

Kelley, Dayton, ed. *The Handbook of Waco and McLennan County*. Waco, TX: Texian Press, 1972.

Lamkin, Adrian, Jr. "The Gospel Mission Movement within the Southern Baptist Convention." PhD diss., The Southern Baptist Theological Seminary, 1979.

Lancaster, Daniel. *The Bagbys of Brazil: The Life and Work of William Buck and Ann Luther Bagby*. Austin: Eakin Press, 1999.

Lasseter, Amanda Slamcik. "Politics, Patriotism, Pageantry: Performing Power at the Texas Cotton Palace, 1910–1930." Master's thesis, Baylor University, 2014.

Leonard, Bill. *Baptist Ways: A History*. Valley Forge, PA: Judson Press, 2003.

Lomax, John Nova. "The Apostle of the Devil." *Texas Monthly*, June 3, 2016. https://www.texasmonthly.com/the-daily-post/the-apostle-of-the-devil/.

Lukes, Steven. *Power: A Radical View*. New York: Palgrave Macmillan, 2005.

MacCulloch, Diarmaid. *Silence: A Christian History*. New York: Penguin Books, 2014.

Malloy, L. C., T. D. Lyon, and J. A. Quas. "Filial Dependency and Recantation of Child Sexual Abuse Allegations." *Journal of the Academy of Child and Adolescent Psychiatry* 46 (2007): 162–70.

Marques, Danilo Luiz. "Um Covil de Escravos Fugidos: A Cidade de Maceió na Década da Abolição." Paper presented at História e Democracia, UNIFESP/Campus Guarulhos, September 3–6, 2018.

McAlister, Melani. *The Kingdom of God Has No Borders: A Global History of American Evangelicals*. New York: Oxford University Press, 2018.

McBeth, H. Leon. *The Baptist Heritage: Four Centuries of Baptist History*. Nashville: Broadman Press, 1987.

McSwain, Betty Ann McCartney, ed. *The Bench and Bar of Waco and McLennan County 1849–1976*. Waco, TX: Texian Press, 1976.

Mein, John. *A Causa Baptista em Alagôas*. Recife: STBNB, 1929.

Mendonça, P. "Sacrílegas Famílias: Conjugalidades Clericais no Bispado do Maranhão no Século XVIII." Master's thesis, Universidade Federal Fluminense, Niteroi, 2007.

Miller, Eric, and Ronald J. Morgan, eds. *Brazilian Evangelicalism in the Twenty-First Century: An Inside and Outside Look*. Christianity and Renewal—Interdisciplinary Studies. Cham, Switzerland: Palgrave Macmillan, 2019.

Miller, Steven P. *Billy Graham and the Rise of the Republican South*. Philadelphia: University of Pennsylvania Press, 2011.

Mindlin, Jessica, Leslye E. Orloff, Sameera Pochiraju, Amanda Baran, and Ericka Echavarria. "Dynamics of Sexual Assault and the Implications for Immigrant Women." National Immigrant Women's Advocacy Project (NIWAP). https://niwaplibrary.wcl.american.edu/wp-content/uploads/2015/CULT -Man-Ch1-DyanimcsSexualAssaultImplications-07.10.13.pdf.

Modes, Josemar Valdir. "Antônio Teixeira de Albuquerque: O Ex-Padre Facilitador e Potencializador das Capacidades de Bagby e Taylor." *Revista Via Teológica* 20, no. 39 (July 2019): 15–35.

Moore, Christopher C. *Apostle of the Lost Cause: J. William Jones, Baptists, and the Development of Confederate Memory*. Knoxville: University of Tennessee Press, 2019.

Moreton, Bethany. *To Serve God and Wal-Mart: The Making of Christian Free Enterprise*. Cambridge, MA: Harvard University Press, 2010.

Nash, Robert Norman, Jr. "The Influence of American Myth on Southern Baptist Foreign Missions, 1845–1945." PhD diss., The Southern Baptist Theological Seminary, 1989.

Niebuhr, Reinhold. *Moral Man and Immoral Society: A Study in Ethics and Politics*. New York: Charles Scribner's Sons, 1932.

Nogueira, Severino Leite, Mons. *O Seminário de Olinda: E Seu Fundador o Bispo Azeredo Coutinho*. Recife: Governo de Pernambuco, 1985.

Nolasco, Edriana. "Por Fragilidade Humana: Constituição Familiar do Clero, em Nome dos Padres e Filhos." Master's thesis, Universidade Federal de São João del-Rei, 2014.

Oliveira, Ana Maria Costa de. *O Destino (Não) Manifesto: Os Imigrantes Norte-Americanos no Brasil*. São Paulo: União Cultural Brasil-Estados Unidos, 1995.

Oliveira, Betty Antunes de. "Antônio Teixeira de Albuquerque." *Jornal Batista* 77, no. 26 (June 26, 1977): 7.

———. *Antônio Teixeira de Albuquerque: O Primeiro Pastor Batista Brasileiro*. Rio de Janeiro: self-published, 1982.

————. *Centelha em Restolho Seco: Uma Contribuição para a História dos Primórdios do Trabalho Batista no Brasil.* 2nd ed. São Paulo: Edições Vida Nova, 2005.

Oliveira, Zaqueu Moreira de. "Perfil Histórico da Educação Teológica Batista no Brasil." Paper presented at the 14th Congress of the Associação Brasileira de Instituições Batistas de Educação Teológica, Fortaleza, 2000.

Oosterbaan, Martijn. *Transmitting the Spirit: Religious Conversion, Media, and Urban Violence in Brazil.* 1st ed. University Park: Penn State University Press, 2019.

Park, Benjamin E. "The Centrality, Diversity, and Malleability of American Religion." In *A Companion to American Religious History*, edited by Benjamin E. Park, 1–8. Newark, NJ: John Wiley & Sons, 2021.

Parker, Julie Faith. "Blaming Eve Alone." *JBL* 132 (2013): 729–47.

Parsons, Mikeal C. *Crawford Howell Toy: The Man, the Scholar, the Teacher.* Macon, GA: Mercer University Press, 2019.

————. "Rufus Burleson and the Brazilian Girl." *Baptist History and Heritage* 56, no. 1 (March 2021): 26–38.

Pereira, J. Reis. *História dos Batistas no Brasil, 1882–1982.* Rio de Janeiro: JUERP, 1985.

Porterfield, Amanda. *Corporate Spirit: Religion and the Rise of the Modern Corporation.* New York: Oxford University Press, 2018.

Prado, Evilásio Rodrigues. *Conquistando Alagoas para Cristo: Breve História dos Batistas de Alagoas.* Maceió: E. R. Prado, 2008.

Price, Karla. "Slavery in Waco." Waco History Project. Accessed January 4, 2021. http://wacohistoryproject.org/Slavery/slaveryshadows.htm.

Randolph, John. "The Apostle of the Devil: A Biography of William Cowper Brann." PhD diss., Vanderbilt University, 1939.

Redding, Jonathan D. *One Nation under Graham: Apocalyptic Rhetoric and American Exceptionalism.* Waco, TX: Baylor University Press, 2021.

Robert, Dana L. "From Missions to Missions to Beyond Missions: The Historiography of American Protestant Foreign Missions Since World War II." In *New Directions in American Religious History*, edited by Harry S. Stout and D. G. Hart, 363–93. New York: Oxford University Press, 1997.

Robertson, Archibald Thomas. *Life and Letters of John Albert Broadus.* Philadelphia: American Baptist Publication Society, 1910.

Ryan, Terri Jo. "Crash at Crush." Waco History. Accessed January 26, 2021. https://wacohistory.org/items/show/70.

Said, Edward W. *Culture and Imperialism.* New York: Knopf, 1993.

Santayana, George. *The Life of Reason: Reason in Common Sense.* New York: Charles Scribner's Sons, 1905.

Santos, Silas Daniel dos. "O Jornal Imprensa Evangélica e as Origens do Protestantismo Brasileiro no Século XIX." PhD diss., Universidade Mackenzie, São Paulo, 2018.

Schäfer, Axel R. *Piety and Public Funding: Evangelicals and the State in Modern America.* Philadelphia: University of Pennsylvania Press, 2012.

Schwarcz, Lilia M., and Heloisa M. Starling. *Brazil: A Biography.* New York: Farrar, Straus and Giroux, 2015.

Shaw, Susan M. *God Speaks to Us, Too: Southern Baptist Women on Church, Home, and Society.* Lexington: University Press of Kentucky, 2008.

Shurden, Walter B. *Not a Silent People: Controversies That Have Shaped Southern Baptists.* Nashville: Broadman Press, 1972.

Shurden, Walter B., and Lori Redwine Varnadoe. "The Origins of the Southern Baptist Convention: A Historiographical Study." *Baptist History and Heritage* 37, no. 1 (Winter 2002): 71–96.

Silva, Célio Antônio Alcantara. "Capitalismo e Escravidão: A Imigração Confederada para o Brasil." PhD diss., Universidade Estadual de Campinas, 2011.

———. "Confederates and Yankees under the Southern Cross." *Bulletin of Latin American Research* 34, no. 3 (2015): 370–84.

Silva, Elizete da. *William Buck Bagby: Um Pioneiro Batista nas Terras do Cruzeiro do Sul.* Brasília: Novos Diálogos, 2011.

Simmons, Charles Willis. "Racist Americans in a Multi-racial Society: Confederate Exiles in Brazil." *The Journal of Negro History* 67, no. 1 (1982): 34–39.

Smith, Amy Erica. *Religion and Brazilian Democracy: Mobilizing the People of God.* Cambridge: Cambridge University Press, 2019.

Soares, Rodrigo Goyena. "Estratificação Profissional, Desigualdade Econômica e classes sociais na crise do império. Notas Preliminares Sobre as Classes Imperiais." *Revista Topoi* 20, no. 41 (May/August 2019): 446–89.

Sobreira, Vinícius. "Memórias da Resistência: A História de Dom Helder, o 'Arcebispo Vermelho' do Recife." *Brasil de Fato*, April 10, 2021.

Sorenson, T., and B. Snow. "How Children Tell: The Process of Disclosure in Child Sexual Abuse." *Child Welfare: Journal of Policy, Practice, and Program* 70 (1991): 3–15.

Souza, Alverson de. *Thomas Bowen: O Primeiro Missionário Batista no Brasil.* Brasília: Novos Diálogos, 2012.

Steen, Moses D. A. *The Steen Family in Europe and America*. Cincinnati: Monfort & Co., 1900.

Summit, Roland C. "The Child Sexual Abuse Accommodation Syndrome." *Child Abuse and Neglect* 7, no. 2 (1983): 177–93.

Sutton, Matthew Avery. *American Apocalypse: A History of Modern Evangelicalism*. Cambridge, MA: Belknap Press, 2014.

Teixeira, Marly Geralda. "Os Batistas na Bahia: 1882–1925. Um Estudo de Histróia Social." Master's thesis, Universidade Federal da Bahia, Salvador, 1975.

Usry, John M., ed. *Early Waco Obituaries and Various Related Items 1874–1908*. Waco, TX: Central Texas Genealogical Society, 1980.

Vaca, Daniel. *Evangelicals Incorporated: Books and the Business of Religion in America*. Cambridge, MA: Harvard University Press, 2019.

Virginio, Rafael da Silva. "Seminário de Olinda: Entre o Discurso Religioso e o Liberal." Presentation delivered at the 25th National Symposium of History, Fortaleza, 2009.

Wacker, Grant. *America's Pastor: Billy Graham and the Shaping of a Nation*. Cambridge, MA: Belknap Press, 2014.

"Waco History." Waco—Heart of Texas. Accessed January 26, 2022. https://waco heartoftexas.com/wp-content/uploads/2017/05/Waco-History-2017.pdf.

Wahlstrom, Todd W. *The Southern Exodus to Mexico: Migration across the Borderlands after the American Civil War*. Lincoln: University of Nebraska Press, 2015.

Weaver, C. Douglas. *In Search of the New Testament Church: The Baptist Story*. Macon, GA: Mercer University Press, 2008.

Wellborn, Charles. "Brann vs the Baptist—Violence in Southern Religion." *Christian Ethics Today* 72, no. 33 (2001): 14–18.

Willis, Gregory A. *Southern Baptist Theological Seminary, 1859–2009*. Oxford: Oxford University Press, 2009.

Wilson, Charles Reagan. *Baptized in Blood: The Religion of the Lost Cause, 1865–1920*. Athens: University of Georgia Press, 2009.

———. "Myth, Manners, and Memory." In *Myth, Manners, and Memory*, 1–8. Vol. 4 of *The New Encyclopedia of Southern Culture*, edited by Charles Reagan Wilson. Chapel Hill: University of North Carolina Press, 2006.

Wood, Neil. *Burleson at Houston: A Personality Sketch of Rufus C. Burleson as Revealed in His Personal Writings during the Years of His Houston Ministry, 1848–1851*. Waco, TX: Baylor University, 1957.

Young, Corey Rayburn. "Concealing Campus Sexual Assault: An Empirical Examination." *Psychology, Public Policy, and Law* 21, no. 1 (2015): 1–9.

Index of Authors

Index of Authors

Index of Subjects